Spinning Fantasies

Contraversions
Critical Studies in Jewish Literature, Culture, and Society

Daniel Boyarin and Chana Kronfeld, General Editors

Spinning
Fantasies

Rabbis, Gender, and History

Miriam B. Peskowitz

UNIVERSITY OF CALIFORNIA PRESS

Berkeley · *Los Angeles* · *London*

University of California Press
Berkeley and Los Angeles, California

University of California Press, Ltd.
London, England

© 1997 by
The Regents of the University of California

Library of Congress Cataloging-in-Publication
Data

Peskowitz, Miriam, 1964–
    Spinning fantasies : rabbis, gender, and his-
tory / Miriam B. Peskowitz.
        p.   cm.—(Contraversions ; 9)
    Includes bibliographical references and index.
    ISBN 0-520-20831-5 (cloth : alk. paper).—
ISBN 0-520-20967-2 (pbk. : alk. paper)
    1. Sex in rabbinical literature.   2. Women in
rabbinical literature.   3. Textile crafts in
rabbinical literature.   4. Rabbinical literature—
History and criticism.   5. Sex role—Religious
aspects—Judaism.   I. Title.   II. Series.
  BM496.9.S48P47   1997
296.3′878344′09015—dc20   96-43149
                                                            CIP

Printed in the United States of America
9 8 7 6 5 4 3 2 1

For Rob

From which it follows that the business of thinking is like the veil of Penelope; it undoes each morning what it had finished the night before.

Hannah Arendt, "Thinking and Moral Consideration" (1971)

Contents

Preface

I have always loved classical architecture. Stark seamless buildings with clean lines stood without ever calling attention to the architectonics that make standing possible. Effortless buildings betrayed no sign of their own production. I have loved copies of ancient architecture: family homes with Doric columns, nightclubs with Roman themes, Greek Revival courthouses, the Pantheonic domes of library reading rooms.

But what is this love about, this identification with the architecture of what has become "high" Western culture? In graduate school, I adored my course in Roman architecture, but with a difference. Leaving the classroom I would study ancient building techniques by identifying them, reused, in the Georgian-style buildings on one part of campus. Walking elsewhere, I would see them transformed wildly, almost beyond recognition, in the neo-Gothic architecture on the other side of campus.

Through these walks a different kind of love for antiquity emerged. Regarding something small, I began to recognize its parts and understand how it worked. Increasingly, I could see the repetition of ancient habits in our own time. I could sense that these public repetitions make certain ways of knowing the world seem natural and familiar. And I realized that love for what seems familiar authorizes all sorts of things whose effects range from benign to numbing to horrific. These recognitions changed how I felt about the seamlessness of classical structures. From within a more complicated and critical love, I began to study these classic habits and to unravel the stories we tell about women, gender, and antiquity.

Acknowledgments

To my best friend Laura Levitt goes my deepest gratitude. Many of the twists and turns of this book emerged during our marathon talks about things large and small. Rob Baird's loving companionship accompanied the writing of these chapters, and our late night and early morning conversations shaped an array of critical and creative insights that appear in these pages; my special appreciation goes to him. Susan Shapiro provided inspiration from her outpost in New York, and Wednesday night dinners in Florida with Jay Tribby were an invaluable treat. I thank Daniel Boyarin and Chana Kronfeld for including this book in their series, Contraversions: Critical Studies in Jewish Literature, Culture, and Society. My warm thanks go to Douglas Abrams Arava and his staff at the University of California Press. Various conversations—ongoing, intermittent, or one time only—made parts of this book possible. For insights, critique, and encouragement I thank Daniel Boyarin, Judith Baskin, Gail Labovitz, Naomi Seidman, Jean O'Barr, Judith Hauptman, Leonard Rutgers, Ann Pellegrini, Ross Kraemer, Bernadette Brooten, Judith Romney Wegner, Natalie Kampen, Raymond Liu, Hava Weissler, Larry Silberstein, Adi Ophir, and Irene Fine. At the University of Florida I thank Azim Nanji, Jim Mueller, and Shelly Isenberg. In London, Rebecca Wolman, Robbi Gringras, and Saul Rodansky of the Besht Tellers helped me to imagine antiquity's characters and allowed me to offer ideas for their stage production of Beruriah's life in "Far Above Rubies." I thank students in my seminars at the University of Florida for spirited conversations about women, men, gender, and rabbinic texts. Peg Fulton suggested that I begin the book with Penelope. Shaye Cohen pushed me to think about families. The Cedar Key Historical Society provided a quiet and beautiful place to write. Judy Shaw worked computer wonders. Bob Singerman was, as usual, librarian *extraordinaire*. Three student assistants helped procure library materials: Joyce Orr, Ed Sherrouse, and Arik Sinno. I thank curators and personnel at several museums: Hero Granger-Taylor and Jonathan Tubb of the British Museum; Ruth Peleg, Joe Zias, and Orit Shamir of the Israel Antiquities Authority, Rockefeller Museum, and Israel Museum; and staff at the on-site museum at Ostia, Italy. My ongoing appreciation goes to my graduate professors, for initial training and continuing inspiration: Eric Meyers, Carol Meyers, Ed Sanders, Elizabeth Clark, and especially Kalman Bland.

I am also grateful to the many participants in two projects on which I worked while writing this book: "Engendering Jewish Knowledges," a special issue of *Shofar: An Interdisciplinary Journal of Jewish Studies* (1995), and *Judaism Since Gender* (New York: Routledge, 1997), both co-edited with Laura Levitt. The impassioned arguments that surrounded these projects pushed me to think again about many of my own positions from a variety of angles and to clarify where I stand.

Several endowments, institutions, and organizations provided me with the proverbial "room of my own and five hundred quid a year" along with substantial opportunities to write. Prime among these are the American Council of Learned Societies and the Lucius Littauer Foundation. Additional support was offered by the Samuel H. Kress Foundation and the American Schools of Oriental Research; the W. F. Albright Institute for Archaeological Research; the Annenberg Research Institute; the Nathan Perilman Fund of Duke University's Center for Judaic Studies; the Ann Firor Scott Research Fund for Women's History; and the University of Florida, Division of Sponsored Research.

Finally to my parents, Myra and Daniel Peskowitz, and my brother, Ira Peskowitz, and to the rest of my extended family, I offer my love and gratitude, along with my heartfelt thanks for their enthusiastic support.

Introduction

Stories about Spinners and Weavers

For storytelling is always the art of repeating stories, and
this art is lost when the stories are no longer retained. It is
lost because there is no more weaving and spinning to go on
while they are being listened to. The more self-forgetful the
listener is, the more deeply is what he listens to impressed
upon his memory. When the rhythm of work has seized
him, he listens to the tales in such a way that the gift of retelling them comes to him all by itself. This, then, is the nature of the web in which the gift of storytelling is cradled.[1]

    Walter Benjamin, "The Storyteller" (1936)

PENELOPES

Far from being faraway, ancient times, people, and places are made familiar and close at hand by the telling of stories. But in the process of
storytelling, what cultural work is done? In making the past familiar
and usable, what complexities are flattened and effaced? Whose past
does it become? We create our pasts, in various ways and with various
texts and artifacts. Despite the habit of wrapping history in objectivity
and stability, our pasts are pliable. So too, did people in Roman times
creatively convey figures and events into stories about themselves and
their pasts. Those who are ancient to us crafted for themselves stories
of their own antiquities.

   From whatever standpoint of time they are viewed and read, pasts
are always gendered pasts. To go about finding a past that includes Jewish women, and to find a Jewish discourse on women, men, and gender
in the period of the Roman Empire, I start with stories about spinners
and weavers. These stories were as potent and important in Roman
times as they are in our own years. The meanings of these stories are
stable, and yet they shift, sometimes quietly, sometimes dramatically.

Think about Penelope. In Homer's *Odyssey*, Penelope sits daily at her loom and weaves, and returns nocturnally to unweave. Her weaving is an occupation, an identity, a quotidian event, a conventional sign of her femininity, and an act of resistance to others' plans for her remarriage. Homer uses the loom to represent Penelope's domesticity, fidelity, and loyalty to her missing husband, Odysseus. Although believed dead, in fact Odysseus is merely traveling far from home. But until the story unravels and Odysseus returns, Penelope must make plans to remarry. To prevent, or at least to postpone the plans for her remarriage, Penelope makes known that in order to maintain her reputation among local women, she must weave the shroud for her father-in-law, Laertes. She promises that once the shroud is complete, she will remarry. But in the meantime Penelope sets up her loom to weave a cloth of huge dimensions. For three years she weaves each day and by night secretly unravels the web. Then her trick is discovered by a maid, who reveals it to the suitors who have gathered around Penelope to woo her. In Homer's telling, Penelope now has no choice but to finish her weaving and remarry.[2]

Since her birthing in Homer's *Odyssey*, the heroine Penelope has had an afterlife as a beloved icon of gender and sexuality. Penelope proliferated in new landscapes, monuments, objects, and written texts. A marble relief from Thessaly, dated to the fifth century B.C.E., depicts her weaving at her loom while a maid washes the feet of Odysseus, in his guise as a beggar.[3] A painted vase produced in Chiusi in the early fifth century also depicts Penelope. Facing forward, she is seated in front of a loom whose web contains a detailed pattern of border motifs and winged animals; her son, Telemachus, stands next to her.[4] Homer's literary Penelope became a household image, appearing on bronze mirrors such as those excavated from Hellenistic sites. During the early Roman Empire, artistic images of Penelope coincided with the writings of the elegiac poets, and inside homes, such as those excavated at Pompeii, bas-reliefs and wall frescos depicted events from the story of Penelope's life, to be viewed again and again as ordinary people went about their lives.[5]

In the Roman-influenced Mediterranean, Penelope was already a five-hundred-year-old character. She became part of the landscape. Pausanias's travelogue of Greece describes streets and other visual reminders of Penelope's life. For instance, the race that Penelope's father, Ikarios, held to determine which of the suitors could marry her is commemorated at several places. "As you leave the marketplace by Leaving Street," Pausanias wrote in the mid-second century, "you come to what they call the Cattleprice; but I must first deal with the name of the street. They say Ikarios held a race for Penelope's lovers, and obviously Odysseus won, but the others were left behind in Leaving Street" (3.12.1). The beginning of the race was marked by a statue of "the Starting God" (3.12.1). Another monument, the Aidos statue, is placed between the cities Lakonia and Ithaca. Pausanias recounts that "the local people" reported to him that the statue marks the spot where the young Penelope chose to leave Ikarios's house in order to enter the home of her new husband, Odysseus. When Ikarios gave Penelope to Odysseus, he wanted the couple to settle in Lakonia. Odysseus disagreed. Ikarios begged his daughter to stay, and when she set out with Odysseus for Ithaca, he followed her in a chariot. After some time of being trailed by Ikarios, Odysseus declared that Penelope must choose: she must either stay with her father or continue on with Odysseus. In Pausanias's telling, Penelope relinquishes her voice and replies to her father's entreaties by placing her face inside a veil. The statue that Pausanias describes marks the place where Penelope hid her face (3.20.10–11).

The life and character of Penelope became monuments, to be recognized—or ignored?—in various ways by those who passed by these places or by those who wrote about them.[6] These markings in the landscape contain this paradox: the monuments that depict moments in Penelope's life often refer either to her absence (as in the race for her suitors) or her passivity (as in the meaning of the Aidos statue).[7] By making geography tell history, Pausanias guides his readers through the landscape of Mantinea. In Arcadia, off to the side of one of the roads to Orchomenos, is a high mound "which they say" marks the site of Penelope's grave. The following legend, he tells us, is popular among Mantineans: Odysseus sent Penelope away. She moved first to Sparta and then to Mantinea, where she died and was buried.[8] Yet Pausanias is provocative in that he recalls multiple local tales about Penelope. After reporting on the burial mound, he tells his readers about an alternate story, in which Penelope bears another child for Odysseus and remains in Troy until her death and burial (8.12.5–6). Thus, the landscape tells multiple stories about Penelope. The past matters, but it includes the contentiousness of multiple stories and accounts, including Pausanias's own. Furthermore, the textuality of Pausanias's accounts of traveling in Greece matters. His books were meant to preserve the inheritance of the Greek past, to produce and continue a consciousness of Penelope, Homer, and their world into his present and future.[9]

Penelope multiplies into Penelopes. Looking not for monuments but for a model of morality, the second elegy of Sextus Propertius (born between 54 and 47 B.C.E.) recalled Penelope into his nostalgic vision of his past, and crafted her into an exemplar for his own behavior. Propertius has been recently scorned and rejected by his lover. Yet, he declares that he will continue his one-sided devotion to her. Recalling Penelope's determination to await Odysseus's return, Propertius emphasizes Penelope as an icon of loyalty and faithfulness beyond social expectation. Social, cultural, and personal expectations might change with time. But standing guard against these changes, Propertius is one of many who make Penelope a guardian of essential and unchanging human character. Propertius uses his version of Penelope to invoke a lasting virtue from a past time when "modesty flourished and individuals would put aside the joys of a single night in return for higher ideals of sustained ardor and allegiance." Just as Penelope hoped for and received the return of her husband, so too in the name of this past and in the name of Penelope would Propertius love his woman forever, and await her return.[10]

Interpreters of antiquity must resist stabilizing what was not stable. Several Penelopes appear in Ovid's writing (43 B.C.E.–18 C.E.). In the *Tristia,* Ovid asserts that the spirits of Penelope and Andromache presided over his wife's birth and appearance into the world (5.5). And upon her death, Ovid finds a place for his wife alongside his ancient heroines in the pantheon of perfectly devoted wives: "Your name will be invoked along with those of Penelope and Alcestis for selflessness and the faithful love that cynics doubt but I can swear exists because I have seen it" (5.14). Their forms of femininity become his wife's. Echoing Propertius, Ovid's Penelope is an icon for women who stay faithful despite their husband's absences, even when offered the attentions and desires of other men.[11]

But Ovid offers a more ambivalent Penelope in the *Heroides.* In a letter to Odysseus, Penelope reiterates her identity as his wife: "I Penelope will always be the wife of Ulysses." She will be chaste and faithful, a once and only once married woman who lives the rest of her life devoted to her husband's memory. But at the same time, this Penelope wonders at the sacrifices and anguish that this commitment to the dead Odysseus entails. She complains of days that pass slowly, of her widowed hands that beguile the spacious hours of the night. She worries that their son, Telemachus, needs a father and wonders at the logic of it all. What sense does it make that she remains yearning for her missing husband. Should she wait? Sinking further into her fears, she voices the distrust that is part of her devotion: she is not the young girl he left but an aging woman; will Odysseus's love be as chastely faithful to her as hers is to him?[12]

Penelope's femininity does all sorts of cultural work in several Cynic letters (dating to the first or second century C.E.). In the epistle *To Mnasos,* ascribed pseudonymously to Crates, Penelope marks virtue. Along with Alcestis, Penelope is a figure from the past who adorned herself with the most beautiful of ornaments, decorum. The author of the letter emphasizes the desire for identification with this female icon: "try to hold fast to this advice," the letter reads, "in order, then, that you, too, might become like them."[13] The reader is urged to become like the ancient Penelope or Alcestis. At the same time, icons of femininity were deployed with different, conflicting, and contradictory meanings. Another Cynic letter, *To Ganymedes* (number 23), invents a very different Penelope. The letter is an exhortation to Ganymedes, who wants to live a virtuous life of Cynic abnegation and self-denial but is succumbing to the temptations of luxuries and other desires:

> So long as you fear the cloak and wallet and staff and long hair, and as long as you love purple robes and luxury, you will not cease leading on lovers, as Penelope did her suitors. And so, if such men are not troublesome to you, enjoy the life you have chosen. But if, as I am persuaded, they are not a little troublesome to you, dismiss the other aides through whom you frequently, but without success, tried to drive them away from yourself, and put on the weapons of Diogenes, with which he did drive away those who had designs on him. Rest assured that none of the lovers will ever approach you again.

The period during which Penelope awaited Odysseus's return, weaving and unweaving her father-in-law's shroud, no longer demonstrates her devotion. Instead, through these acts, Penelope displayed the distasteful qualities of teasing and flirtation. In this letter, Penelope is potentially the mythic parallel to Ganymede's condition. As this man is beholden to the insincerity of material possessions, so too did Penelope insincerely lead on her suitors. Far from signifying a virtue to be attained, Penelope becomes a state of being to put aside. Penelope tantalizes. She disrupts one's power to resist the traps of superficial desire. In this letter, *To Ganymedes,* Penelope exemplifies the pre-Cynic personality who cannot yet realize and practice the truths of Diogenes. These examples are striking. Penelope comes to signify a stable and historic notion of womanhood, yet at the same time, the genealogy of Penelope belies any such stability for femininity. As the Penelopes proliferate, the woman Penelope is transformed. The supposition that gender has any essential stability disappears, and the clarity of distinctions between male and female is threatened. The woman Penelope becomes a voice through which male writers speak and identify. Propertius identifies himself with Penelope, and Ovid writes his letters in her name.

Interpreters of antiquity have preferred to see stability and purity in their pasts. Within this desire, Homer's Penelope has been seen as the perfect original, and these Roman readings are seen as subsequent distortions of that original perfection. Within epistemological frames that privilege both origins and stable meanings, the plasticity and pliability of icons is deemed abhorrent. This set of assumptions is crystallized by the author of the following dictionary entry on Penelope. Writing about these Roman-period Penelopes, he protects Penelope's purity: "It was inevitable that inventive and possibly perverted writers would assail this image of perfection."[14] We can speculate that this writer would be appalled at the cultural work to which Juvenal put Penelope. In the second *Satire,* Juvenal (60–140 C.E.) uses Penelope to police and protect certain cultural distinctions: male and female gender, and male/male and male/female sexual desire. Juvenal uses the label "Penelope" as an accusation that identifies men who have strayed into femininity. In this *Satire* the character Laronia is beside herself with the hypocrisy of adulterers who would revive the earlier laws against adultery, the *Lex Iulia de maritandis ordinibus.* Juvenal's Laronia conflates her anger with antiadultery adulterers with another anger. She is furious with men who do not perform sexually and socially in the ways "men" are supposed to. Her fury encompasses male adulterers and male homosexuals, and especially, male homosexual adulterers. She deems the latter effeminate. Laronia's reply to them proffers examples of how "real" womanhood never moves outside the proper boundaries of its sex and gender, and thus how "real" manhood should do the same. Laronia argues that women never invade spaces that are men's—and she lists the domains of legal knowledge, courts, and wrestling. Laronia's women would never contribute to cultural decadence by acting out a nonfeminine gender or sexuality. She thus charges the men with inappropriate "straying." To evoke this more vividly Laronia uses images that all would understand. She describes these men as outperforming women at "women's work": "you men spin wool and bring back your tale of work in full baskets when it is done; you twirl round the spindle big with fine thread more deftly than Penelope, more delicately than Arachne."[15] Through spinning and weaving, Penelope demonstrates and assures others of her appropriate and normative femininity. Mimicking Penelope, these men inappropriately take on the sexual desires and gender roles of women. "Inappropriate" men disturb Juvenal's desire for a gender culture that maintains clear boundaries between male and female (but paradoxically, his own writing contributes much to the gender messiness he overtly abhors).

It is common but incorrect to suppose that ancient people did not think, speak, or write explicitly about gender, to assume that their discussions about these things were innocent or naive, or to imagine that they did not think about the categories of gender and sexuality, their distinctions and meanings. Looking closely at written and artifactual remains, it is possible to see the ways that ancient people negotiated gender culture. These Roman readings of Penelope demonstrate some of the many transformations that were effected on an image of a woman and a female body.[16] A pliable icon of gender and sexuality in the Roman period, Penelope was used by writers to make vivid the proprieties and norms of both. The Roman Penelopes show the many transformations of the gendered and sexed body which male creators of culture fashioned. At least in writing, Penelope was made to mean several, often contradictory things: she was virtuous, devoted, dedicated, and chaste. She could also be dishonest and flirtatious. Her tools of spindle and loom displayed a perfect wifery and womanhood, and thus Penelope could exemplify a role for women to perform. In moments of transgendering, Penelope could also be adapted as a voice for male writers. "She" becomes "he." *Penelope* is a letter by Ovid. She is a reference from Roman pasts as Juvenal writes through Laronia's voice. In these cases gender matters, but it does not constitute an absolute difference. Rather, male is not so clearly distinguished from female, and what we might call "cross-gender" identifications become possible (if we were to think from within a more rigidly oppositional notion of gender); Penelope's devotion and loyalty become Propertius's own. Other times, gender's distinctions matter very much, in very different ways. Juvenal's creation of Laronia's Penelope sets up much more rigid and oppositional notions of masculinity, femininity, and same-sex/"other"-sex sexual desire. In other words, gender and sexuality are not just appropriate (or inappropriate) roles and social performances. They form categories, divisions that are given social meaning and import. They serve as marks of difference. Taken together, these Roman Penelopes are more than just multiple interpretations of a single ancient heroine. They demonstrate a range of overlapping but different discourses on gender. They display various ways that the ancient heroine was used to shape new (and renewed) kinds of knowledge about sexual difference.

Defining gender as knowledge about sexual difference is one way to delimit—temporarily and provisionally—just what it is that is under investigation in this feminist study of rabbis, gender, and history in the period of the Roman Empire. The following definition comes from the historiographical work of Joan Scott. In her landmark 1988 collection of essays, the term "gender"

> means knowledge about sexual difference. I use knowledge, following Michel Foucault, to mean the understanding produced by cultures and societies of human relationships, in this case those between men and women. Such knowledge is not absolute or true, but always relative. It is produced in complex ways within large epistemic frames that themselves have an (at least quasi-) autonomous history. Its uses and meanings become contested politically and are the means by which relationships of power—of domination and subordination—are constructed. *Knowledge refers not only to ideas but to institutions and structures, everyday practices as well as specialized rituals, all of which constitute social relationships.* Knowledge is a way of ordering the world; as such it is not prior to social organization, it is inseparable from social organization.
>
> It follows then that *gender is the social organization of sexual difference.* But this does not mean that gender reflects or implements fixed and natural physical differences between women and men; rather gender is the knowledge that establishes meanings for bodily differences.[17]

Much study of women in antiquity and women in ancient religions has focused on the images that remain of these women. It has inquired into the structural oppressions that shaped women's lives and has found examples of female resistance to masculinist culture. It has examined the status of women in different regions or communities and has focused on the literary and cultural constructions of female bodies. Scott's formulations push historians of women, gender, and religious culture to examine ancient societies and ask how notions of gender were produced. This definition stresses the ways that gender is integral to other relationships of power. With some debts to Foucault, Scott's writing makes it impossible to look at society and history and see any stable male and female subjects that predate the social expression of masculinity and femininity. Scott challenges assertions that these are stable or essential qualities in humans. In an antiessentialist move with which I am aligned, male and female are wrested from conceptualizations that would tie gender to biological difference, since the privilege and meaning accorded to biology are themselves part of gender and not prior to it. Scott's formulation also interrupts commonly held notions in which gendered bodies are imagined to hold stable meanings. Instead, it points us toward the variety of knowledge—institutions and structures, everyday practices as well as specialized rituals—through which meanings of gender are stabilized. Again, gender is not simply how men or women perform being different from each other; rather, gender is that which "establishes meanings for bodily differences" in the first place. This kind of definition pushes us beyond looking at static images and ambiguous assessments of women's status. Instead of stressing any essential necessity of gender, it points out gender's contingency and evitability. It makes it possible to search antiquity for those mechanisms that made certain notions of masculinity and femininity—and the differences between the two—seem persuasive, ordinary, and natural.

Writings about Penelope were one way that gendered knowledges were produced in Roman antiquity, in the regions and societies that surrounded the Mediterranean. I use "knowledges" as an explicitly plural form precisely because different knowledges about gender and sexuality circulated simultaneously. These circulated between and within regions, groups, classes, cities, and towns. It seems that whereas multiple knowledges circulated, certain notions and knowledges were privileged over others. Privileged knowledges had more influence and authority, and proffered greater cultural pressures. I use the plural "knowledges" to resist suggesting that there was one singular hegemonic gender culture in "the Roman world," or (moving toward the specific focus of this book) "the world of early rabbinic Judaism and Roman Palestine." Especially when I turn to study the texts of rabbis and other Jews from Roman Palestine, I read these texts from an ethos that recognizes multiple notions of gender, and looks for both their texture and contests. One recurring problem will be to resist flattening out differences of power and influence among these differing conceptions and practices of gender. Although it is attractive to find either ancient utopias or dystopias for women, in most cases we are stuck with relatively little evidence to support either, or any other, broad answer. And so close, careful, and critically creative readings of ancient evidence are in order.

Assessing the distribution of ancient knowledges helps to establish a discourse, or discourses, of gender. The example of Penelope shows that these knowledges were distributed visually—among landscapes, monuments, and household decorations—as well as through writing, speaking, reading, and hearing the languages of travelogue, poetry, and prose. These texts might have been read—or heard during their recitation—at places ranging from schools to dinner banquets. Penelope—and many of Homer's characters—would have been well known to educated schoolchildren, mostly boys, and the adults they grew to be. Homer's texts were used pedagogically, memorized by students in Mediterranean regions such as Palestine where Hellenistic culture became and remained important. Homer's characters were a kind of cultural *lingua franca* in the Roman Empire. Accused of elitism, Stoic philosophers would refer to lines from Homer "to show that their philosophy accorded with the common conception of people," and Homeric poems were used as textbooks for learning Greek up into the Byzantine period.[18]

If Jews living in Palestine had available to them a Roman culture of gender, as well as a newly forming rabbinic one, they also had a set of meanings associated with spinners and weavers from their legacy of biblical texts. These were known and repeated in an array of languages beside the original Hebrew. Biblical books included stories such as the wife depicted in Proverbs 31, who works at her spinning well into the night, or the curse leveled by David against the House of Joab, afflicting it with sons who will spin (2 Samuel 3.29).

Pasts are gendered, in several senses and in multiple layers. Pasts are gendered by virtue of the practices that were part of the societies and places under study. And pasts are gendered through the constructs, narratives, and tropes that are used to make those pasts into "history"—into our expressions and reflections. In this second way, the making and telling of history is another site for the production of gendered knowledges.[19] Thus, in the relations of Romans with Greeks, the relations of Roman-period Jews with other aspects of Roman culture, the relations of Roman-period Jews with their biblical and Hellenistic legacies, and in our relations with ancient Romans and Jews, there is always a double (at least) gendering at work: the gendered knowledges in the "sources," and the gendered knowledges and desires—as well as the gender—of the modern reader/scholar, who crafts these "sources" into a history of gender culture. In all cases, the gendering of each reader and layer is at the same time similar, different, and overlapping, and all of these are necessary subjects of inquiry. As we study how "they" produced gender in history, gender is produced as well for our time.

STORIES ABOUT SPINNERS AND WEAVERS

Stories about spinners and weavers—men and women who were, among other things, trustworthy matrons, promiscuous wives and daughters, reliable witnesses, thrifty single women, ragtag rebellion leaders, and pious men spinning ritual fringes—are not the only way to tell stories about gender in Roman and Jewish antiquity. But they are a starting point. Spinning and weaving were simultaneously tasks done as everyday work, and cultural images that proffered social meaning. Looking at spinning and weaving in Roman and Jewish culture, then, is to find examples of how gender was made to work, and to find out how gender was made *at* work, as part, parcel, and product of some of the most ongoing, continual, and repetitive acts that human beings do. Traces of women and telltale signs of gender's construction can be found in the fragments of texts and artifacts that remain of Jewish life in Roman Palestine during the first three centuries C.E. Traces remain of the details of femininity and of masculinity; of gender's production, reproduction, repetition, and reiteration; and of the contests and questions over gender's definition. But finding these traces means learning how to look and to see. It means learning to read fragments. These traces and signs are found articulated in written texts, as social performances, and otherwise as tacit and unarticulated knowledge. Examining the fragments of antiquity, the distinction between written and other texts starts to fade, as it should when considering societies whose modes of literacy were quite different from our own. The word "text" expands beyond a meaning that privileges writing. "Text" refers to the many places where social imagination and practice are articulated: law, literature, tools, clothing, media, burial sites, art, economic and legal documents, architecture, and much more. All of these things conveyed social and cultural meanings to any number of ancient people. It is a modern conceit to divide and segment evidence into distinct subjects of study, and these divisions seem at odds with ancient experiences that would not so easily have separated the meanings of things.

Gender was made in all these places and in all sorts of ways. Produced at many sites, gender eludes the division of society and culture into rubrics such as law, social roles, literary representations, art, and divisions of labor. Performance, too, is crucial to gender's repetition. Performances of ritualized activity and everyday life—(and this distinction too will start to disappear as the chapters unfold)—are gendered. These performances, and the viewing of ordinary and extraordinary performances, are themselves social texts. Both written language and daily performance were, and are, key sites for the production of gender, and are not as separate as their distinction here would suggest. Both as social contest and as repetition, traces of gender become visible within individual texts or when various texts are examined together. In some texts, traces of gender are apparent and overt; others must be read against their grain, or against their many grains. In different combinations and read with different types of critical tools, these textual remnants from Roman Palestine provide clues to how early rabbis made bodies into genders, and crafted gender into "sense."

From Roman-period Judaism, stories about spinners and weavers are found scattered throughout the Mishnah and Tosefta—the extensive religio-legal texts produced by rabbis in Galilee in the late second and third centuries—and in the midrash that was produced contemporaneously. In the form of archaeological artifacts, they are found among the grave goods buried with the dead in Palestine and in funerary epitaphs in Asia Minor. They reside in archaeological deposits of tools, in the work of travel writers such as Pausanias who recorded their visits to Palestine, in imperial documents, in multivolume treatises on technology such as Pliny's *Historia Naturalis,* in papyrus contracts for cloaks and blankets, and in manuals for the interpretation of dreams. These stories may be read in Hebrew, Aramaic, Latin, and Greek writings transmitted from antiquity through generations of scribes, as well as in texts and artifacts buried in antiquity and uncovered centuries later. Reading these different types of evidence in various relations with each other has another effect. The find sites, to use an archaeological term, of these stories and icons level some of the differences of authority between privileged and canonical texts on the one hand and those considered popular and common. While today and for centuries the Mishnah and other rabbinic texts hold special status among some Jews, and carry respect from others, in the second century these were texts in process. Even upon its publication, or promulgation, in the early third century, the Mishnah remained in the domain of a small circle of relatively uninfluential rabbis in Galilee. Conversely, twentieth-century archaeologists emphasize the monumental finds and relegate small artifacts—"minor objects"—such as spindles, spindle whorls, and loom parts to low priority. Yet small tools such as these were crucial in the Roman period. They facilitated the production of material resources at the same time that they conferred popularly known, variable, but widespread meanings of gender and other relations of power.

Telling stories about spinners and weavers in Roman and Jewish antiquity is no easy task. Stories about spinners and weavers were stories about women and men and about various kinds of social relations. Simultaneously, metaphors of spinning and weaving were used as
tropes—or repeated patterns—in writing, thought, argument, and the
production of texts. Abstracted from male and female bodies, tropes of
spinning and weaving became stories about the telling of stories. An example from Cicero makes the point. In the *Academica* (2.95) Penelope's
unweaving of the web is a metaphor in an argument against a mode of
doing science that destroys at the end the steps that came before. That
is, in Cicero's terms, Penelope's weaving is the sign of "bad science."[20]
Representing bad science with Penelope's unweaving marks its badness
as feminine. In contrast, "good" scientific practice, and hence "science"
itself as well as the category of trustworthy knowledge, become masculine. In rabbinic texts later than the Mishnah, the image of the distaff
is the vivid emblem of the separate wisdom of women, of the difference
of female knowledge from that of men; and the woven cloth on a loom
provides the general title *masseket* for the talmudic tractates.[21] Stories
about spinners and weavers do many kinds of cultural work, and part
of that work entails making various kinds of ideas into gendered practices.

EARLY RABBINIC AND ROMAN-PERIOD JUDAISM

In a book that calls attention to the gendering and constructedness of
history, it would be disingenuous to simply narrate an historical background of Jews and Judaism in Roman Palestine to serve as a context
for an inquiry into gender culture. First of all, the term "background"
has a particularly problematic history with regard to the study of Judaism in the first few centuries.[22] In scholarly accounts, studies of Judaism
in this period were often framed as background for the development of
Christianity. Second, the relation between background and foreground
shifts, depending on what we want to know. And furthermore, the
background that could be provided would rely on reconstructions of
the period that ignore female experiences. The problem with the currently available accounts of Judaism in these centuries is that few consider women's lives, reflect on how gender mattered, or analyze men's
lives and religion as specifically male, not as universal Jewish experiences applicable to all. Hence nearly all of what could be used as background knowledge is itself in need of reconsideration. At the same, it

would also be dishonest to pretend not to want to be able to offer a straightforward history of this moment and place in time. In the midst of this tension, I suggest one way to start reconsidering the period of the Roman centuries in the history of Judaism.[23]

Discussions of history are anchored around notions of periods. Hence, the names and divisions of these periods of time are clues to the starting assumptions from which written history is crafted. In the regions inland of the Mediterranean's Eastern shore, Jews lived (and rabbis produced their texts) in various relations to Rome, that is, to Roman culture, as this might have been experienced from the perspective of the provinces. Rabbinic writings were produced in environments shaped by direct Roman rule, by people who had relations both with the bureaucracy of Rome and with the idea of Rome. Relations with aspects of Rome were part of the lives of Jews in Roman Palestine, and thus are necessary parts of our discussions of their lives. In studying the gender culture of this period, these relations must be foregrounded. Setting aside more commonplace and traditional names for the period in the history of Jewish religion and culture, I use the moniker "Roman-period Judaism."

One traditional name for the period that includes Judaism in the first few centuries is "Greco-Roman Judaism." This name is problematic for several reasons, the first being that it conflates at least eight centuries of changing Mediterranean culture into something more singular. The name Greco-Roman functions in similar ways as does the more modern term Judeo-Christian. Both terms efface the differences within. Judeo-Christian effaces the "Judeo" and elides it too easily and seamlessly into the "Christian," invoking a supercessionist narrative in which Judaism ends with the advent of Christianity.[24] Although the order of the terms "Greco" and "Roman" are reversed, a similar elision happens. The "Roman" is elided into the "Greco," erasing the Roman in favor of the Greek, which Western thought regards as the more original and innovative culture. Within the narratives that have come to shape our visions of the ancient world, Rome is widely regarded as a cultural copycat which mimicked and repeated the Greek "masterpieces" that had preceded them in time. Thus, the nomenclature of Greco-Roman Judaism seems also to contain an element that favors origins. This element has its own origins in Enlightenment-based practices for the study of Judaism, where a Euro-Christian privileging of moments of origin came into use as a framework to study Judaism, despite the visible lack of fit.

The second term used to describe Judaism of the first few centuries is "talmudic (or rabbinic) Judaism." This term is sometimes used as the opposite of Greco-Roman Judaism. This usage would separate a more "pure" form of talmudic (or rabbinic) Judaism from what is seen as a more syncretic, adulterated, Hellenized Judaism. The problems that inhere in the need to posit this kind of purity should be apparent to most readers. This naming evaluates a religion based on a standard that grants a privileged status given to "the pure," as opposed to studying ancient Judaism in ways that allow us to see syncretic practices. Conceptions of religion as pure contain a devaluation of what is deemed syncretic, "a term of disapprobation denoting the confused mixing of religions."[25] Historically speaking, this conceptualization can ignore the adoption of Roman and Greek gestures into rabbinic Judaism, and hence can miss seeing ways that Jews interacted with a range of cultural possibilities in forming their own practices. Using the term "talmudic Judaism" as a description of Judaism in the first six centuries C.E. also makes nonrabbinic Jews disappear from history. Although the vast majority of written evidence transmitted to the modern period was produced by rabbinic Jews, a wider range of Jews and Jewish practice existed as well. This diversity of Jews disappears from historical accounts of the past conceptualized as "talmudic Judaism."[26]

Problems with this term continue. Meant to describe the first six centuries, it invokes the term "talmudic" for centuries where most Jews would not have known what a Talmud was, since the documents themselves were not finished until at least the fourth century. It takes a text whose influence and authority were not felt by most Jews until much later and refracts earlier Jewish history through this lens. As a result, a religious unity is created where none existed.[27] Furthermore, the term "talmudic Judaism" erases material conditions and region. Where were these talmudic Jews, one must ask. The term erases the differences between Palestine and Babylon, the two main centers for rabbinic Judaism. It imposes a false unity that forecloses investigating very real differences between various rabbis, Jews, and their communities. It forecloses asking how material conditions matter, how place and neighbors make a difference. It also suggests that Judaism comes entirely from Jews, that as a religious culture and cultural practice Judaism is not ever formed in reaction to others.

The phrase "Roman-period Judaism" emphasizes some of the material conditions within which Judaism emerged anew in Palestine after the destruction of the Jerusalem Temple. This broader name assumes that the religion of the rabbis was one of many different forms of Judaism. It decenters the assumption that early rabbis and rabbinic Judaism were central to Judaism in the second and third centuries, even in Palestine. It leaves room for considering other forms of Jewish practice, discourse, and culture, even if remarkably less evidence remains for these. This seems important: both "talmudic Judaism" and "rabbinic Judaism" are names that are used to describe contemporary practices and ideological conceptions of Judaism. Their current use forges a connection between present and past in Jewish religiosity. In such a situation, their use to describe part of a Jewish past masks contention and conflict. And, the use of the same names to describe both present and classical forms of Judaism makes it too easy to forget that—in a modification of Kalman Bland's efficacious title "Medievals Are Not Us"—ancient rabbis are not "us."[28] Framing this study as Roman-period Judaism enables (but of course does not ensure) seeing the time, conditions, and people of early rabbinic Judaism and Roman Palestine as different from our own.

Since the available terms contain so many assumptions or references that are problematic, I use the phrase "Roman-period Judaism." This name is not perfect. It does not resolve questions of the relation of Jews, Judaism, and Jewish culture in Palestine to Rome so much as it puts them up for reconsideration. The term does enable a more pointed acknowledgment of how imperial Rome might have mattered in the history of Judaism. After all, if the Mishnah was edited and promulgated by Judah ha-Nasi, then it becomes significant that rabbinic stories also make him the man who represents the Jews to Rome. This early form of what would become classical rabbinic Judaism emerged in close, although complicated, relation to imperial Rome and its culture and in relation to a Roman legal tradition that, like that of the early rabbis, also emerged during the second century.

Hence, the emphasis is on the "Rome" in Roman-period Judaism, but with a difference.[29] Traditionally, histories of Judaism emphasize the increasingly direct control of Rome over Palestine, from the march of Pompey to Jerusalem's gates in 63 B.C.E. to the First Jewish Revolt, to the appearance of additional legions in the late first or early second century, and to the reorganization of Palestine as a province attached to the domain of the governor in Syria. Also emphasized and studied are Jewish military resistances to Roman rule, in the form of the rebellions against Rome: the First Jewish Revolt of 66–73, the Diaspora Revolt of 115, and the Second Jewish Revolt of 132–135. Yet, the inquiries I have in mind are about how the relation of rabbis and Jews to the

Roman Empire's culture framed their concerns with society, family, and religion during a time when many of these things were up for question. For instance, Romans claimed that their organization of the family made them unique in all the world. In light of Roman use of family to sustain a notion of cultural uniqueness that was simultaneously augmented by the social status of the Empire, we can see early rabbinic prescriptions for family relations as a definition of Jewishness within the setting of imperial culture. Especially after the early third century, the rabbis in Palestine were simultaneously a subaltern class and a local elite with loyalties to Roman bureaucracy. While many of these questions may remain unresolved, these shifts will open up new areas for study. For example, it becomes possible to ask how—within these emerging relations—rabbinic texts from Roman Palestine may have used the bodies of Jewish women to negotiate and imagine their relation to Rome.

Recognizing the Rome in Roman-period Judaism has a converse effect: recognizing the Jews and Judaism in both the Roman Empire and in the modern meanings of Rome. Rome reentered the modern West through the writings of Enlightenment philosophers searching for a usable past for a new Europe. Replacing the legacy of the Christian medieval period with this "pagan" antiquity became a popular mode of writing about the past, although Enlightenment-based scholarship continued an interest in Christian history. At least one result of this remains with us: the tendency to ignore the Roman Empire's different ethnic and religious groups.[30] Although new scholarship attends more carefully to the regions and culture of the entire Mediterranean, including Africa and the East, it is still the case that these are marginalized. Seeing the Rome in Roman-period Judaism also means seeing the Jews in the Roman Empire, and is part of a revisioning of antiquity that narrates the Empire with tales of its minorities.[31] Furthermore, by emphasizing the place of Jews in the Roman Empire, the history of Jews can be imagined as one of many possible histories of Palestine, a region in which Jews were but one of many groups and people who lived there during the era of the Roman Empire.

As a change from the expected, the renaming elicits some questions and reflections. I suggest Roman-period Judaism as a temporary title for a historical time and place for Judaism and Jewish culture. The name change points out some political and religious commitments of prior scholarly research in this field, and brings some new interpretive possibilities to the fore. Jewish history and the history of Jewish religion have been organized into periods that begin and end with military events: the monarchy in Jerusalem, the Exile to Babylon, the return to Yehud, the Hasmonean (Maccabean) rule, the entrance of Pompey into Jerusalem, the reign of Herod the Great, and the destruction of the Second Temple. Although religion and culture and social change are interrelated, periods based exclusively on military and political events force the study of religion and culture into uncomfortable, predetermined boxes. For example, the growth of early rabbinic Judaism is often narrated as emerging out of, and responding to, the catastrophic loss of Jerusalem and the Temple in 70 C.E. Yet, perspective matters a great deal: the destruction of the Temple, the cessation of offerings and sacrifice, and the displacement of the priesthood would have entailed many and multiple things to different Jews in Judea and/or Palestine, and to Jews living throughout the regions of the Mediterranean. The destruction of the Jerusalem Temple forced major changes to Judaism. The Temple was the legitimate place for Jews to bestow offerings and sacrifices through the priests to their God, to celebrate festivals, atone for sins, and mark other events in their lives. For many of its priests, the destruction of the Temple meant the end of the institution and rituals that provided them with their power and influence, and we can imagine, provided them with their most immediate and familiar sense of relation with the divine and with other Jews. Yet, this version of the origins of rabbinic Judaism not only erases women's experiences, it flattens out very real differences among Jews in the first century. For example, not all priests agreed equally that the Jerusalem Temple was the legitimate center for Jewish ritual life, as witnessed by the challenges of those who settled at Qumran or those priests who organized temples such as that at Heliopolis that were also devoted to a Jewish God.

The narration of the Temple's destruction as despair often moves quickly to Judaism's rebirth as the religion, ritual, and halakah (or, law) of the early rabbis (Tannaim). As Baruch Bokser observed: "It is a commonplace that rabbinic Judaism heightened the importance of extra-Temple practices such as prayer, charity, and acts of loving kindness as part of a response to the destruction of the Second Temple and the end of the sacrificial system."[32] However, interest in these ancient disasters is rendered more resonant through the highly charged remembrance of modern disasters for Jews, in particular the genocide of European Jews in 1939–1945. The ancient atrocities are highlighted, and made to stand in for, concern with more recent events.[33] Writing the history of Judaism in the ancient world has been entirely enmeshed in a range of social and political and cultural desires, whether this has been conscious or less than conscious.

But when the period after the Temple's devastation in 70 C.E. is explained with recourse to the theology of genocide, as is common, the powerful metaphors of rupture and destruction tend to obscure more mundane and local responses. The narration of a history of Judaism "from Temple to Tannaim," from one form of Judaism dominated by men to another, leaves little room for asking how these changes might have mattered to women. It misses asking how constructions of gender figure in historical and popular narratives about this time, or for querying how in this shift gender was used and reconfigured, placing women in new relationships vis-à-vis men, and vis-à-vis Judaism.[34] The destruction of the Jerusalem Temple and the ending of ritual sacrifices and offerings directly interrupted the lives of only certain groups of Jews, men mostly, priests, Levites, and those laborers who depended on the Temple and its pilgrimage trade for their livelihood. Outside of Judea, the destruction of the Temple and the cessation of sacrifices meant different things. For some it may have seemed like a rupture to the sense of a sacred center. More materially, the possibility of making pilgrimage on the thrice-annual festivals ceased. The half-shekel Temple tax incumbent upon Jewish men was replaced by the Imperial tax to Jupiter Capitolinus, and male Jews might have noticed this bureaucratic change in the tax's collection and destination.

But what becomes visible when we privilege the daily lives of women and men as a standpoint for thinking about the period 70–250 C.E. in Jewish history and the history of Palestine? Whereas the destruction of the Temple will figure prominently, we can surmise that Jews in Palestine would have noticed other types of changes. They might have noticed that the name of their region was changed from Judea to Palaestina and that it was made part of the province of Syria-Palaestina. They may or may not have known that the equestrian governor was replaced by a man of the senatorial class. Most Jews would likely have noticed the increased Roman military presence in many but not all areas of Palestine. Jews and other inhabitants of the region would have experienced the construction or improvement of roads by Roman soldiers, and the new links these provided between cities and towns. They might have heard or passed along news of the intrigues at Caesarea, or at Damascus, or talked about sightings and experiences with Roman soldiers. They would have seen or heard about the installation of a new legion and its various *cohors* at nearby military outposts. They might have served soldiers at local inns or gotten to know the soldiers billeted at their homes through the onus of *hospitium*.

In 71 and the years and decades that followed, changes in Jewish life ensued. Cues for thinking about these changes arise by posing very specific scenarios. For instance, what did a man and his son do on the festival of Sukkot once they could no longer make their way among the throngs of people gathering at the Jerusalem Temple? And what did a woman devoted to practices of ritual purity do after childbirth to replace the ritual of sending her husband to Jerusalem with a sacrificial turtle dove? How did priestly families maintain themselves without a constant supply of *terumot* entering the Temple and their dinner tables? What new economies replaced the substantial ones that had surrounded the Temple, its tourism, and its ongoing construction projects? But amid changes and uncertainties such as these, there were also continuities, such as Sabbaths, Holy Days, certain ritual practices of kashrut, and meetings for prayer and reciting biblical passages. For Jews living in Palestine, some things changed while others stayed the same. The critical question is, what happens when we set aside terms that demand one thing or its opposite ("rupture" or "continuity"), and allow that society, religion, economy, and community, and the meanings associated with all of these, both change and remain the same, and that these things may be perceived and represented in complicated ways? And since our evidence from this period is always mediated by texts, we must ask what things "stayed the same" but were understood by the sources upon which we rely as having changed. What changed but was represented nonetheless as unchanging, and as always present?

GENDERING THE ORDINARY

When you get right down to it, both religion and culture are slippery concepts, and it is tempting to look for them in what is big, monumental, extraordinary, special.[35] It is tempting—and in some ways necessary—to look for gender and notice its most visible manifestations in egregious displays of sympathy and empathy; in instances of misogyny, privileging of men, and structural oppressions of women; or in examples of women who entered domains and roles that were usually defined as belonging to men. An initial feminist study of Jewish women in these centuries was Bernadette Brooten's *Women Leaders in the Ancient Synagogue* (1982). From the evidence of inscriptions, Brooten argued for women's roles as leaders in some synagogues and Jewish communities. Her groundbreaking research located women among positions of religious and communal leadership that, for centuries, scholars and others have argued were occupied solely by men. Brooten found evidence that placed women inside the synagogue and participating in its rituals. Using the excavated evidence from synagogues of the Roman and Byzantine periods, she argued against the belief that in these centuries women at worship were separated from men through a special gallery. Placing this archaeological evidence alongside early rabbinic passages that also located women in these synagogues, Brooten's work forced a critical reimagination of ancient synagogues as places that included both women and men. While the evidence for women's leadership was not widespread but limited to a few synagogues and communities, Brooten's work interrupted prior assumptions that communal leadership was solely the domain of men.[36] Other scholars, too, began in the 1980s to find and include information about women, especially in books whose focus was social history. Yet, these books often treated women as extra or additional. While women were included, they were still marginal to the history being told.[37] Their presence did not change the kinds of questions asked about Judaism and Jewish communities in the Roman period. Some information about women's lives was included, but scholars did not query the terms or limits of these inclusions, nor did they use new information about women to question the critical practices of the scholarly field. The historical studies by Brooten and by Ross Kraemer were produced alongside literary and textual studies of rabbinic writings. Work by Judith Hauptman, Judith Baskin, Daniel Boyarin, and Judith Romney Wegner catalogued images of women, analyzed these, drew differing assessments on the status of women in rabbinic traditions, and in the case of Wegner, investigated the categorization of women in early rabbinic law.[38] Much of this historical and literary research provides a context for this book, which is perched on a boundary that connects historical, literary, textual, and archaeological study.

However, gender can be most powerful in its ordinariness, in things that become common, nearly invisible, until they seem to be natural. Walter Benjamin, in the passage used as an epigraph to this introduction, provides one of many possible starting points for thinking about gender and the ordinary. In this passage from "The Storyteller," Benjamin highlights the ideological power of repetition. Stories are told and retold during events that are themselves repetitive. It is during the rhythm of work that stories are told, again and again, to listeners who become self-forgetful. Storytelling, and the circulation of culture, happen within modes of production. Stories are told by spinners as they spin, by weavers as they weave, by workers as they work. Stories are cradled in webs, as Benjamin invokes a long-standing tradition in which images of textile production become metaphors for culture. Work is a mode of production of culture, as it produces talk, tales, notions, beliefs, and other conversations. Stories are neither told nor heard in isolation. They are not necessarily heard consciously. They happen not as special or extraordinary moments, but are embedded in the ordinary. Spoken and heard, stories come tangled with other intersecting stories, visions, and tales. They are heard in different ways, in various combinations, states of consciousness, degrees of attention, wholly or in fragments. They take place amid, and as part of, what is ordinary and banal, ubiquitous and mundane.

Images of spinners and weavers, their products and their qualities, appear in the niches, corners, and crannies of early rabbinic writing. They pop up, sometimes unexpectedly. A spindle whorl evokes the size of a fetus's head, or a spindle thrust into a wall becomes an example of distances over which a movable object can communicate impurities.[39] Wool shearings, bundles of combed flax, and strips of purple wool become examples of finds that must be proclaimed publicly, in hopes of alerting the owners and enabling their return.[40] The tasks of textile production are counted as twelve of thirty-nine acts prohibited on the Sabbath (Shabbat 7.2, 13.1–4). The tools involved become part of rabbinic discussions of how impurities were transmitted: into and through flax combs, dyers' gloves and woven cloth, spindle whorls, thread, and loom parts. And worker's bodies are examined: a woman in *niddah*—menstrual impurity—spins flax, and men with genital fluxes weave together using different types of looms.[41] These recurring images are neither dramatic nor prominent. Yet, taking a cue from Benjamin, their very ordinariness and seeming meaninglessness is what calls attention.

Images of spinning and weaving also appear when rabbis write about women, work, sexuality, and femininity. Wool work becomes an icon of matronly domesticity, as Rabbi Eliezer opines that a married woman must always perform her wool work, even if she had sufficient slaves or servants to do the work for her. Skeins of spun wool measure the work that a wife must do for her husband, and specific terms distinguish between the necessary number of lighter woof threads from the heavier yarn for the horizontal warp. Elsewhere a woman spins in the *shuk*, or marketplace, in the presence and vision of onlookers, as this act of public spinning is placed among those things which allow the woman's husband to divorce her without a *ketubbah* payment (marriage settlement).

Metaphors for work were simultaneously metaphors for sexuality. Yet, our tendency *not to see* how work is simultaneously a gendered and sexed category makes it difficult to talk about work and sexuality in tandem. Work, sexuality, and gender were integrally linked in the Roman-influenced antiquity of which early rabbis were a part. Seeing these things as imbricated—by which I mean things that intersect, are intertwined, and hence not reducible from each other—also signals a renewed concern within and for feminist theory, a return to consider a way not taken in recent research. In 1979, Joan Kelly argued for the necessity of seeing *"the simultaneous operation* of relations of work and sex, relations that are systematically bound to each other—and always have been so bound" (58). Since the early 1980s, feminist research has moved away from considering work, labor, and women's working bodies. Bodies are not only about sex and gender. Rather, in Roman-period Jewish culture, sex, and gender and labor and work were intimately entangled.[42]

Ironically, studying gender and examining the ordinary takes rabbis partially at their word. Early rabbinic writings concentrate in part on what is ordinary, on the details of what is ostensibly uninteresting. They sacralize the ordinary by making it part of a life lived by halakah. Biblical mitzvot (commandments) were expanded into a myriad of everyday rites and relations. This element of early rabbinic Judaism understood the power of embedding religious ideology in the mundane and repetitive events of daily life. They showed an awareness of the significance power of the minutiae of everyday life, even if early rabbinic writers would not quite have described themselves in this way.

Because the ordinary too is a cultural product—it is never a neutral backdrop or background—I look not just for the gender in the ordinary but for the gendering of the ordinary. In other words, how was ordinariness crafted into gendered experience? Sometimes the study of everyday life in antiquity is used as a background that would enable a fuller and richer reading of ancient religious texts. Yet, in this book, the everyday is not a background but a cultural product in its own right. Here, I am following Henri Lefebvre, although with a change. Lefebvre writes that "the everyday is a product . . . the most universal, and the most unique condition, the most social and the most individuated, the most obvious and the best hidden."[43] However, Lefebvre excludes labor (as well as religion) from these social experiences of everyday life. The notion of everyday life in my investigation of Roman Palestine includes labor as part of what is habitual and repetitive. Modes of production—work, labor, economy, religion—matter, these daily activities that consume much of the time of most people. The perpetual presence, practice, and constant (re)valuation of work is a prime part of what I consider "ordinary." Like gender, work itself is constituted in part through stories told and retold, about the work itself and in the course of working. Work is not background. Work is not limited to a description of occupation, a demographic portrait. It is a signifier that engages the ordinary in other ordinary and extraordinary meanings. And as a signifier, the meaning of work is never simple, stable, or unchanging. As much as everyday life is a cultural product in its own right, it is at the same time a site for the construction of regional, religious, and sexual difference(s) and similarities. If everyday life, work, and gender are imbricated and entangled, then neither of these can be used as an explanation of the other. The practical ramifications of this point will become increasingly clear and significant as the chapters of this book progress. Neither category is prior to the others, and all were sites for early rabbinic imagination. Thus, conditions of everyday life cannot be used as a functional explanation for certain legal innovations regarding the relations of women and men. Nor can references to "preexisting" relations of gender be used to explain rabbinic representations of the everyday. Although conceptually difficult, it will be necessary to imagine and to investigate the gendering of the ordinary as a process entangled in making gender ordinary.

MAKING GENDER

This book is about how the early rabbis used fantasies about spinning and the spinning of fantasy to make gender into sense. In the economy of Roman Palestine, the production of wool and linen textiles ranked among the region's top few industries, along with the production of olive oil and wine.[44] Weaving and spinning were but two stages in the process of textile production. In different ways, Jews in Roman Palestine performed these acts, wrote about them, saw them done, talked about them, imagined them, heard about them. In understanding and producing their cultural world through these things—and of course in combination with many other things—social meanings of gender were naturalized, made to seem familiar, commonplace, natural, expected, and very, very ordinary.

Gender was one of the major changes wrought within Judaism in the century that followed the destruction of the Temple and the displacement of its priesthood. From different angles, the following chapters examine various combinations of evidence. Each engages these traces of gender and antiquity with different critical tools, as a way to think about how female and male humans were imagined in early rabbinic Judaism and in other, perhaps intersecting, formulations of Roman-period Judaism. Together, these chapters demonstrate that Jews in Roman Palestine lived amid a gendered landscape. Following the Judean revolts against the Roman Empire, and within a cultural environment that included both Rome and other Jews, rabbis in Roman Palestine created, altered, and gave new and renewed meanings to gender and its differences. They did so in ways that were complicated, changing, contested, as well as occasionally contradictory. It is to these complexities that I now turn.

CHAPTER ONE

Patriarchy's Ordinariness

Rightfully and passionately, we feminist scholars of religions argue back and forth about where to look for women, men, and gender. Do we seek new sources from outside the classical traditions transmitted by male hands and elite interests? Can we find archaeological artifacts, and when we do, what is it that we are finding? Do we look to the few and fragmentary samples of writing by women? To papyrus documents that detail some of the legal and economic transactions of specific women? To rituals performed by women alone, or by women along with men? Do we survey traditions that are sacred and canonical and which, for the most part, privilege men? And when we scrutinize these traditions, what do we look for, and how do we look? Do we proffer examples of misogyny, sexism, and other gender-based oppression of women? Probe for systemic gender hierarchies? Highlight moments of sympathy? Do we sketch the familiarities of the quotidian? Locate ironies? Note male projections of women? Find moments when women resisted oppression, with the knowledge that these moments come to us mostly through the writings of the men they were resisting in the first place? Do we examine polemics of gender, list roles for men and women, show transgressions, trace moments of gender fluidity? Do we demonstrate gender's constructedness—and its contingency? Do we show the intellectual habits that have structured how we interpret and explain evidence? Do we want to find heroines and role models for the present, metaphors for the future? Or undermine common beliefs that gender is inevitable?

And, choosing any combination of these strategies, do we tell happy
stories? Horror stories? Both? All?[1]

A passage from the mishnaic tractate Ketubot offers a starting point
for working through these questions. The earliest rabbinic legal texts
were produced by rabbis in Palestine around the turn of the third century. These writings—the Mishnah and slightly later, the Tosefta—
were put together several decades after the end of difficult relations between the Roman Empire and its Jews. In the Jewish revolt of 66–70
C.E., the Jewish Temple in Jerusalem was destroyed and its aristocratic
and priestly ruling class sundered. Another revolt, centered in Judaea in
the years 132–135 C.E., also resulted in Roman victory. Rabbinic Judaism is a Jewish tradition that developed in Palestine in the aftermath
of these revolts against Rome. By the late second century, relations between Rome and Palestinian Jews had calmed, but the Empire itself was
embroiled in ongoing tensions. Imperial succession was hotly contested,
military prowess faltered, and the earlier desire to expand Rome's borders gave way to attempts to defend what territory the Empire already
held.[2] Outliving its reputation as a hotspot of Roman military attention, by the turn of the third century Palestine and its inhabitants faded
as a problem for Rome. Both Jews and the region of Palestine also fade
from the attention of ancient chroniclers. One result of this is that much
remains unknown, barely known, or unknowable. Little is known with
much certainty about the lives of Palestine's women and men, about
the circles of rabbis who produced the Mishnah and Tosefta, about its
Christian communities, about people who were not part of the Jewish,
Christian, or Jewish-Christian communities, about the individual rabbis and others who appear in early rabbinic texts.

According to rabbinic tales of their origins, the Mishnah was edited
by Judah ha-Nasi in Sepphoris, a small Roman city on the southern
edge of Galilee, whose population included Romans, Christians, and
Jews. Still under excavation, year after year more of Sepphoris is dug
from the dirt. Although Sepphoris was a small city, it was well connected with other parts of the eastern Mediterranean, and with the Empire. The excavated city reveals a Romanized culture, with a theater of
major proportions, and well-planned city sections and roads. Its everyday art included hand statues of Roman gods. Mosaic floor pavements
displayed mythological heroes, folktales, motifs of other Mediterranean cities such as Alexandria, as well as beautiful women and naked
men. Palestine and the region of Galilee were relatively unimportant to

Rome's history. But the local version of Roman culture was certainly important common knowledge for the people who lived in Sepphoris.

The Mishnah is composed of select discussions, arguments and opinions, recollections, and brief narratives. It contains infrequent references to the Bible but is built on a thorough knowledge of biblical books. The Mishnah has an authorial voice mixed with anonymous statements and with positions attributed to specific rabbis. Although it was edited in the early third century, the men who appear in the Mishnah lived in the years between the first century and the early third century.

The Mishnah contains a radically new vision for Judaism, one that developed in Palestine a century after the destruction of the Second Temple. This vision replaced the more extraordinary, visceral, and perhaps burdensome rites of the destroyed Temple with halakah, or religious law. In this law, *the everyday and the extraordinary are merged.* The Mishnah uses similar tones for the imagined world of the extinct Temple and for the equally imagined realm of the ordinary and the interpersonal. Promulgated in the early third century, the Mishnah became the basis of the talmudic commentary tradition. The Mishnah's first commentary was the Tosefta, a Palestinian text that features mostly the same group of early rabbis (called Tannaim, or "Repeaters"), and which dates (most likely) to the middle of the third century. This first commentary was followed by the two Talmuds: the Babylonian Talmud (ca. 500) and the Palestinian Talmud (ca. 400). Although it was the first finished, the Palestinian Talmud never gained the prominence and authority of the Babylonian Talmud. Eventually, rabbinic halakah became influential and authoritative for Jews. The study and explication of talmudic traditions became a ritual and social practice for literate men in some Jewish communities. Forms of rabbinic Judaism became widespread among Jews, although the details of this spread and its meaning for ordinary Jewish men and women are largely unknown. The texts that the early rabbinic circles produced in a small Roman province on the edge of the Roman Empire are usually read *now* as part of a classical tradition. But in its own time, the early rabbinic movement that produced these texts was relatively small, its influence restricted to small communities of Jews in northern Palestine.[3]

As part of a classical tradition for our world, the images of ancient rabbis and the ways to read the Talmud are both largely overdetermined. For centuries and generations since talmudic texts were composed, they were read almost entirely by men. Due to this tradition, for women and for many men, several things combine to make talmudic texts difficult or intimidating to approach: the religious authority invested in them, their mystique in a modern world, and the difficulty of talmudic modes of expression. These texts come with fairly strict traditions for reading and making sense of them. For us, these texts come with inherited paths of religious study and critical academic study, each of which carries its own possibilities, its own variety, and its own restraints. Furthermore, the Talmud is usually classified as a legal text. As such, its "legalness" can be conflated with modern Western notions of law. This association brings with it notions about the authority, inaccessibility, and "dryness" of the text. We tend to read legal texts for their directions and counsel, seeking straightforward answers to specific questions. Reading the Talmud as law privileges legal answers, in as much as it usually assumes that there is only one kind of legal reading. But why indeed should we limit legal texts to a legal reading? Why examine these texts as lawyers? All sorts of assumptions about the Talmud tend to shield it from certain questions: how its tractates work ideologically, how passages work as stories, how it became part of a naturalized ethos for everyday life, to name only a few. These inheritances preclude a whole range of critical and creative concerns about how legal texts make their meaning. Locating the contours and limitations of the available traditions for interpreting the Talmud and other ancient texts can clear some space for other ways of reading these texts to emerge.[4]

The written texts of early rabbinic Judaism are an example of what happened when an all-male Jewish elite turned its attention to the economy and relations of the everyday. Reading these we can see how this movement made certain possibilities of gender imaginable and real. One feature of everyday life—and one site for the construction of gender—was marriage between men and women. Tractate Ketubot attends to the intersection of women, men, property, and marriage. Reading the following passage slowly and closely I experiment with different kinds of feminist ways to read rabbinic texts. The text of mKetubot 8.1 translates as follows. In general, all translations are my own, unless otherwise noted. Brackets—[ ]—add words and phrases that are not in the Hebrew text but which are helpful and even necessary to make the grammatical terseness of the Hebrew comprehensible in English. Parentheses—( )—offer explanations of pronouns, contexts, and concepts that help readers new to these texts make "basic" sense of the passage;

parentheses also hold occasional transliterations (in italics) of Hebrew terms that might be of interest to more advanced readers.[5]

> Regarding the woman to whom property fell before she was betrothed: Shammai's House and Hillel's House agree that she may sell and/or give it away, and it (her act) is valid.
>
> [If property] befell her after she was betrothed: Shammai's House says she may sell, and Hillel's House says she may not sell.
>
> They (the Houses) agree that if she sold or gave it away (after she was betrothed and before she was married), it is valid.
>
> Recounted Rabbi Yehudah: They said before Rabban Gamliel: Since he (the husband) has authority over the woman, will he not have authority over the [woman's] property?
>
> He (Gamliel) said to them: Concerning the [ownership and control of] new [property] (*haḥădāšîm*) we are embarrassed [by the lack of legal justification], and you would burden us with [halakah for the ownership and control of] the old [property] (*hayĕšānîm*).
>
> [If property] befell her after she wed: Both Houses agree that if she sold it or gave it away, that the husband may take it from the hands of the buyers (since he owns and controls it and the wife had no right to sell or give it away).
>
> [If property] befell her [after betrothal but] before she wed, and she wed: Rabban Gamliel says, if she sold or gave it away (after she wed), (her act) is valid.
>
> Recounted Rabbi Hanina ben Aqabya: They said before Rabban Gamliel: Since he has authority over the woman, will he not have authority over the [woman's] property?
>
> He (Gamliel) said to them: Concerning the [ownership and control of] new [property] we are embarrassed [by the lack of legal justification], and you would burden us with [halakah for the ownership and control of] the old [property].

Mishnah Ketubot 8.1 is a legal story about a woman's relation to property, both during betrothal (the period that precedes marriage) and during her marriage.[6] But although I have introduced mKetubot 8.1 as a passage about women and their property, this is not the most accurate description. The passage is not so much "about women" as it is a compact story about male rabbis who debate the legal conditions for a woman's relation to property. Hence, the passage is really about men and property. To describe it as "about women" effaces the presence and power of the men who produced this text. It renders invisible the ideological frame that organizes the tractate's contents. In mKetubot 8.1, male rabbis argue about property. They offer various arguments to extend—or resist the extension of—a husband's privilege to own and control his wife's property. A husband's privilege could be extended in either of two ways. The first is chronological. The man's authority as a husband would begin during the betrothal period that precedes marriage. Second, his husbandly authority to own and control would be strengthened to cover additional types of his wife's property, specifically, any property she gained before their marriage. From these extensions, rabbis and other Jewish men profit. Male rabbis discuss the general extension of men's legal privileges over the women who will be their wives. Since in their Jewish societies, rabbis were also men, these extensions of male privilege would have augmented the privilege of individual rabbis. Along with other men, rabbis too would gain ownership and control over more parts of their own wives' estates.

In focusing critical attention on the men in rabbinic passages that are also about women, I do not want to let women disappear. In fact, women are part of what this passage produces. The women of mKetubot 8.1 are constructs, rabbinic fictions, one-dimensional personae named by their legal status and their relations to men. The women of mKetubot 8.1 have names like "betrothed woman" or "married woman." These female identities are first and foremost fantasies of halakah, not "real women." So, rather than searching ancient rabbinic texts for fictions of "real law" or "real women," I read this passage to show the difficulty that rabbis encountered as they made gender. I catch rabbis in the act, so to speak, of producing characters for women and men, and forming them into an economy for marriage. I find them crafting male and female humans who will fit appropriately into a rabbinic vision for Jewish marriage. This part of Ketubot reveals traces of rabbinic uncertainty, and I focus on it for this reason. As a matter of course, religio-legal texts from early rabbinic Judaism contain debates and different opinions. But the admission of uncertainty found in mKetubot 8.1 is rare, even when it functions, as I will argue, as part of a polemic to reassure rabbis and their readers that fundamental security is possible.

ON PROPERTY

Property is part of a complex set of social relations. A woman's relation to property—land, animals, metals, money, clothing, and other possessions—shifts with her legal relation to different men. Her legal potential to own and control property changes with marriage. As a wife, a woman may still *own* some kinds of property, but her *control* is curtailed. Her husband gains control over the property, and he owns the profit from most of the types of property that belongs to her. In other words, for married women, ownership is not always synonymous with control. Depending on the gender of the owner, ownership does not necessarily include control over the property that is owned.

In early rabbinic law, once a woman is married, the degree of control her husband maintains over her property depends on how her property was designated. One distinction classified property as either "new property" or "old property." New property is what a woman gains during the marriage, primarily through her own labor. This differs from property she gains from inheritance or other gifts. New property results from anything she finds, from wages she earns as a worker, or from profits on property she owns and controls. Old property refers primarily to gifts, private holdings, and family inheritances she received before she married. Old property includes gifts her family gives to her on the occasion of marriage, as well any inheritance or gift she receives during her marriage. In early rabbinic law, old property contains a further set of distinctions. When a woman marries, her property is designated as either *zon-barzel* or as *mulug*. Over *zon-barzel* property, the husband has almost absolute ownership, and he takes responsibility for its diminution or loss. With *mulug* property, the wife maintains the title. She owns the property, but the husband controls it and has usufruct (the "rights of fruit"). In more vivid terms, a married woman might own a field of olive trees, but she does not always own the harvest of olives these trees produce. Further, since the husband has usufruct (the rights to the profits from the property), he can prevent his wife from selling the property or giving it away. If his wife sells the property, he can retrieve it, since her sale interferes with his rights to profit from usufruct. A third distinction includes gifts that are given to a married woman on the condition that both the property and income are hers to own and control.[7]

Both the husband's ownership of his wife's new property, and his control of her old property designated as *mulug* were innovations of early rabbinic law. Neither are found in the Bible. Mishnah Ketubot 8.1 shows an initial moment at which rabbis formulate innovations that strengthen a husband's control over his wife's property and write these innovations into early rabbinic halakah. Mishnah Ketubot 8.1 begins

with the question of whether the husband's legal control over a
woman's property begins with betrothal (*kiddushin/erusin*) or with
marriage (*nesuin*). Its question is this: Does a man control his wife's old
property during their betrothal, or must he wait until their marriage?
Underlying this first question is another: Which legal conditions of marriage take effect at betrothal, and which must wait until the formal cere-
monies of marriage itself to take effect? These quandaries are the predicament within which the first half of mKetubot 8.1 is set. A man
betroths a woman. The woman owns old property that the man will
control upon marriage. Does he control it during their betrothal?[8]

To answer these questions mKetubot 8.1 offers several cases. Each
case elicits historical rabbinic positions. The legal history begins with
debates attributed to two pharisaic opponents from the mid-first century, the Houses of Hillel and Shammai. The first case establishes that,
potentially, a woman may own and control property. If before her betrothal a woman gained property, then her ownership of that property
includes control over it. The first-century Houses of Hillel and Shammai agree that if a woman gained property *before* she was betrothed,
then as a betrothed woman she retains control. She can sell it, give it
away, or profit from it in other ways, and her acts are legally valid. In
the next case, the betrothed woman gained property *after* her betrothal
but before the ceremony of marriage, and she wishes to sell or give it
away. Here, the Houses take different positions. Shammai's House
maintains that the betrothed woman controls her property. But Hillel's
House disagrees: the betrothed woman owns but does not control this
property. The position of Hillel's House treats the betrothed woman as
if she were already married and thus separates ownership of property
from its control.

In the third case, uncertainty about the rabbinic innovation of
extending a husband's authority prevails. If the betrothed woman sold
property or gave it away, neither House will allow the future husband
to reclaim the sold property from its new owner. Neither House will
extend the man's privilege this way. Only once he is formally married
can the husband retrieve such property. But the position is slippery, even
murky. The betrothed woman is not supposed to sell or give away property she gained during the period of betrothal (according to the House
of Hillel's position in the second case). But if she did so, her act is legally valid.

The gist of these three cases is that womanhood was conceptualized
to entail any number of changing relations between women and prop-

erty. These relations were contingent and situational. They depended upon a woman's legal relation to her husband or her father. Answers to questions about a woman's relation to property could be answered by pointing to her relation to a particular man. In this way, early rabbinic notions of gender imagined that womanhood included various relations to property. But twisting around a bit and looking differently, something else becomes clear. Property ownership was one node in the construction of sexual difference. Both gender as well as distinctions among women's states—unmarried, betrothed, married, widowed, and divorced—were constituted (in part) through assessing their relation to property. In early rabbinic law, the definition of men's relation to the ownership and control of property is stable. A nearly unassailable part of masculinity was the legal right and social potential to own property. For women, the legal capacity to own and control property was variable. Early rabbinic ideas about womanhood did not include the idea that property ownership and control was a necessary element of female being.

READING HISTORICALLY

It is always tempting to read a passage such as mKetubot 8.1 as documentary and to assume that it unfolds in an historic progression from early to late. This temptation should be turned around. Passages from the Mishnah begin in the early third century and work backward, and they should be read this way. Mishnaic passages move forward and backward among the positions attributed to various rabbinic and pharisaic ancestors—such as the Houses of Hillel and Shammai—over a period of roughly one hundred and seventy years. The Mishnah is a formal selection of rabbinic argument. It is a fictionalization, a product crafted by a third-century storyteller and narrator of halakah. The Mishnah is never a transparent record of "real discussions" among rabbis, but a text that fashioned rabbis and instaurated a rabbinic movement. The Mishnah is heavily edited and known only through manuscripts from periods much later than the third century, manuscripts that contain some later interpolations, along with slight variations in words and phrases. Temptations to read the Mishnah as a simple and straightforward text—and to read its contents as moving progressively from start to finish—must always be thwarted.

The first three cases of mKetubot 8.1 feature the first-century Houses of Hillel and Shammai. To follow these, mKetubot 8.1 introduces

Rabbi Yehudah. According to rabbinic chronology, Yehudah was active among the third generation of early rabbis, in the mid-second century. Yehudah adds a more specific argument to the debate about men,
woman, and property. His contribution addresses the legal murkiness
that was revealed in the third situation: a betrothed woman should not
sell property she gained during betrothal, but if she did, then after the
fact her act is valid, and the future husband cannot reclaim what she
sold. The section that begins with Yehudah attends less to the details of
the third case and more to the sense of murkiness and uncertainty. In
this middle section mKetubot 8.1 presents the second and third tiers in
its legal history of the issue at hand. Having begun with debates from
the mid-first century, the early third-century narrator produces a response by introducing a second-century rabbi who will introduce a late
first-century rabbi, the authoritative Rabban Gamliel. Including these
rabbis asserts a lineage for thinking about a husband's authority and a
betrothed woman's property. Paradoxically, by presenting this lineage
as an authority for resolving the debate, the passage portrays the debate
as powerful enough to have continued for over a century and a half,
unresolved.

In this story about a legal argument, Rabbi Yehudah tells a tale in
which his rabbinic ancestor Rabban Gamliel questions the halakic justification for a husband's authority over his wife's property. To discuss
this, I will repeat a section from the middle section of mKetubot 8.1:

> Recounted Rabbi Yehudah: They said before Rabban Gamliel: Since he (the
> husband) has authority over the woman (his wife), will he not have authority
> over the [woman's] property?
>
> He (Gamliel) said to them: Concerning the [ownership and control of] new
> [property] we are embarrassed [by the lack of legal justification], and you
> would burden us with [halakah for the ownership and control of] the old
> [property].

The context of the debate is betrothal. In this middle section, "they" —
an unnamed group of sages—present a two-part argument before Rabban Gamliel. The first part claims that the husband has authority over
his wife. The second part builds on the first. Because the husband has
authority over his wife, he also has authority over her property. In his
response, Gamliel does not question their first principle. A husband's
authority over his wife is not the point that is up for debate. Their basic
premise holds. Gamliel responds only to the second part of their argu-

ment, the expansion of the basic principle. The sages have argued that since the husband has authority over the wife, he also has authority over her property. In this context, he would control her old property during the period of their betrothal. In the Mishnah's version of Ye-hudah's tale, Rabban Gamliel raises some concerns.[9]

To the sages' desire to expand the husband's authority over his wife during the period of betrothal, Gamliel demurs. Not offering a simple agreement or disagreement, instead he raises a broader concern and calls attention to the lack of legal justification. He reminds his interro-gators, as well as readers like us, of a larger contour of early rabbinic debate about husbands, wives, and property. Gamliel understands that early rabbinic halakah places a woman's old and new property into the economy of marriage, but he wants his fellow rabbis to ascertain reli-able legal foundations for their innovation. Rabban Gamliel argues that the legal justification of a husband's ownership of his wife's new prop-erty must precede any attempt to expand the husband's authority over the woman's old property. To his mind, the sages have not yet presented an adequate justification for the husband's control of the wife's old property, and he is embarrassed. Gamliel's dissent is built on the de-mand for legal justification—whether through scripture or rules of exe-gesis or from the rulings of pharisaic ancestors or elsewhere. It is on this account that Gamliel refuses to give a husband-to-be rights to his wife's property during the period of their betrothal.

Gamliel will reappear in the next and last part of mKetubot 8.1. This last section turns from the betrothed woman to consider the married woman. The section's first case begins with a consensus position that is attributed to the first-century Houses of Hillel and Shammai. A married woman gains old property (i.e., inheritance or gift). She sells it or gives it away. Both Houses declare that her act is legally invalid. As a result, her husband can nullify the sale and retrieve the property from the buyer or recipient. The husband controls the wife's old property, and the wife cannot undercut his control and his rights to its profits by re-leasing the property to others.

The section's second case is more complicated. A woman gains old property during betrothal. She marries, and then sells the property or gives it away. On this point, the Houses' consensus turns to disagree-ment, and Rabban Gamliel is introduced again. He permits the wife the right to sell or give away the property she gained during betrothal. Ac-cording to Gamliel, the husband does not control the old property she gained during betrothal. Gamliel does not allow the husband to act as if the property were under his control and does not permit him to reclaim it. Property that the wife gains during betrothal remains hers alone; upon her marriage it will be neither *zon-barzel* nor *mulug*. Gamliel's position maintains that a woman's legal ability to own and control property during betrothal is markedly different than the restrictions that apply once the marriage is fully consummated. Furthermore, the fact of when the woman acquired the property outweighs the factor of the time at which she sells it.

With Gamliel's second appearance, the Mishnah begins to build an argument that reaches its conclusion at the end of mKetubot 8.2. In his first appearance, Gamliel was placed clearly in a position of authority. The argument between Gamliel and the sages ended the discussion of property during betrothal. His point about the lack of legal foundation explains the ambiguity of the case in which a betrothed woman did release her property: she should not have done so, but the husband has no legal recourse. Gamliel's second appearance is followed quickly by his third, a word-for-word repetition of the earlier exchange with the sages. In this recounting, the exchange between Gamliel and the sages is cited by Rabbi Hanina ben Aqabya, a contemporary of Yehudah's in the rabbinic circles of the mid-second century. In this new context, both Gamliel and the sages "say" the same words. Only now, the topic has changed from betrothal to marriage. Although the words are repeated verbatim, the exchange means something different. In the earlier exchange about betrothal, Gamliel ended the argument and refused to extend the principle of a husband's authority over his wife so that he controlled her property during betrothal. In the repetition, Gamliel is the one who is refuted and refused. The relations between Gamliel, the sages, and the mishnaic narrator shift. Gamliel's authority is more ambiguous. He is no longer the authoritative speaker who satisfactorily answers the sages. Instead, Gamliel's argument becomes a minority stance. The Mishnah refuses Gamliel's position. The sages speak against him, and their argument is victorious.

I reproduce the exchange once again, this time to make a different set of points. As the passage yields its legal story about how to extend the privileges of husbands, it reveals a rabbinic anxiety about the foundations for their law. When these lines from mKetubot 8.1 are read in this way, the repetition of Gamliel's argument with the sages becomes an ambivalent, questioning refrain.

Recounted Rabbi Hanina ben Aqabya: They said before Rabban Gamliel: Since he (the husband) has authority over the woman (his wife), will he not have authority over the [woman's] property?

He (Gamliel) said to them: Concerning the [ownership and control of] new [property] we are embarrassed [by the lack of legal justification] and you would burden us with [halakah about the ownership and control of] the old [property].

The refrain is repeated, and this repetition displays a rabbinic activism on behalf of a husband's authority. But as the repetition displays their active interest, it simultaneously betrays a rabbinic anxiety about gender and male authority. If they needed to argue for it, masculine authority was not an entirely automatic and naturalized part of life. If it were, it would be an unspoken assumption and not a topic of discussion. The fact that their argument is necessary means that male authority is desired but its details still are under question, a privilege to be actively maintained by those who coveted it. In articulating an argument to extend a husband's privileges, the Mishnah implicitly acknowledges the plasticity of masculine privilege. Now, the technological invention of plastic appears many centuries after these rabbis, but it provides a vivid way to talk about how they took human life and shaped specific forms of gender. As a substance, plastic can be shaped into an almost unlimited array of forms. As a critical term, it can describe what people do with ideas, acts, and culture. Plastic can be shifted, reshaped, manipulated into different forms. As opposed to something which is thought to be defined by an essence, plasticity refers to the sense in which ideas and practices are shaped and changed. Thus, when mKetubot 8.1 alters the legal conditions of women's and men's lives, it tacitly admits the constructedness of gender.

In the act of changing the legal and economic relations of a man with the woman to whom he is betrothed or married, the assenting rabbis reshape (one part) of what it means to be a man. In reshaping they attest to the changeability of masculinity, to its plasticity. Shaping masculinity and providing law for certain visions of women and men, those who wrote rabbinic passages were not mere vessels for their halakah but responsible for these visions of human life. To describe this in language that rabbis in Roman Palestine certainly did not use, the passage's polemic witnesses their engagement with (if not their awareness of) the constructedness of gender. And, it shows their active commitment to

influencing these constructions, to remaking men, women, and the social relations of gender.

In mKetubot 8.1 and elsewhere, gender and the relations of women
and men were something that mattered very much to the early rabbis.
Rabbinic writers of this text were conscious, more or less, of their
experiments with changing the relations of Jewish men and Jewish
women. But rabbis who produced the Mishnah and other texts did not
transmit exactly what they inherited; rather, they consciously created
something new. They did not seamlessly pass along a heritage (not that
transmissions of heritages are ever seamless). These were not inheritances that less than consciously became part of the new rabbinic Judaism. Rather, the parameters of marriage were up for discussion. Within
certain limits, the details of marriage were debated and the foundations
for legal innovations were parsed.

If gender mattered, and it did, the question at hand is how the rabbis
conversed about gender. For instance, mKetubot 8.1 is overtly concerned with the economic relations of women and men. The inter-
change offers two sides to a debate about male privilege. The sages are
overt in their desire to extend a husband's privilege, and their argument
addresses this directly. Rabban Gamliel's position can be read as a defense of women against this incursion of male privilege. But in this passage, Gamliel's response is not based on a direct argument about the
relations of women and men. The issue at hand is gender—the various
ways that women and men will be constituted as separate and distinct
through different powers over property. Yet gender as such is not directly addressed. Gamliel objects on the grounds that he and his fellow
rabbis must find a foundation for their legal innovation, in order to
make the new law legitimate. As his words are recounted by Yehudah
and Hanina ben Aqabya, Gamliel wants the plasticity of men and masculine privilege to be grounded in legitimate rabbinic forms of legality.
(This is the Mishnah's perspective as well and provides a partial reason
for its inclusion of the position attributed to Gamliel). Gamliel's dispute
is based on the desire that halakah have recognizable and authoritative
foundations.

Gamliel's argument can be part of a polemic about men, women, and
marriage. His refusal to extend a husband's power can be read as a defense of women. But Gamliel's position is not articulated as a demand
for greater justice for betrothed women and wives. It does not suggest
that this goal will be achieved if elements of their husbands' control
over property are contained. Rather, Gamliel's position is articulated as

a quest for juridical certainty and better law. The debate is about how halakah for marriage will craft men and women into different types of property-owning subjects. The sages' words address this rather directly. Gamliel's response to them does not. In Gamliel's critique of the sages, gender is present as a topic but is not deployed as the basis for an argument. His defense of women may be just an inadvertent, even ironic, effect.

Gender can be as powerful in its apparent absence as in its presence. This recognition is what prompts me to look two places at the same time: at the overt results of rabbinic deliberation and at the multivalent process they used to arrive at conclusions, even when this process seems barely visible.

In a culture built on distinctions between women and men, in a religious law grounded in the pervasiveness of sexual difference, clues about gender are never too far away. A closer reading of mKetubot 8.1 finds traces that makes gender visible in Gamliel's position. I look again at the refrain—"He said to them: Concerning the new we are embarrassed, and you would burden us with the old." But now my attention turns to the phrase I have translated as "we are embarrassed," or *ʾānû bôšîn*. The phrase contains a personal pronoun and a verbal participle in the first person plural. The phrase does not speak only for Gamliel as an individual. It was not written in the singular: "I am embarrassed." The plural places Gamliel with a group larger than himself. The tantalizing question of who is included in the "we" with whom Gamliel speaks must be set aside, since the plural may be used to convey a greater sense of Gamliel's authority to speak not only for himself but for rabbis more generally.

There are additional meanings in these sparse words given to Gamliel. Philologically, the root for "embarrass"—*bôš*—refers to human bodies that are exposed and injured. Built from this root, the term used to describe Gamliel's sensibility slips in and around a range of meanings that include shame, abashment, insult, exposure, and disgrace.[10] Abstractly, this injury and these feelings of disgrace can apply to both women and men. However, gendered meanings are situational. In mishnaic tractate Ketubot, the term makes vivid an emotional state that is very precisely gendered. The root appears in several passages that precede mKetubot 8.1. In these places, the root refers to the shame, disgrace, and loss of dignity the rabbis attribute to a woman as a result of her rape by a man.[11] These nearby meanings would be available and familiar to those who wrote, edited, read, discussed, or listened to mKetubot 8.1. These meanings give a certain cast to Gamliel's embarrassment by linking it with the emotions and power relations surrounding male rape of women. Choosing the word "embarrassment"—*bôšîn*—the Mishnah presents Rabban Gamliel's position through its gendered meanings. Gamliel's dissent is expressed as the undesirable position of a woman who has been raped. Voiced through language that is associated with a raped woman, Gamliel's character is one whose position is acknowledged, forsworn, and indirectly recompensed, but one who nonetheless loses.

HOW IT KNOWS WHAT IT KNOWS

Gamliel's embarrassment has long fascinated me. Becoming more vivid through my own repeated readings of this text, Gamliel's words in mKetubot 8.1 seemed heroic. I applauded his refusal to extend a husband's authority over his wife's property. I savored the way he stood in the way of other rabbis who wished to do so. His admission of insecurity about the foundations of halakah merged with my own interests in finding the traces of how gender and law were produced. It was simpatico with my desire to locate the seams of production that, once closed, make gender and its details seem natural, normal, and even inevitable. I was in sympathy as his character reached for an argument about foundations, this strong legal and literary weapon that always asks *how* something is known. Although differences of opinion are the insignia of mishnaic and other rabbinic writing, the kind of metacritique in Rabban Gamliel's statement is relatively rare. His bewilderment about the foundation for this specific halakah indicates a rabbinic desire for the security of legal ancestry. And at the same time, his bewilderment shows the very manufacture of ancestry and genealogy. If in this early stage, the rabbinic movement needed to make its foundations seem authoritatively self-evident, these traces are the text's own evidence that its law is neither inevitable nor self-evident. In short, I saw the argument between Gamliel and the sages as a conceptual tool offered by the Mishnah for its own deconstruction.

Highlighting the passage's uncertainties about how it knows what it knows is my entry point into a discussion of different feminist relations with these ancient rabbis and rabbinic texts. This passage is a vivid moment in the production of early rabbinic law. It can be analyzed in many ways. How one analyzes this and other rabbinic passages depends on a whole series of prior assumptions. For example, if one assumes that the

Mishnah (and the rabbis who produced and used it) favored indeterminacy, then the uncertainty articulated through Rabban Gamliel (in mKetubot 8.1) becomes part of what rabbis wanted to say about the foundations of law for marriage and property. To find and highlight this uncertainty is to read with the rabbinic grain. It means that we have found something the Mishnah's editors would have wanted their readers to know: that they wished to highlight the insecurity of legal foundations.

Another kind of reader could assume that the Mishnah wanted to privilege stable meanings and secure foundations. This assumption would reject the idea that the legal text surreptitiously helps its readers effect its own unraveling. According to this second possible way to read the passage, the expression of uncertainty in mKetubot 8.1 is a less-than-conscious bulge in the text's seams. Thus, finding this trace of indeterminacy amounts to reading against the rabbinic grain. Reading this way makes visible something embedded in the text's logic, and it shows something the text might have wished to keep under wraps. The expression of uncertainty about legal foundations pressures the Mishnah to reveal its own arbitrariness. Against its own desires, the text is made to show the unnatural, constructed status of the law, of gender, of masculine privilege and women's relation to property. Pretty major differences, these, that all depend on what we readers assume about the world, about the rabbis, and about how writing works.[12]

Of course these are not the only two options for making sense of the passage. In reading for women, men, and gender, both options focus on how the Mishnah comments on its own status as law. Delving into these metacritical questions about law and text are not the only queries someone might bring to this and other mishnaic texts. Sometimes, more readily accessible answers about women are desired. But this desire, too, is complicated and built on different assumptions about interpretation. A panoply of feminist readings of rabbis, early rabbinic Judaism, of "women in the Mishnah," and of the Mishnah's women are possible. One reading, for instance, might focus on the specific resolution offered by the Mishnah on the issue of women's property rights and the extension of husbands' authority. Such a reading would seek and find answers to questions about the status of women in early rabbinic law.[13]

Another kind of reading could emphasize individual rabbis. The textual frame around these ancient rabbis is set aside. We could forget that it matters that Gamliel is narrated by Hanina ben Aqabya and Yehudah, or that Hanina ben Aqabya and Yehudah are narrated by the Mishnah's editing writers, and so forth. The crafting of ancestral voices and arguments could be forgotten in favor of plucking out individual rabbinic voices that are deemed usable for feminism. In letting our attention drift from the written-and-transmitted quality of the Mishnah, the named rabbis seem to come alive, magically released from the constraints of the text. Individual rabbis become a pantheon of "real people" with lives independent of the characters that early rabbinic writing has created. This way of reading can result in a collection of redeemable rabbis and rabbinic heroes, a group to which Rabban Gamliel can belong.[14] Depending on the reader's desires, Gamliel would be a double hero. Not only does he deconstruct the law's authority, in his sympathies he defends betrothed women and wives against the extension of a husband's authority. For Jewish women and feminists in communities that are committed to halakah, Rabban Gamliel can be used as an ancient and authoritative ally in arguments for increases in women's rights. Gamliel's position and his critique of his colleagues can be read as marking a road not historically taken by rabbinic Judaism, but a more positive road still located within the parameters of the Talmud.[15]

I see the attractions of this Gamliel. But I am not searching for heroes among the rabbis, and this kind of detextualized and decontextualized reading perturbs me. Seeking ancient rabbis as friends for feminists, it can become too easy to forgive them their patriarchy. Thus, another kind of feminist reading might emphasize the structural inequities and the intransigence of masculinism expressed in early rabbinic texts. Here, Gamliel's heroism falters. Within an economy of marriage that is already restrictive, Gamliel's position grants women in some circumstances greater control over certain types of their property. He argues against extending the husband's rights—to the period of betrothal, to the control of a wife's old property gained during betrothal—but only until the proper halakic foundations can be asserted. But these are details at the margins: a husband still has legal rights that directly curtail the rights granted to his wife. This position protects a wife only from an extension of a husband's rights over her and her property. Gamliel's mishnaic words do not contest the basic hierarchical premise of a husband's authority over his wife. Reading this way, Gamliel is not so heroic. He is a patron who remains patronizing. Whether once live in the flesh or given birth only from a scribe's ink pen, he is not someone that I would want as an ally for long. But when I read this passage now, this is the Gamliel that I see.

DEMANDING ANSWERS

All of these readings are organized as referenda. In the end, individual rabbis, or rabbis in general, or the entirety of rabbinic halakah is announced as either positive or negative. They are either good or bad, redeemable or not. The rabbis and their law are worthwhile, useless, or dangerous. But there is a problem with needing the rabbis and their texts to be either good or bad, with seeing profeminism, protofeminism, absolute villainy, or good news for Jewish masculinity in these texts. The problem is that any of these answers can allow too quick a move away from the process of figuring out how these ancient rabbis painstakingly made certain notions of gender, men, and women imaginable as "common" sense. My quandary in reading rabbinic texts for answers and for temporary allies is that it allows the broader power of masculinist culture to slip too easily from view. Looking at individuals and their positions can allow the general assumptions of these writings to go unchallenged. The specific masculinist relations they imagine in their views of the world become both invisible and universal. Reading for details, the underlying claims about women, men, and about rabbis themselves can be too easily accepted as truths. Reading rabbinic texts this way, as readers and thinkers we gain no practice in looking closely at evidence, in taking apart its assumptions and logics, in finding historic contexts, and in figuring out the mechanisms of how masculinism worked. The demand for truths and answers from early rabbinic texts can ignore the ambiguity within rabbinic texts. It can presuppose that these texts always had specific answers. Reading these texts is always in part a reflection of ourselves. Demanding these kinds of answers situates us as people who will countenance no ambivalence and little complexity. It constructs us as people who can only navigate the starkly opposite possibilities of the *either* and the *or.*

The practice of plucking out individual characters—whether heroes, fallen heroes, or villains—removes from view the broader rabbinic culture out of which these texts were produced (and which in turn was produced by these writings). Plucking out heroes removes from view the rabbinic writers whose work produced these texts, these "voices," and these arguments, and whose efforts transmitted characters and legal stories in these forms and configurations, and not in others. It removes from view the ordinary and unnamed rabbis who repeated, read, heard, and commented upon this text. Although he may have lived and

participated in rabbinic gatherings, the "Rabban Gamliel" of mKetubot
8.1 is not an individual. Gamliel's "voice" does not exist historically
outside of these textual renditions. The figure of Gamliel is proliferated
through this, other, and later rabbinic texts. Early rabbinic men are fig-
ments of their creators and their readers. As a necessity of life in the
twentieth century, it is possible to claim him as heroic, or at least, as
helpful. But the Mishnah is not a transparent record, nor does it transmit even a fraction of early rabbinic conversation. It crafts both rabbis
and words into fantasy, into stories about law and life. As significant as
Gamliel may have been within the early rabbinic movement or as important as he became in later Jewish traditions, Rabban Gamliel is at
the same time part of early rabbinic fictions for real life. Remembering
that texts are mediated, feminist desires for rabbinic allies cannot claim
a historical truth about any real Gamliel.

ORDINARINESS

Here is what happens when we bring back into view those who produced the Mishnah, crafted mKetubot 8.1, and constructed this version
of Rabban Gamliel. A mishnaic passage never records opposite positions on an equal footing. Its arguments are never really arguments as
we know them, between colleagues, friends, strangers, and opponents
who maintain their own stances, think on their feet, react and respond,
and change course. Mishnaic arguments are highly staged. Although
at times the relations of opponents are unclear, majority and minority
voices and voices of dissent are often noted as such, in various ways.[16]
The debates of mKetubot 8.1 are not about the rabbis involved, so
much as they are about a mishnaic argument writ large. In other words,
the position attributed to Rabban Gamliel marks a point along the way
to the resolution of the predicament of mKetubot 8.1: the shaky foundations of some of the halakah for marriage and property. Gamliel's
position is emphasized through repetition, but it means something different each time it appears. Mishnah Ketubot 8.1 concludes with the
second repetition of Gamliel's embarrassment. In one way of reading,
this would indicate support for Gamliel, through sheer numbers of
repetition and through the fact that he alone is named. But perhaps we
are caught in the habit of emphasizing individuals, of attending to those
characters whose writers gave them names. The reiteration of this refrain does not emphasize Gamliel's position alone. Far from it, the repetition allows both sides a second hearing. With Gamliel, the unnamed

sages too get their moment. Gamliel's critique is repeated, but so too is the basic premise of patriarchal marriage—that a husband has authority over his wife—repeated and authorized through the unnamed sages, whose very anonymity may be interpreted as consensus.

When we broaden the context for analyzing this passage, it becomes clear that the resolution of the debate in mKetubot 8.1 actually appears in the mishnah that follows. There the tractate finds one legally viable foundation for the husband's control over property that his wife received before their marriage. As will become clear, mKetubot 8.2 partially attends to Rabban Gamliel's concern about legal justification, but on new and different terms. To demonstrate this I repeat the end of mKetubot 8.1, followed by mKetubot 8.2:

> Recounted Rabbi Hanina ben Aqabya: They said before Rabban Gamliel: Since he has authority over the woman, will he not have authority over the [woman's] property?
>
> He (Gamliel) said to them: Concerning the [ownership of] new [property] we are embarrassed [by the lack of legal justification], and you would burden us with [halakah for the ownership and control of] the old [property].
>
> Rabbi Shimon distinguishes between kinds of properties. Properties that are known to the husband, she may not sell. And if she sold or gave them away (as a married woman), the act is void. [Properties] that are unknown to the husband, she should not sell, but if she sold or gave it away (again, as a married woman), her act is valid.

Rabbi Shimon distinguishes between property about which the husband knows, and property about which he is ignorant. A married woman can own and control property she gained during betrothal, if her husband is unaware. If her husband knows about her property, then he has rights to it, and she may not sell it, give it away, or otherwise deprive the husband of its usufruct. Now, according to Gamliel's priorities, his rabbinic colleagues must attend first to the problem of justifying a husband's claim to his wife's *new property*, that which she gains during their marriage. But in mKetubot 8.2, Rabban Gamliel's priorities are ignored. His becomes the minority view. Gamliel had demanded that they justify first the husband's authority over new property gained during marriage. In contrast, in mKetubot 8.2, Rabbi Shimon prioritizes finding a foundation for the husband's control of the woman's *old property*. Shimon supplies a principle to justify extending the husband's authority: his knowledge of the woman's property. If he *knew* about the woman's property, then he has the right to control that property and to profit from it. Shimon resolves the problem of extending a husband's privileges over his wife and her property by locating the basis for this extension in a man's knowledge.[17]

In telling this story about rabbinic men who make laws that privilege men and constrict women, the repetitions highlight an underlying principle in their notion of marriage: "They said before Rabban Gamliel: Since he has authority over the woman. . . . " As a character in this tale, Gamliel serves the rabbinic extension of husbandly authority well. Gamliel does not argue against this aspect of male authority. He merely wants its legal authority to be established appropriately. The refrain of the husband's authority over the wife provides a prior context for Shimon's reliance on the authority of a man's senses. The repetition stresses the principle of male authority and makes it familiar. This makes reliance on male eyes seem like ordinary and common sense.

In this way, mKetubot 8.2 and Rabbi Shimon offer a circular argument. The principle that a husband has authority over his wife envisions a man as powerful, a woman as less so. Based on this already established authority, his knowledge (of her property) is deemed authoritative. This authority is transformed into a viable legal foundation for a further rabbinic extension of a husband's authority. The exchange between Rabban Gamliel and the sages presumes a man's authority over a woman in marriage. This is precisely the portion of the refrain that remains consensual, familiar, and uncontested. That it is even possible for a feminist or any other reader not to notice this immediately points to the relative invisibility and ordinariness of what is, from another frame of reference, an absolutely extraordinary claim.[18]

CHAPTER TWO

Daily Labors

Textile trades were trouble. Across the Roman Empire, in places as diverse as Alexandria, Galilee, Pompeii, and Palmyra, the daily labors that produced blankets and towels, tunics and caps, cloaks and curtains, hairnets, headcoverings, ropes, nets, wall-hangings, napkins and more, were ubiquitous. To the elite writers who captured textile workers in words, these trades often were stigmatized as labor for lower classes, whether freeborn, freed, or enslaved. But this economic otherness was not the only source of their distress. Labor was one of many places where gender was imagined and institutionalized as a difference that mattered. Textile laborers in particular were caught in the construction of gender and sexuality. Metaphorically, in these trades gender and sexuality were less controlled and their distinctions less than clear. At tasks such as dyeing, spinning, and weaving, women and men might work together. As shepherds, men might be together too intimately. Gender boundaries were blurred, and sexual desire was not limited to interchanges between women and men. Textile trades were trouble because the category of gender—with its primary commitment to demonstrating distinctions between "women" and "men"—was on unsteady ground.

Textile troubles yielded a variety of solutions. On a workshop wall at Pompeii, eighteen names of spinners and weavers were inscribed as graffiti, and then memorialized by the volcano that buried that Italian city in 79 C.E. In this workshop of M. Terentius Eudoxus the seven *textores*—Vebius Tamudianus, Felix, Ephebus, Zanthus, Successus, Faustus, and Florus—were all men. The male weavers' names were scribbled near those of eleven female spinners: Vitalis, Florentina, Amaryllis, Iuanuaria, Heraclea, Maria, Lalage, Damalis, Servola, Baptis, and Doris.[1] The graffiti make immediately visible a gender division of labor. Women spun yarn that men used to weave cloth, or at the very least, graffiti described them this way. Divisions of labor were one way to express gender in the repetitive motions of the quotidian. In this workshop, women and men worked in the same physical place, but they did different tasks. Through graffiti scribbles we see both the gendering of work and gender at work.

A six-week's ship ride from Pompeii and a century later, a rabbinic passage responds in its own way to a similar problem of work, sex, and gender. As tractate Qiddushin draws to a close, it instructs that "a man whose livelihood takes place with women should not be alone with women, and a man must not teach his son a craft practiced among women" (mQiddushin 4.14). This rabbinic instruction was part of a sensibility that circulated through the Roman Empire. Placing it in this wider context, it can be more easily understood. Ideas about sex and gender were conveyed through work and through stories about workers. In both the Pompeii graffiti and in this fragment of rabbinic legal writing, gender is a set of differences to be demonstrated and displayed. Pompeii and Palestine may seem far from each other. However, the Empire's regions were linked through merchants and trade, soldiers, traveling artisans, religious preachers, and philosophers, as well as tax collectors, bureaucrats, and census takers. From region to region there were variations and differences, as well as shared features. These bits of evidence from Palestine and Pompeii pay homage to a culture of gender in which differences between women and men were performed repeatedly, at work, at tasks that were ordinary, familiar, and routine.

As work, textile labors were highly visible and widely known. People who did not themselves work as weavers, or dyers, or tent makers, still saw cloth articles being produced, knew people who did this work, purchased them at a market, wore clothing, or used in daily life the results of someone's labor at these trades.[2] As repetitive and unthought-about as these daily work tasks probably were for those who did them, they were used continually by writers to comment upon society and to intervene into culture. For writers, artists, and others who produced public images, portraits of labor were ways to explain the social relations and the people of their worlds. But there is a circular relation between these explanations and the people they explain, especially as the explanations take on lives of their own, and as humans start acting according to (or in opposition to) the explanations. The tasks of textile production were transformed into a range of human traits. The transformation of combed cotton fibers into continuous spun yarn would signify feminine sexual chastity and marital loyalty. The weaving of yarn into cloth would indicate men who were neither sexually trustworthy nor respectable as men. The transformation of task into trait is as remarkable as it was familiar. But in this case, the extraordinariness is masked in some of the most ordinary, mundane, and banal acts imaginable.

Gender and its distinctions were crucial to the writings of early rabbinic Judaism. In forming a new vision of Judaism after the destruction of the Jerusalem Temple, differences of gender—and what it meant to be a woman or a man—were deemed significant in new ways and were made part of all facets of this new tradition of everyday life and ordinary labors. In this chapter I look closely at passages from Mishnah and Tosefta Qiddushin to consider how differences between women and men were to be manifested in daily life and how gender was prescribed anew as the basis of sexual desire. In reading passages from the end of Qiddushin and locating them within a more widespread Roman discourse, I am fascinated by these fantasies of work, sexuality, and gender. The tendency in reflecting on these things is to place them into cause-and-effect relations (examining, for instance, the effects of workplace separations on gender, or the effects of a specific organization of gender on ideas and practices of sex, and so forth). But instead of assuming that work, gender, and sexuality are separate and can "cause" each other, I will follow the lead of the rabbinic text and examine them as intertwined, as things that take place simultaneously, and as tensions that only sometimes are resolved. Each is inextricable from the others, and I do not want to simplify the rabbinic construction to fit our modern terms. In tractate Qiddushin, the regulation of sex is inextricable from the regulation of gender, and all these things are inextricable from the regulation of labor. In a word, these things are imbricated with each other, and gender was imbricated with nearly every other topic of rabbinic concern. Reading rabbinic texts, we must learn to see these textures, so that in the future it will be unimaginable to read a passage from this corpus and not see how gender is present and working.

CATTLE HERDERS

Near the end of tractate Qiddushin, the rabbis use cattle herding to consider gender and sexuality, and of course, use gender and sexuality to
think about cattle herders. Their query is how to apply these distinctions to daily labors. Part of mQiddushin 4.14 translates as follows:

> Rabbi Yehudah says: An unmarried man should not herd cattle, and two
> unmarried men should not sleep beneath one cloak. But the sages permit
> [this].

As this chapter progresses, this passage will unfold in various directions. Each section introduces different kinds of evidence and provides
an increasingly rich texture of meanings in this short and succinct passage. In this way we move away from the tendency to read early rabbinic texts in isolation, or through the lens of later talmudic writing.

   With these lines from mQiddushin 4.14, we enter the middle of a
discussion that has already begun. The unmarried cattle herder and the
men who sleep beneath a single cloak are part of an immediately preceding discussion of *yiḥud*. The rabbinic principle of *yiḥud* is usually
described as the combinations in which men and women may be together and the instances in which they must be separated. Having
discussed the principle in more general terms, the rabbis consider how
yiḥud applies to labor and workplaces. They also consider how a principle directed at women and men might apply to groups of men. The
usual way to explain the example of the cattle herder and the men who
share a cloak is that it provides an extreme, even silly, way for the principle's limits to be established.

   What becomes visible when we gaze a different way? Instead of reading "the usual way" I begin in the middle. Doing so provides a new
vantage point for seeing the rabbis and their cattle herders. It helps to
overturn the usual explanations and expectations and assumptions
about reading. Had we started where Qiddushin begins its discussion of
yiḥud (at mQiddushin 4.10), we would have begun with what the text
sees as normative: male–female desire (or what we might call in modern
terms heterosexual desire). According to *yiḥud*, humans must have
erotic desires for the "opposite" sex, and at the same time, these desires
must be limited to the opposite-sexed humans to whom they are married. All other desires, which the rabbis acknowledge are present and
part of life, must be contained and controlled. In the usual explanation,
to prevent illicit sexuality, unmarried women and men may be together
in the same place only in specific conditions and combinations. Had we

begun at their beginning, we would have moved with a rabbinic eye from this treatment of *yiḥud* among women and men, to what it imagines to be nonnormative and extreme, male–male desire (what we might call homosexuality). We modern readers tend to read this and other rabbinic passages as if we were rabbis and shared their positions as men. We have tended to discuss *yiḥud* as if it were about women and their dangers to men. Reading this way with the rabbis means accepting their unspoken truisms as truths. It means that we are always gazing heterosexually with the rabbis at women's bodies.

But instead of giving priority to the male rabbinic eye, following the text's order, and beginning with mQiddushin 4.10, by starting elsewhere—in the passage's middle—we can more easily locate rabbinic tensions about gender and sexuality. We have jumped into the middle of a rabbinic interdiction against unmarried men sleeping close together under a single cloak. From this point of entry, we may consider different explanations of *yiḥud*. Beginning with male–male desire makes visible how this passage reassures its readers of the familiarity and normalcy of male–female desire. Starting our reading with the cattle herders and unmarried men sharing a cloak shows the process by which rabbinic texts fashion gender as an opposition and male–female desire as the norm.

In the case of these unmarried men, the rabbis apply the assumptions of *yiḥud*—that gender must divide humans into women and men, and that sexual attraction upholds this distinction between them—to a case where only men are involved. Through Rabbi Yehudah, mQiddushin 4.14 states that unmarried man should not herd cattle, and that unmarried men should not share a cloak to cover them as they sleep. This restriction resonates with the Torah's prohibition on bestiality and male–male sexuality (Leviticus 18.22–30).

Yehudah's statement is followed immediately by a negation. Despite Yehudah's prohibition, the sages give their permission. The difference between Yehudah and the sages is generated by two competing assumptions about the sexuality of Jewish men. In Yehudah's opinion, Jewish men, like other humans, are driven by various kinds of sexual desires. He imagines that their desires and practices can in some situations be "suspect." The suspicion works in several ways. First, Jewish men can be suspected of not limiting sexual desire to the women they have married. And second, Jewish men can be suspected of not limiting their desires to heterosexual acts. As Yehudah understands Jewish men, male–male desire is part of sexual feeling. It is also illicit. As a result Jewish men might need rabbinic regulation to "control" themselves. Thus, Ye-hudah would preempt an instance where men's desires for other men might be combined with the conditions for acting on these desires. Hence, he would apply to them a form of *yiḥud*.

By contrast, the sages do not consider Jewish men to be sexually sus-pect. Their vision of Jewish masculinity entertains no room for sexual desire between men. Hence, there is no reason to prohibit unmarried men from sleeping near each other, their bodies close as they share a single cloak. Rather, Jewish men, even unmarried Jewish men, set the standard for trustworthy and reliable sexuality. Their desires are di-rected only at women, and limited to their wife or wives. The trust-worthiness of Jewish men is in contrast to that of Jewish and non-Jew-ish women and that of non-Jewish men. As the Mishnah recounts, the sages permit unmarried men to herd cattle. What is possible for unmar-ried men in Yehudah's vision, is impossible in theirs. Thus, the unmar-ried men are not regulated, since the assumption of sexual attraction which is the basis of *yiḥud* does not apply.

Out of the tension between Yehudah and the sages, the first posi-tion—that unmarried Jewish men are not sexually trustworthy—did not become part of a rabbinic consensus. The second supposition—that they are—prevailed. But I am less interested in the resolution and more interested in pressing the underlying difference between these two com-peting assumptions about gender and humanity.

Reading for gender in early rabbinic Judaism often means searching for tensions such as this between Yehudah and the sages.[3] For this task, the Tosefta is crucial. When scholars look for evidence of Judaism in Roman Palestine, they turn most frequently to the Mishnah. As the ba-sis of the Talmud, of all the early rabbinic writings it is the most famil-iar. The Tosefta is the Mishnah's first commentary. It was probably pro-duced within several decades of the Mishnah's appearance. The Tosefta's orders and tractates are organized alongside those of the Mishnah. By and large, it refers to the same set of rabbis named in the Mishnah. The Tosefta tractates have different relations to the Mishnah; they can cite the Mishnah, gloss it, rephrase it, ignore it, serve as the basis for the Mishnah, or provide a good deal of material only tangen-tially related to it. The Tosefta is important not because it provides either a more positive or negative view of women. Rather, when read in certain ways alongside the Mishnah, passages from the Tosefta provide alternate modes through which rabbis produced the category of gender and asserted its details. The Tosefta often expands the evidence of the Mishnah to show the multiple ways that rabbis went about imagining men and women. These doubled readings can provide examples of counterarguments, of different resolutions to similar problems, or of different senses of what constitutes a problem. In the passage from tractate Qiddushin, the more loquacious Tosefta adds a vividness as it glosses the Mishnah's characteristically more terse account.[4]

Here is what happens when the Mishnah and Tosefta are placed together, and furthermore, when the brief sentences about cattle herders are placed back into the longer discussion of *yihud*. The Mishnah appears along the left side of the page, the Tosefta along the right:

A man must not be alone with two women, but one woman may be alone with two men. (mQiddushin 4.12)

Even if both are Samaritans. Even if both are slaves. Even if one is a Samaritan and one is a slave. Except for a minor. For (a woman) is shameless about having sexual relations in his presence. (tQiddushin 5.9)

Rabbi Shimon says: One man may be alone with (just) two women, so long as his wife is with him. And he may sleep with them at an inn because his wife guards him. A man may be alone with his mother and with his daughter, and he may sleep with them, with their bodies near. But if they are grown, this one must sleep in her clothes, and that one must sleep in his clothes. (mQiddushin 4.12)

As to his sister and his sister-in-law and all those women in a prohibited relationship to him, according to Scripture: he must not be alone with them, except before two (witnesses). But she should not be alone, even with a hundred non-Jews. (tQiddushin 5.10)

An unmarried man may not teach *sofrim*, and a woman may not teach *sofrim*.
Rabbi Eliezer says, Even one (who is married but) his wife is not near him may not teach *sofrim*. (mQiddushin 4.13)

Rabbi Eliezer says: Similarly, he who has a wife and children, but they do not live with him, he should not teach *sofrim*. (tQiddushin 5.10)

Rabbi Yehudah says: An unmarried man should not herd cattle, and two unmarried men should not sleep beneath one cloak. But the sages permit [this]. (mQiddushin 4.14)

And the sages say: Israelite men are not suspected in such a matter. (tQiddushin 5.10)

The debate about unmarried Jewish men is resolved with the resounding certainty of the sages' permission. In mQiddushin 4.14 the lone influence of a single rabbinic attribution is allayed by the collective authority of the sages. In its consideration, the Tosefta (5.10) agrees with the sages' position and articulates it as a principle: Israelite men are not suspected in such a matter. The Tosefta weighs in on the side of the sages, and in doing so clarifies the contours of these clashing views of male sexuality. It refuses to let stand Rabbi Yehudah's understanding that Jewish men have a continuum of desires, of which rabbis might trust some and be suspicious of others. And, it expands the notion of the trustworthiness of Jewish men beyond the priestly caste. Its phrase—"Israelite men"—makes Jewish men of all religious castes, whether priest, Levite, or Israelite, into a singular standard for sexual reliability.

The usual way to think about the halakah of *yiḥud* is that it addresses the topic of women and men whose sexual desires are already established and already known, and then regulates them. However, *yiḥud* looks different when we allow that it constructs the gendered subjects that it seemingly only regulates. The regulation contributes to an ethos in which it becomes natural to believe that women and men are certain ways, and that they act accordingly. As the regulation becomes part of law and part of the repetitions of rabbinic learning, so too are these assumptions about human beings enmeshed in a rabbinic consciousness. Thus, as it regulates, the assumptions in the law become stories told about men and women.

Returning now to the passage's beginning, it becomes clear that *yiḥud* originates in a discussion of physical space and sexual desire between women and men. The general principle from Qiddushin is this: "A man must not be alone with two women, but one woman may be alone with two men." A woman may be in a place with two men. But one man must never be in the same place with two women, unless one of these women is his wife. If the man's wife is not present (or, if he does not have a wife), then he must make sure that no less than three women are present.

In this vision Jewish men are more sexually trustworthy than are Jewish women, *tout court*. Jewish men will stop each other from transgressing rabbinic sexual codes. The same presumption is not extended to Jewish women, who must be more directly regulated. The Tosefta's comment supports and strengthens this vision. Citing the Mishnah's "a woman may be alone with two men," the Tosefta adds: "Even if both [men] are Samaritans, even if they are slaves, even if one is a Samaritan and the other a slave." The exception is "minor" men; the passage suggests that women are sufficiently shameless that the presence of a male youth would not prevent women from having sex.

This extends the range of men considered trustworthy. It includes not only free Jewish men of all religious castes but also Samaritan men and slaves, groups often treated with suspicion by rabbinic law. The Tosefta's vision introduces another element, that Jewish women have an ordinary sense of shamelessness. Their behavior must be regulated by adult men because women may dominate younger, minor men. Women are not bound by internal notions of correct behavior, the transgression of which will bring on a feeling of shame, and for whom the determination to avoid this sense of shame will prevent transgression. If Jewish women have no sense of shame, then the presence of an adult man— Jewish or Samaritan, free or slave—is necessary to deter women from transgression when they are near a minor male, who may himself not yet have the discipline to resist or the strength to prevent her. Discipline by men stands in for the interior mechanism of shame that Jewish women are assumed not to have. An adult man's presence becomes the equivalent of a woman's (absent sense of) shame.

To demonstrate how *yiḥud* will work in a specific instance, mQiddushin 4.12 evokes the closed quarters of a room at an inn, and continues on in the voice of Rabbi Shimon. One man may be alone with just two women, even to the extent of sharing a room and a bed at an inn, so long as one of these women is his wife. In this vision, one woman might be sexually impulsive and predatory. But in that event, a wife will protect and guard her husband. A man may share a bed at an inn with female relatives, including his mother and daughter. A man may be alone with his mother, and with his minor daughter, even to the extent of sleeping next to them in positions where their bodies touch, and even if each is naked. But age will change this. If the daughter is adult, she and her father may sleep together in the same bed only so long as each is clothed. The example attends to men, women, and families on the road, away from home.

In writing about *yihud,* rabbis, and anyone who wrote or repeated or read or heard these texts, can contemplate a number of situations and possibilities. Here are some of the passage's assumptions, its assumed truisms of human life. Two women desire the same man. A married man is still attractive to women other than his wife or wives. If two women fight over one woman's man, his wife will defend her privileged relation to him. A married Jewish man is always desirable by women other than his wife. Men are coveted, and women are cast unfavorably as those who covet.

The string of illustrations moves from inns and bedrooms and turns to schoolrooms, workplaces, and trades. Unmarried men may not teach *sofrim* (in this context, the term refers to young students who would be learning Torah as their curriculum). Nor can a woman teach *sofrim.* Rabbi Eliezer adds to this: a man who is married, but whose wife is not nearby, may not teach. He is considered the same as an unmarried man, a man who has no wife to guard him from other women. This example is concerned both with teachers—male and female workers—and the physical places where they work. These two factors—types of labor and workspaces—become significant concerns as the passage continues.

From a schoolroom of teachers and students the passage proceeds to where we began, the outdoor field of cattle, the cattle herder's body, and the nighttime bivouac of two unmarried men. The first examples had assumed that sexual desire would operate along the lines of gender. If gender would construct women and men as opposites, sexuality too was directed at a member of the opposite sex. *Yihud* imagines a sexual economy in which men desire women and women desire men, and in which these sexual desires constitute gender identities. However, in the case of the unmarried men a notion of gender as opposites still holds, but the parallel notion of sexual desire breaks down. The desire that men are to direct toward women (but only when married to them) is instead directed among men. Sexual desire has broken free from the dictates of gender.

This discussion of whether unmarried Jewish men may herd cattle or sleep together beneath one cloak, articulates the possibilities of bestiality and male–male desire that Jewish law prohibits to Jewish men. The goal of this passage is not to promote usable law nor to offer a specific regulation or permission. The case is intentionally extreme, a test of *yiḥud*'s limits. But reading for gender makes clear that the disagreement between Rabbi Yehudah and the sages is not just limited to the details of a principle, and to the ramifications of whether or not unmarried men can herd cattle or share a cloak. Nor is the passage limited to demonstrating two contrasting visions of the sexuality of Jewish men. Amid all these things the passage questions whether the dictates of *yiḥud*—with its basis in male–female desire—should ever be applied to men. The answer is both certain and ambivalent. Underlying the question and its resolution is the desire to protect the category of gender and to keep the largely arbitrary social meanings assigned to women and men rigidly clear. The disagreement between Yehudah and the sages does not revolve only around competing assumptions about Jewish men's sexuality, but around somewhat different notions of how gender operates and about how its series of distinctions should matter. The sages' trouble with Yehudah's position is that he can imagine a Jewish masculinity that overlaps with femininity, in which Jewish men can sometimes be "like women." In contrast, the sages propose a form of gender in which distinctions between women and men are more permanently rigid.

Can men ever be "like women"? In the case of the unmarried men, no women are present. Yehudah's examples contain only men. Men are the lone cattle herders. Men share cloaked coverings as they sleep. In other words, since no women are present, the standards of *yiḥud* have already been met. When he places some men in positions that early rabbinic texts usually accord to women, Yehudah imagines the possibility that adult Jewish men can in fact be "like women." Generally, the sexuality of women is regarded with suspicion. So too these unmarried men are made "like women" in that they are regarded with the same kind of suspicion. The unmarried male cattle herder is trusted no more than a woman. Yehudah's prohibition is built on the belief that women and men might share some character traits, traits which other rabbis and Jews might prefer be linked either to one or to the other. In this passage, Yehudah believes that unmarried Jewish men can act with the impetuousness of women. Ideally, strict distinctions between women and men are preferred, but in some instances in the lives of women and men, gender distinction might not be so rigid and strong. Yehudah recognizes the category of gender, regards it as partially unstable in practice, and moves to prevent some ramifications of this instability.

In the halakah according to Rabbi Yehudah, there is a tension between the ideal and the messiness of human life in which in some circumstances, men can be like women. The position of the sages, on the other hand, does not recognize the category of gender as potentially unstable. The way they see it, Jewish men are not ever like women. The sages share a similar stance with Yehudah in one regard, that ideally, such fluidity and overlap are not desirable. But the sages' vision of humanity and gender will not allow them to see these possibilities when they look at real people. Their more stable notion keeps male and female separate. Their stance will not allow Jewish men to be positioned as women, even if this overlap is temporary, as in the case of the men who are caught unprepared and tired, and share a cloak to sleep. The sages will not sanction the idea that the characters of men and women are largely similar. They do not want to imagine men as sexually irresponsible and shameless in the same way they will imagine women. Neither will the sages discipline men with the kinds of controls they use to regulate women. Their answer to the question of whether Jewish men can be like women is unambiguous, and negative.[5]

WORKING FANTASIES

Peering at unseen and unguardable fields of cows and herders, and gazing upon the imagined bodies of unmarried men, this rabbinic passage is concerned with questions of what men and women should do—or not do—as the case may be. At the same time, the passage has more conceptual interests: what will women and men *be,* and how will they be different.

From this debate about the relative rigidity of gender, tractate Qiddushin leaves the overt discussion of *yiḥud* and turns to consider how these strict notions of gender distinctions will be part of ordinary work and daily labors. The principle of *yiḥud*—a man must not be alone with two women, but one woman may be alone with two men—is restated and developed in terms of workplaces, types of work, and the bodies of workers. Here are the translated texts:

And [a man] whose livelihood [takes place] with [the] women should not be alone (*yityaḥēd*) with (the) women. And a man must not teach his son a craft practiced among women (*ʾûmānût bên ha-nāšîm*). (mQiddushin 4.14)

For example, netmakers, those who prepare fibers, weavers (*gardiyîm*), peddlers, millstone grinders, tailors, haircutters, launderers. (tQiddushin 5.14)

Rabbi Meir says: A man should always teach his son a clean trade,
and pray to Whom riches and property belong. (mQiddushin 4.14)

Rabbi says, A man should always
try to teach his son a trade that is
clean of thievery and easy. (tQiddushin 5.15)

In this rabbinic vision, Jewish men will distinguish themselves from
Jewish women and non-Jews through the daily labors they refuse to do.
The Mishnah directs that a man not teach his son a craft practiced
among women. In support, the Tosefta gives the names of trades it considers especially problematic: netmakers, those who prepare fibers,
weavers, tailors, launderers, and peddlers, as well as millstone grinders
and haircutters. The list of trades adds texture to the Mishnah's interdiction. It clarifies how the Tosefta gave meaning to the phrase "crafts
practiced among women." And it links these rabbinic texts from Palestine with a broader Roman discourse.

The rabbinic instruction is caught in a tension between what they see
as current practice—in which crafts are not gender-segregated, and a
utopian desire—in which they will be. As much as men should not be
alone with unrelated women in the course of a day's work, and as much
as young men should not be taught crafts practiced among women, it is
clear that these things are very much the case. For the passage to cast
these trades as work that men should not do is clearly utopian. The
passage envisions a society in which habits of work and gender were
much more clear than the rabbis' own. For each of the listed trades,
other references in the Mishnah and Tosefta indicate a messier and less
clearly defined situation, in which rabbis imagined and wrote about
Jewish men who worked at these "crafts practiced among women." Although the netmaker appears rarely, men who process flax and wool
or who comb the fibers in preparation for spinning appear repeatedly.[6]
Male weavers are found throughout.[7] Men working as peddlers, grinders, and barbers, as well as tailors and launderers/fullers all appear,
usually in contexts where rabbinic texts regulate their practices or their
products.[8] If the Tosefta's list expands the Mishnah's meaning, the logic
of both falters when pressed. If this is not description, but vision, then
what happens when the logic of the vision is expanded? If in communities of Jews these labors should not be done by men, then who will do
them? Will they be redefined as women's work, to be done by Jewish
women? Should they be done by people who do not adhere to Jewish customs, women and men who are not members of Jewish families?

This instruction from the Mishnah and Tosefta takes a strong rhetorical stance, but then retreats from pressing the ramifications of its ideal.

The vivid details of tailors, peddlers, and millstone grinders lend the passage a sense of accuracy and practicality. Reading it, I can almost hear the hustling chatter of artisans and customers at the marketplace. But this is a seduction. Most modern interpreters of rabbinic writing have considered words about work to indicate something that approximates real life. Yet, acknowledging the utopianism in this description means that the passage is not an example of real life, and that all real life is located within a continuum of fantasy. It is easier to admit degrees of fantasy in texts that are explicitly about sex. Indeed, in common language, fantasy often seems linked inextricably to sex, as if by definition all fantasies are about sex and sensuality. There is an ethos, a set of operative assumptions, in which work is presumed to be material and physical, and in which things that are material and physical are seen as more truthful and real. I want to break down this habit of imagining the ancient world. Used as a critical term, *fantasy* works more broadly. It calls into question the more pedestrian ways in which words about work are usually understood. Images of work can be as metaphoric, as symbolic, and as rich as images of sex and gender. This is especially the case because sex, work, and gender are imbricated, each enmeshed in how the others operate in a given society, place, and time. In the written and repeated and listened and read context of Qiddushin these trades are not limited to truthful accounts of physical labors. They form a discourse of work and workers that is also a discourse of gender and sexuality. Stories about ancient sexual bodies are highly valued as imaginative, exciting, and titillating.[9] These passages from Qiddushin contain fantasies about laboring bodies, and they are every bit as interesting.

CRAFTS PRACTICED AMONG WOMEN

The problem of making history out of rabbinic sources extends beyond the habit of ignoring the levels of fantasy in these representations. A whole range of ideas about how the world works undergirds how ancient sources are crafted into histories of ancient people and communities. When these models—which are actively misogynist at their worst and mildly stereotypical at their best—become "the past," there are drastic results. For instance, the most commonly found explanation of the passage from Qiddushin is that it prohibits male workers from engaging with women who might be purchasing the materials that these

men have produced, or engaging the services they offer. Those who read
the passage this way assume that the economy of Roman Palestine
was divided so that men were producers and women consumers. Hence,
men should not engage in trades that will bring them into contact
with female consumers. They must stay away from trades that produce things that women need, require, or buy. An example comes from
Moshe Aberbach's *Labor, Crafts and Commerce in Ancient Israel*
(1994). Commenting on mQiddushin 4.12–14, he writes:

> It was because of such excessive moral considerations that a strong recom-
> mendation was made that "a man should not teach his son a craft which is
> practiced among women." . . . The list of such trades is formidable indeed.
> It includes goldsmiths who made trinkets for women; carders who combed
> wool for women's garments; tailors whose clientele inevitably included ladies
> (not all of whom would make their own dresses); handmill cleaners who
> would visit homes and offer their serves to housewives; netmakers who pre-
> sumably sold their products to women for various uses; peddlers who sold
> ornaments, spices, and toilet articles to women . . . launderers whose cus-
> tomers were almost exclusively women . . . barbers to whom women (who
> did not indeed attend beauty-parlors which were, as yet, for better or for
> worse, unknown to womankind) would bring their children for haircuts.
> (202)[10]

Interpretations such as this rest upon a series of oppositions. Men
produce, women consume. Men are active workers who are paid for
their labors, women are domestic and unpaid workers. Men produce
money, women spend money that they themselves do not earn. Women
buy ornaments, spices, and gold trinkets, they commission dresses from
tailors, summon the help of millstone sharpeners, bring dirty garments
to launderers, and chaperon their children to the barber. Women consume what men produce, purchase what men sell, and use the services
men proffer. Women depend on men's labors. One ramification of this
logic is that it makes the categories of "women" and "worker" conceptually incompatible. Within this logic, only men can work. The assumption that "work" and "worker" are masculine categories is found in
almost all scholarly and popular reconstructions of early rabbinic Judaism and Jewish communities in Roman Palestine.[11] In this conception
real work is equated with waged work, and waged work is equated with
masculinity. From this emerges the notion that men performed paid labor while women engaged in unpaid labor—domestic or household
tasks—which is ambivalently understood as "work." This logic builds
on a set of stereotyped ideals about what men and women do and do

not do. When gender is constituted as a set of opposites, men and women must do the reverse of each other's acts. Thus, if men work, women cannot.

Wage-producing labor was part of Jewish women's lives in Roman Palestine, and it was part of how rabbis wrote about Jewish women. However, rabbinic texts are not consistent. Reading the corners and niches of rabbinic writing, we find women at work. Women do various tasks and jobs, in instances in which they are, like men, engaged in a waged economy. They worked as merchants, selling textiles, bread, calves, clothing, and olives. Women worked as artisans and producers. They baked bread, prepared oils and wines, worked as baking assistants, ground grain at millstones, spun yarn, and wove yarn into cloth. Women organized egg-hatching enterprises. Women manufactured wool and flax. Recent research has identified women as glassmakers in Roman Palestine. Women did other kinds of service work, including wet nursing and midwifery, textile laundering, teaching, hairdressing and innkeeping. They were associated with certain ritual work regarding burial, although this last may not have been considered paid labor.[12] Women seem to have worked at fewer types of jobs than men, or, fewer types of work were recorded for women than for men, but nonetheless, it is clear that women undertook a broad range of paid labors.

The evidence for working women in Palestine—or at least, the evidence for how women's lives as workers were represented—easily undermines the reigning notion that men worked and women consumed, or its variant, that only men did paid work and women were restricted to domestic labor at home. This demands that nearly all accounts of Roman Palestine must now be corrected. But it also has major implications for interpreting the last phrase in the dictum from Qiddushin that "a man must not teach his son a craft practiced among women." "Crafts practiced among women" does not refer only to situations in which male producers provided services to predominately female clients. With this new research on the range of work by women, the phrase takes on other meanings. There was significant overlap in work done by women and by men. This overlap includes several of the trades listed in tQiddushin 5.14. According to rabbinic knowledge, men prepare wool and flax for weaving, and so do women. Women sew and mend clothing, as do men. The same is true for hairdressing and for laundering and fulling. Men weave, and so do women. In fact, netmaking and peddling are the only two trades on the list for which I can find no examples in which the task is performed by a woman.

Women worked. At times, they did the same work as men. The phrase "crafts practiced among women" refers, at least in part, to trades which were done by both male workers and female workers. When we can admit that women as well as men were engaged in a range of labors, and that both were—at various times—paid workers, the passage takes on a different and additional cast. Crafts and trades that a father should not teach his son is not explained by claiming that a man—unaccompanied by his wife—might be surrounded by multiple women, and might find it difficult to uphold the conventions of *yiḥud*. This may be a partial answer for some of the trades. In peddling, for example, we find no references to women peddlers. A male peddler might sell to women, but then again, wouldn't he sell to men as well? After all, there is no reason to assume that men did not buy items from peddlers. Read differently, with selections of ancient evidence for female labor tempering modern stereotypes, "crafts practiced among women" refers to the possibility that in certain trades—those that a father should not teach his son—a man would likely work alongside women workers. And even if he was not actually in physical proximity to other (female) workers, still he might be doing the same kind of labors as women.

In other words, the passage is concerned with both physical space and with the sense of being that one's vocation expresses. Read this way, the passage is not primarily concerned with the relations of buying and selling, nor with the specific conditions in which some male workers might occupy the same physical space as women. This conception of labor follows the logic of *yiḥud*. Knowledge of *yiḥud*'s regulations was as important as and inseparable from its effects of keeping unrelated women and men physically apart. In fact, this knowledge was its strongest effect. The principle of *yiḥud* reminded Jews of the underlying social and personal meaning of gender. It marked gender in the ordinary spaces that women and men traverse. In a similar vein, the majority of troubling trades are those which were done by both women and men. When men and women engage in similar or the same trades, this overlap blurs the distinctions of gender that the division of labor might enforce. In these passages, the rabbis need work to demonstrate the rigid differences of gender. In a world where "women's work" and "men's work" might overlap, fathers are asked to help enact gender as a rigid difference. They are asked to help decrease the confusion by not transmitting certain trades to future generations of Jewish men.

At stake is the desire to separate what "women's work" means from

what "men's work" means. If preparing fibers for spinning is considered to be a feminine task, then a man who washes and combs wool
himself becomes feminine. Doing work that women do, men become—
temporarily and conceptually—like women. Work ceases to clarify the
distinction of gender. In this early rabbinic sentiment, men must never
not be men. One way to insure this is for fathers not to train sons in
trades they share with women. Separating the acts and performances
of "women's work" from "men's work" diminishes the chances that in
daily life, Jewish men will ever be effeminate, that they will ever act like
women.

There is more. Not all the listed trades are overtly deemed "feminine." But some trades place "men's work" confusingly near "women's
work" in other ways. For instance, some of these labors can be confused with domesticity. Men who use millstones for grinding share the
domestic task of grinding grain which rabbis direct wives to do for their
husbands.[13] Male launderers overlap with the domestic laundering assigned by rabbis to wives, who wash their family's clothes. Male weavers and men who prepare fibers for weaving might perform the task of
wool work that rabbis associated most insistently with a Jewish wife.
By doing these tasks, a man could be too closely identified with domesticity and with wifeliness. Any of these tasks bring men too near to being like women, and as a result, all of them are troubling.

WEAVERS WHO KISS

In these passages from Qiddushin, men must refrain from doing—or
being taught—certain types of suspect labor because their labor must
demonstrate distinctions of gender. But if this brief list now seems
immeasurably more textured than when we began, there are still more
ways for it to unfold. In a list of workplace metaphors and fantasies, no
less than five of the eight trades—weaving, tailoring, netmaking, peddling, and fiber preparation—were part of the production and distribution of textiles. The prominence of textile trades places this rabbinic
text into a much broader vocabulary in which scenes from these trades
formed a common language for gender, sexuality, respectability, degra-
dation, and shame. Images of spinners, weavers, dyers, even tanners and
those who worked with hides were very popular, highly charged icons
of gender culture. Consider Clement of Alexandria, who decried these
trades because they undermined strict distinctions of gender and sex.
For Clement, workplaces where textiles were produced were filled

with "crafty women and effeminate men, who blend these deceptive dyes with dainty fabric, [and] carry their insane desires beyond all bounds."[14]

Studies of Jews in the orbit of Hellenistic culture and Roman rule have been undertaken as if there were only two choices. Either Jews were thoroughly immersed in these universal dominant cultures. Or, they showed a particular adherence to Jewish tradition. In other words, the ancient world is described in the peculiar terms that modernity offers its minorities. In these oppositional terms, ancient Jews are "Hellenized" or "Jewish."[15] Seeing this pattern and putting these binary terms to rest, we can start to consider the nuances of cultural difference and similarity.

In this period after two revolts against Rome, and on the eve of the extension of Roman citizenship throughout the Empire, the writings of early rabbinic Judaism both state what makes it distinctive and show it to be part of the Empire. When the rabbis write about work and about workers' bodies in ways that convey notions of sex and gender, they are part of a wider Roman discourse, one with similarities—and variations—throughout the regions that the Empire linked. Part of what the writings of early rabbinic Judaism demonstrate when they use gendered images for work and family is their relation to Roman standards and structures. Rabbis employed notions of appropriate gender and sexuality to demonstrate that they belonged within Roman culture. Their differences as Jews would be expressed in other ways.[16] Admitting that the rabbis—long considered the most Jewish of Jews and those who set the standard for Jewish practice—partook of Roman culture when they desired opens the door for letting go of the standard of purity for judging Jews as much as it allows us to see the nuanced uses of gender in these passages from Qiddushin.

Daily labors were potent metaphors through which gender, sex, and other cultural distinctions were expressed. The visual sights, spoken and heard stories, and written texts in circulation gave meanings of sex and gender to men and women of different classes. Male weavers were sexualized in ways that placed them outside the gender ideals for elite and respected (or respectable) men. Among Suetonius's (born 69 C.E.) biographies is the tale of the grammarian Quintus Remmius Palaema. The home-born slave of a woman, in his first vocation Remmius Palaema was a weaver. Later, he worked as a *paedagogus* and educated himself while accompanying his master's son to school. Remmius Palaema's social status rose with his intellectual achievements as a grammarian. Still, the biographer Suetonius cannot forgive him his lowly origins. Remmius Palaema is promiscuous. He kisses everyone he meets—including men—and about this point Suetonius is emphatic. The grammarian is presumptuous and self-centered. He overspends his income. The explanation for all this imprudent and indiscreet behavior lays in Remmius's initial station as a weaver. Weaving is both a labor and a character trait. It becomes an essence. An education in weaving, it seems, provides an unavoidable and unchangeable moral seasoning.[17]

For anyone in contact with the expressions in Martial's (38–104 C.E.) epigrams, the fear of weavers and men kissing men would have been familiar. One epigram features a returning traveler around whom "all the neighborhood" crams. In a scene Martial describes as loathsome, the returning man is surprised by kisses from several workers—a bristly farmer, a cobbler whose lips had been recently on an animal hide, a fuller/launderer, and a weaver. The loathing has a specific, sexual cast: male weavers and other low-status workers kiss one another upon greeting. Any man who ventures near them risks the physical offense of an unwanted kiss, as well as the unsavoriness of being near what these men represent.[18]

To call a man a weaver casts aspersion and suspicion on his masculinity. Spinning too was a trope of transgression. When Juvenal, through his character Laronia, critiques men for spinning more deftly than Penelope, he chastises men who do not uphold the proprieties of masculinity. The masculinity of these men does not establish sufficiently clear differences between them and women's femininity. Another effect of this discourse is to portray men of nonelite classes as feminine. Weavers were lower-status workers, whether slave, freed, or freeborn. Written into life with a distinctively sexualized timbre, these men are different from elite men, and as such, help to establish the masculinity that makes elite men superior.

The discourse on female spinners and weavers worked somewhat differently. Spinning, weaving, and wool work were icons for those upper-status women who eschewed luxury and promiscuity in favor of simplicity, sexual chastity, and loyalty to the men they married. These reminders were widely available. Walking on a road outside the city, one might have seen grave markings such as this, in which the buried woman was described as "a wool worker (*lanifica*), pious, modest, frugal, chaste, domestic."[19] Or been arrested by this longer epitaph: "Stranger, what I have to say is short. Stop and read it through. This is the unlovely tomb of a lovely woman. Her parents named her Claudia.

She loved her husband with her whole heart. She bore two sons, one of which she leaves on earth; the other she has placed beneath the earth. She was charming in conversation, yet her conduct was appropriate. She kept house, she made wool."[20] The ideal and idealized woman was domestic, and she showed it by working wool. This woman attended her home and raised children. She was loyal and affectionate toward her husband, chaste before marriage, and faithful during. Similar versions appeared throughout the Empire. The rhetoric of a eulogy, the so-called "Laudation of Turia" expresses similar notions of womanhood: "Why should I mention your domestic virtues, your loyalty, obedience, affability, reasonableness, industry in working wool, religion without superstition, sobriety of attire, modesty of appearance? Why dwell on your love for your relatives, your devotion to your family? . . . You have innumerable other merits in common with all married women who care for their good name."[21] Other funerary monuments left not words behind, but instead were decorated with images of women holding spindles and distaffs. And spindles were among the goods buried with women in their graves. In their funerary commemorations, women do not stray from these idealized ways of explaining wifeliness to living women.

Tombstone inscriptions portray a seemingly unambiguous message of wifely perfection. But in other accounts, the spindle and distaff are more ambivalent. Writing in the early second century, Suetonius offers snippets of the lives of the daughter and granddaughter of Caesar Augustus. As girls they were taught spinning and weaving. They were educated in a feminine morality that they were to model for other women. They should be productive. They should keep their voices low and attend carefully to the words they spoke. Their discussions were to be restricted to things that "might be recorded in the household diary," and they were kept from meeting male strangers. Caesar himself chastises men who venture too close. According to Suetonius, Caesar Augustus once wrote to Lucius Vinicius, a man of stature and reputation, to tell him that he had "acted presumptuously in coming to Baiae to call on my daughter."[22]

But this tale of discipline holds a surprise. Despite his attempts to educate the girls in the virtues of spindle and loom, Augustus fails. The two Julias, daughter and granddaughter, engage in vices of all kinds. In the end spinning was not a foolproof tool for training women into femininity. It could not guarantee that a woman would be "safe" for elite society. This ambivalence was found in somewhat earlier expressions.

In "The Lady of Andros" (written in 166 B.C.E.), Terence's elderly gentleman Simo describes the shortcomings of Chrysis: "At first she lived a modest life with thrift and hardship, struggling to make a living by distaff and loom; but when a lover came on the scene offering a price, first one and then another, as the human mind always runs downhill from toil to pleasure, she took the offer and afterwards set up in the trade." The material and metaphoric profits of working thread into cloth were not sufficient to prevent Chrysis from becoming a prostitute.[23]

The ambivalence about women and wool work runs in several directions. Spinning could not protect society from errant women, nor protect women from themselves. Neither could it protect women from society. Another version of this womanly ideal also ends in failure. In the oft-repeated tale of Rome's origins, Lucretia was the model wife. Livy (59 B.C.E.–17 C.E.) recounts the following. One evening at the front, the princes were trading bets on whose wife was the best. Collatinus boasted of his wife, Lucretia, and sang her praises. To give each husband a chance to prove his claim, the princes challenged each other to a horseback ride back to the princesses' palace. Paying a surprise visit, they found all the other princesses banqueting extravagantly and drinking wine. But Lucretia sat tucked into her quarters; "though it was late at night, [she] was busily engaged upon her wool, while her maidens toiled about her in the lamplight."[24] Ovid fills his version of Lucretia's story with more detail. In her chambers she is surrounded by baskets of soft wool. Lucretia urges the women servants to work quickly, as they were preparing a new cloak for Collatinus. Despite their royalty and wealth, Lucretia produces homespun for her warrior husband to wear. Both Lucretia and Collatinus embody the imperial ideals of simplicity and thrift. Ultimately, her spinning, her loyalty, and her chaste demeanor were of no avail to Lucretia (although they were powerful ways for writers to express imperial values).[25] In a later episode, Tarqinius visits the house of Collatinus and encounters Lucretia's performance of chastity. He is filled with lust and desire. That night, sword in hand, he enters Lucretia's room to rape her.[26] Spinning does not and cannot insure a woman's safety.

These stories of women and wool work were familiar and durable. These ideas were not restricted to the literate and reading elite. They circulated much more widely, appearing in places as varied as funerary stones, graves, and formal literature. In Rome, images of wool work and female domesticity were displayed in architecture, as in Domitian's monumental Forum Transitorium. Completed by early 98, the frieze of the Forum Transitorium depicted images of wool-working women in a pictorial rendition of Arachne's insubordination and insolence to the Goddess Minerva. The art and its images were part of Domitian's project of renewing Rome after the destruction caused by the fire of 80 C.E. These bas-reliefs of women working at their looms were part of an enclosed piazza for Domitian's Temple to the goddess Minerva.[27] The frieze and the piazza were located in a busy, well-traversed area. The Forum Transitorium was the entry point to the Roman Forum, the city center, from the "teeming, squalid" quarter of the Subura. As d'Ambra argues persuasively, the frieze sculpts devout wool-working matrons of "traditional" Roman society. Their wool work becomes the metaphor of an imagined past that was so central to Domitian's ideology of Empire.

These public images of womanly perfection were necessary precisely because perfect womanliness was not natural, not consensual, but an ideology up for question. Simplicity, chastity, and loyalty may have been desirable, at least by some, and some women may have been simple, chaste, and loyal. Yet metaphorically, the productivity and sexual restraint of (elite) women in their homes was to prevent the decadence that was associated with the current state of human affairs. Through these metaphors women's lives were narrowed and simplified, and made to symbolize a utopian desire based on an invented past of self-sufficiency and thrift. Femininity and sexuality were not just important for individual women, for families and local communities. They were enmeshed in larger notions of Empire. Wool-working women were familiar metaphors for building one's society and renewing its culture. Women's working bodies were—for some—a microcosmic display of a collective self. They were a nostalgic emblem of a selectively imagined past. But the boldness of the ideology is undermined by ambivalence. These emblems of controlled women point to the ways that the conjunction of women, wool work, and sexuality still could not control women. Metaphorically and materially sculpted in stone, one finds the disciplinary tale of how the weaver Arachne was punished by the goddess Minerva for her indolence and insubordination. But as the frieze demonstrates the punishment and as it dedicates itself to Minerva, it repeats the story of female disobedience to authorities.[28]

These tales of textile workers—and there are more—from around the Empire form a discourse in which early rabbinic writers took part. From these widely shared ideas of what women and men should do and be, and of how they should be different, rabbis in Palestine shaped this discourse into their own. In doing so, they also worked with their other inheritance, biblical chapters such as the story of David and Abner in 2 Samuel 3.29. In this ancestral tale, Abner, son of Ner, has abandoned Saul and has offered to serve David at Hebron. When David's men return from a raid, they are told of Abner's presence. Joab in particular is enraged. Seeking revenge for Abner's murder of his brother, Joab sends a message that Abner should meet him at the city gate. When Abner arrives, Joab motions him into one of the gate's inner spaces and stabs him fatally in the chest. When David learns that Joab has murdered Abner, he is aghast. David affirms his own innocence in Abner's death and proclaims a curse upon the murderer: "May the house of Joab never be without someone suffering from a discharge or an eruption, and may it never be without a male who handles the spindle (*maḥazîq ba-pelek*), or a male slain by the sword, or a male lacking bread." Among the curse's disgraces is a son with a spindle, a feminine son. Such a son does women's work. He is unable to perform elements of this version of masculinity: self-protection, care of one's needs and health, and distinction from women. In David's curse, the spindle is a specter of femininity from which men must abstain. The tool is the concrete sign of that version of gender.[29]

Part of a region-wide trade in textiles and other products, rabbis in Palestine were also part of an Empire-wide trade in images and meanings for textile workers, women, and men. They shared in the widespread, but not inevitable, sense that textile trades were a gender problem. When rabbis give prominence to these trades—and not others—they are bringing evidence and showing proof of things that were already established in the worlds in which they lived. Evoking these things appealed to a familiar sensibility and used it to express their own cultural desires. With images such as these, they displayed an adherence to Roman notions of gender respectability and simultaneously showed a Roman-period Jewish development of an ancient, Israelite icon.

A CLEAN AND EASY TRADE

Rabbis in Palestine used gender in many ways, and as a result labors were made to mean all sorts of surprising and unsurprising things. They used gender to show their similarities to others around them, especially to those with more bureaucratic power and those with greater cultural capital. And they used gender to express what made them different:

their distinct reform of Israelite religion and Temple-based Judaism. In other words, from amid this Empire-wide trade in products and ideas, rabbis found their own resolutions.[30]

Near the end of tractate Qiddushin, the charge that a father not teach his son a craft practiced among women is followed by the admonition that a father should always teach his son a clean and easy trade. The Tosefta makes a slight addition: a father should teach his son a trade clean *of thievery* and easy. The rabbis have already asserted that daily labors be made part of ordinary respectability. This respectability is always underwritten by codes of gender and sexuality, by the relations of provincials to Imperial culture, and by notions of status, character, and wealth. Both versions of Qiddushin now begin to link a man's labors to his respect for God—"And let him pray to Whom riches and possessions belong." As tractate Qiddushin moves toward a close, it turns from men and women whose bodies are in close physical contact and begins a discussion of men, work, and merit before God.

The discussion of clean and easy work is rancorous. Which trades and professions should be excluded from this category: camel drivers? shopkeepers? sailors? shepherds? donkey herders? doctors? butchers? From the rancor emerges Rabbi Nehorai's position. If in one sense it is necessary to compare and distinguish daily labors, in another, all comparison and distinction is moot:

> I gather together all the crafts that are in the world, and I would teach none to my son other than Torah, for a man eats the reward in this world, and the essence remains for the world to come. And with all the rest of the crafts, this is not so, for a man came to the hands of sickness or to the hands of age or to the hands of troubles, and he may not engage in his work, and behold, he dies of hunger. But the study of Torah is not like this, rather, in his youth it guards him from all evil, and in his old age it gives him a future and hope. (mQiddushin 4.14)

The question of truly appropriate work for men is moved from the messy cauldron of hairdressers, camel drivers, weavers, and bachelor schoolteachers. Attention turns to the practiced utopia of Torah study, the clean and easy trade *par excellence*. The rabbis resolve the problem of work, trades, and gender in the masculine and homosocial space of the study house. According to Rabbi Nehorai's utopian vision, of all the world's crafts only Torah shall be taught. In the craft of Torah alone, only the reward is used now, and the principal remains for the world to come. In all others, the reward disintegrates slowly—with sickness, aging or other troubles—and all rewards end at death. Only Torah study guards the young man from evil and offers the older man hope for the future. The products and profits of all trades are ephemeral. Only Torah study staves off hunger and ill health, and provides for a man in the world to come. According to Rabbi Nehorai, the problems of this world are resolved in a look toward the rewards of the next. Ending this way makes gender one of the ephemeral troubles that can be left behind when Jewish men remove their laboring bodies from the workshop, schoolroom, and marketplace, and repair to the study house.

VISIBILITY

The move to the study house means to resolve the problem of work, *yiḥud,* and gender, and in effect, to leave these problems behind. The resolution is a bit too easy, and even the Tosefta's version shows some discomfort with it. Gender is not really "left behind." The absence of women from the study house does not make it an ungendered place. Gender is still present, only, in this resolution it has been rendered invisible. It is a misnomer to say that the passage has left gender behind. To do so mistakenly conflates "gender" with "the presence of women." It is in moments of tension that the traces of the construction of gender are most visible. In their resolutions, the traces fade into normalcy, operating invisibly until they resurface elsewhere and later. Critical and creative study of the rabbis must provide explanations, conclusions, and insights that the rabbis themselves could not have foreseen. I end this reading of tractate Qiddushin with three brief examples that make the invisibility of gender visible.

First, in this resolution, the ideal for Jewish men's labor is Torah study. However, as talmudic traditions develop, the tension has not yet really been resolved. The character of the Jewish man inhabiting the study house is still defined against several opposites. The learned man is the opposite of the feebleminded male who holds the spindle.[31] His wisdom is still defined in opposition to that of women, whose wisdom is cordoned off in the emblem of the spindle: there is no wisdom for women except in the spindle.[32] These opposites are part of what defines the man of the study house and sets him apart. These icons from biblical, Roman, and rabbinic culture still operate to define the study house's others.

Second. In one sense the passage solves the problem of gender when men enter the segregated realm of Torah study and its rewards. Rabbis move men out of spaces inhabited by women. To accomplish this, they must make domains belong to men, in part by moving women away. A man studying Torah is never in danger of engaging in work with women or in women's work.[33] In this way, men's Torah study resolves the problems of gender.

But if women have been removed, gender has still not been left behind. The study of Torah is a mitzvah (commandment). By the time one reaches the end of tractate Qiddushin, the entire structure of mitzvot has already been gendered. Qiddushin's first chapter (1.7) articulates the early rabbinic innovation that took biblical mitzvot and placed them onto a grid of cross-cutting attributes. All commandments are classified as either positive (one must . . .) or negative (one must not . . .). And each commandment is classified as to whether its observance depends upon a certain and specific time (for example, morning prayers are bound to that time), or whether its observance was not bound to a specific time. These two classifications are combined to form four categories: time-bound positive commandments, non-time-bound positive commandments, time-bound negative commandments, and non-time-bound negative commandments. All four groups are incumbent upon adult male Jews. For men's Jewish practices, these divisions are largely superfluous. There is no direct halakic result. Whether or not a commandment is positive or negative, time-bound or not simply does not matter.

In this new rabbinic system, mitzvot are enmeshed in gender. The four divisions have more specific ramifications for adult female Jews. Women are held to only three of the groups. They are released from the fourth, commandments that are time-bound and positive. The labor of studying Torah was classified as a positively commanded and time-bound mitzvah. From Torah study and other mitzvot in this category, women were exempt. Women received no merit from Torah study, and hence, had no reason to be near the masculine house of study. Notions of gender were organized such that this mitzvah was incumbent upon men alone. As much as it excluded women, this system sets aside a series of highly valued ritual acts that will be incumbent on Jewish men alone. The effect—if not the reason for—this system is the production of rigid notions of gender; it creates certain mitzvot and ritual practices in which the distinction of gender will always be clear.

Within this new gendered structure of ritual labors, an innovation of early rabbinic Judaism, the labor of Torah study was limited to men. By the end of tractate Qiddushin, this domain is already—structurally—masculine. It is part of a halakic structure that divides and genders ritual labor. So, even if women are absent from the study house, Torah study is still implicated in gender, and effectively, still troubled by it. As part of this new system of mitzvot, gender will start to seem ordinary and invisible, its distinctions a normal part of the rituals of everyday life.

Third, in our world of modern concepts, we like to imagine that things are divided into zones of the "spiritual" and the "material." We organize these zones as opposites, so that something cannot be simultaneously spiritual and material. Within this conception, religion as we know it is defined through the first of these sets of terms. Religion is spiritual and not material. Our modern and western conceits incite divisions that did not work in quite this way for early rabbinic Judaism. To understand, finally, what is at stake in the gendering of daily and halakic labors, modern notions of the difference between ordinary labor and religion must be upset. From beginning to end, tractate Qiddushin links together ordinary productive and service work with ordinary ritual work. The distinctions of gender that were made part of daily trades, tasks, and labors were also used to structure mitzvot. The distinction between women and men was made inextricably part of, and also silently invisible in, the ritual labors that were part of everyday life and ordinary existence.

Everyday life entailed repetitive performances of gender. But these repetitions were not just about the materialities of work, production, and consumption. Nor were they only about the religiosities of Torah study and other mitzvot. In early rabbinic Judaism halakah, work, and gender were integral parts ordinariness. In the rabbinic imaginary, mitzvot were as ordinary, as material, and as gendered as any other daily labor.

CHAPTER THREE

Weavers at Their Looms

Sometimes stories about weavers and spinners had a certain flair. From Rome in the first century C.E., hearing of Cerinthus's affair with another woman, Sulpicia proclaims, "For you, toga and strumpet loaded with a wool-basket may be worthier of your preference than Sulpicia, Servius's daughter. But they are distressed on my behalf, to whom this is the greatest cause of pain, that I may yield my place to an ignoble rival." Unlike the aristocratic Sulpicia, Cerinthus's lover—the "ignoble rival"—is of a lower class, and the wool basket is proof.[1] Sometimes these stories exhibit the heroism of the ordinary, as in Tobit's Anna, written somewhat earlier in Palestine, about an imagined Assyria. One night after subversively burying murdered Jews, Tobit sleeps outside. Bird droppings fall into his eyes and cause a four-year blindness that doctors cannot cure. During that time, his wife, Anna, keeps the family alive through her "women's work" (*ergois tois gunaikeiois*). One day when she finishes her labors, removing the web from the loom and delivering it to her usual buyer, she receives not only her usual wage, but the added bonus of a goat. Anna's dedication and hard work pays off, and she and the family are aptly rewarded.[2] In another story, from the late second century, Artemidorus of Ephesus in Asia Minor offers interpretations for looms that appear in one's dreams. His dream readings have their own prosaic élan as they combine the fantastical with the mundane. Implements attached to the loom signify anxieties, complications that will be resolved but at great length and with difficulty. If a woman moves to and fro at the loom, this signifies trips abroad. Since a loom resembles life itself, dreaming about a loom with a web ready to be cut indicates a short life ahead.[3]

From northern Africa in the mid-second century comes a similar tale, but with a twist. In his *Metamorphosis,* Apuleius recounts a story heard at an inn about a woman and two men. One day, the husband, a construction worker, returns home unexpectedly early. Discovering the door bolted shut, the husband congratulates himself upon his wife's supposed chastity and self-protection. He knocks and whistles to gain her attention. But behind the locked door, the wife trysts with her lover. Hearing her husband outside, the wife quickly hides her lover in a half-buried storage jar. She then opens the door and shouts angrily to her husband. Why was he not at work, she wants to know. They were so poor, and had barely enough to eat. He walks around idly, her harangue continues, while she stays home, her days and her nights spent wearing her fingers to the bone spinning wool so that they could afford at least one lamp inside their tiny home. The husband counters. To their fortune, he has just sold the storage jar for six denarii. The wife responds that she has already sold the jar, for seven denarii, and that the new owner is inside, checking it for cracks. Invoking her spinning, the wife demonstrates her fidelity. After all, some women, literary reports announce, carried a spindle or distaff proudly at their wedding processions, or draped woolen fillets over the doorposts of their new homes.[4] But Apuleius twists the image into ambivalence. Instead of serving the ideal of a woman's loyalty to her husband, the spindle becomes a poor woman's tool to cover up her extramarital sexuality. Although home—and the home with a bolted door at that—was set in contrast to the lecheries of the marketplace, in this tale home does not insure a wife's fidelity; it is the very location of her treachery. In Apuleius's hand, the spindle is not sexual truth, but trick.[5]

Despite these tales of playfulness, piety, and pain, the repetitive tasks of the quotidian were not nearly as exciting as they were ubiquitous. Stories such as these mask the tales of tedium that can also be recounted about weaving, spinning, and other tasks of textile production. The *Naturalis Historia* of Pliny the Elder (23/24–79 C.E.) provides a different kind of guide and presents a different kind of challenge for making visible how gender worked:

> With us the ripeness of flax is ascertained by two indications, the swelling of the seed or its assuming a yellowish color. It is then plucked up and tied together in little bundles each about the size of a handful, hung up in the sun to dry for one day with the roots turned upward, and then for five more

days with the heads of the bundles turned inward towards each other so that the seeds may fall into the middle.

Linseed makes a potent medicine; it is also popular in a rustic porridge with an extremely sweet taste, made in Italy north of the Po, but now for a long time only used for sacrifices.

When the wheat-harvest is over the actual stalks of the flax are plunged in water that has been left to get warm in the sun, and a weight is put on them to press them down, as flax floats very readily. The outer coat becoming looser is a sign that they are completely soaked, and they are again dried in the sun, turned head downwards as before, and afterwards when thoroughly dry they are pounded on a stone with a tow-hammer. The part that was nearest the skin is called oakum—it is flax of an inferior quality, and mostly more fit for lampwicks; nevertheless this too is combed with iron spikes until all the outer skin is scraped off. The pith has several grades of whiteness and softness, and the discarded skin is useful for heating ovens and furnaces.

There is an art of combing out and separating flax; it is a fair amount for fifteen [. . .] to be carded out from fifty pounds' weight of bundles; and spinning flax is a respectable occupation for men.

Then it is polished in the thread a second time, after being soaked in water and repeatedly beaten out against a stone, and it is woven into a fabric and then again beaten with clubs, as it is always better for rough treatment.[6]

The task is to find gender in the tedium, in what is ordinary, apparently insignificant, or difficult to see.[7] Pliny's account marks neither romantic betrayal, care of the family, nor the pursuit of dreams. Instead, it pays homage to picking flax stalks and bundling them together to dry, removing the seeds, plunging the stalks into warm stagnant water, breaking the dried stalks with wooden mallets, skutching them with a heavy blade, separating the outer layer from the inner pith, combing the inner pith, and manufacturing it into fibers to be spun. But embedded in the chatty tedium of Italian flax production lays a surprising statement about men.

Part and parcel of Pliny's description is a concern with who will do this work. And questions of "who" are always gendered. Buried in an account of technique and tools that seems otherwise divorced from social relations is a fragment that argues that men can spin flax, and moreover, they can spin flax and still be respectable as men (*linumque nere et viris decorum est*). Pliny's sentence should be read as a polemic, one that recuperates flax spinning as a possibility for male workers. This recovery was no small matter. Although men dominated the production of flax and linen, in the culture Pliny knew, spinning was feminized. Pliny intervenes into a gender culture that attributed spinning and wool work to women, girls, and effeminate men. His culture was marked as much by the princess Lucretia's decorous wool work as by Juvenal's accusations that effeminate men spin more deftly than Penelope and by the division of labor at Pompeii between male weavers and female spinners. Text after text and image after image made spinning and other kinds of wool work into work for women, and into metaphors for womanhood and femininity. The second-century tract by Hierocles, "On Economics," provides a vivid statement of spinning's irrespectability, the irrespectability of men who spin, and spinning as a physical mark of men who are already irrespectable: "For such men as pay great attention to neatness and cleanliness will not conceive the spinning of wool to be their business; since, for the most part, vile diminutive men, and the tribe of such as are delicate and effeminate apply themselves to the elaboration of wool, through an emulation of feminine softness."[8] These fragments evoke the culture into which Pliny offered his words.

The culture Pliny knew used work to formulate notions of gender and sex, and used gender and sex as ways to talk about work. Practically, labors were separated into what were considered gender-appropriate divisions. Gendered work tasks demonstrated what men were and what women were, and they showed the clean distinction between the two. Pliny's text seeks to modify these distinctions, at least in one small way. In the case of delegating spinning to women, the logic of gender difference had not worked in the best interests of men. One result was that in flax production, men would have to compromise the proprieties of masculinity by spinning. That Pliny recovers and seeks to defeminize flax, and not wool, is significant. Flax and linen were more highly valued than wool. Recuperating flax spinning for men, Pliny intervenes in a gender culture that might deny a lucrative work task to some men. Linen commanded higher prices than comparable types of wool. And workers who specialized in flax and linen were paid more than workers of wool. According to Diocletian's *Price Edict*, published in 301, linen weavers were to earn 20–40 denarii for a day's work, in contrast to the lower wage (15–40 denarii) to be paid to weavers of wool.[9] Pliny seeks to modify gender culture so that men can participate in the productive economy with greater privilege and ease, and without transgressing gender respectability. To do so he foregoes distinctions between trades, tools, or technologies, and focuses on the difference of fibers, by letting rest the traditional association of women and wool, and retrieving flax for men.[10]

This concern from Italy appears in writings from other parts of the Empire, including rabbis from Palestine. In Palestine, if textile production was not the top industry, it was one of the top three, along with the manufacture of grapes into wine and olives into oil. Textile production occupied the time and energy of women and men, girls and boys. This was especially so as trades tended to be done by whole families, together.[11] The production of cloth was commonly seen and commonly known. The tools that these workers used—looms, spindles, whorls, combs, shuttles, baskets—were similarly common and commonplace. Cultural commitments to gender had to be naturalized into the ordinary and everyday. But tales about textile workers were not monolithic. These commitments were made real in their variety. In many, myriad, and minute ways gender and its differences were made part of the repetitive world of work and production.[12] The idea of gender was embedded in things used daily, in things that were background and commonplace, in acts that were so boring that, in Benjamin's terms, the retelling of their meanings is not conscious, but comes "all by itself."

Early rabbinic texts attend to details. Within these attentions and their tensions, work was a site for the construction of gender. But in the case of weaving, this was no easy or simple task. Metaphorically speaking, weaving was "women's work," despite the fact that both women and men used looms to weave cloth. When human bodies could no longer convey gender differences, the mark of difference was placed somewhere else. Where both women and men wove, tools and technology replaced the human body as a means for sustaining the idea of gender. The bodies of textile workers were sites for the production of gender. But so too, this chapter shows, were the tools of textile production crafted into tactile signs of women, men, and the distinction of gender.

LOOMS

A search through the nooks and crannies of rabbinic literature and the remains of excavated loom parts finds something that seems peripheral and small. Finding the effects of gender in the minutiae of daily life requires the historical equivalent of careful detective work: searching the present remains of antiquity for clues, finding evidence whose initial meaning is unclear, making connections, and forming a story. It means interpreting the obscurities of eighteen-century-old texts and setting these texts into conversation with clay and stone loom parts excavated after centuries of burial beneath layers of sand and dirt. In Roman Pal-

estine, both women and men wove cloth, and the technology they used
was the loom. The looms they used were part of the gender culture in
which they lived. Three passages in early rabbinic literature mention
both the gender of the weaver(s) and offer clues to the type of loom
being used. I read these three passages alongside other information
about the technology of weaving and looms in the Roman period. Then
I read the archaeological remains: loom weights that were hung to keep
the vertical warp threads tense and straight.

To hint at the conclusion, this snooping around antiquity's remains
leads to the following argument. In representing weavers at their looms,
early rabbinic texts sequester women to a specific type of loom. This
association segregates women to an older form of loom that was very
possibly extinct by the time these rabbinic texts were circulated as the
Mishnah, Tosefta, and later commentaries. Men, on the other hand,
were represented weaving at both kinds of loom. Getting to this conclusion will take some time and will journey through diverse kinds of
evidence—ancient texts reprinted as published books, excavated artifacts stored in wood flats and cardboard boxes, illustrations from antiquarian journals—things that are shelved in libraries and stored in museums, and somehow can be used to compose histories which history
did not see fit to transmit.

The historical juncture is important. The first and second centuries
saw a change in loom technology that predated by only a few decades
the production of the rabbinic texts in question. In different regions
around the Mediterranean, the technology of weaving shifted from the
warp-weighted loom to the two-beam loom. Some information about
looms and the technologies of weaving in Roman Palestine is necessary
to decode the three rabbinic passages. Roman-period looms were bulky,
space-consuming machines. The warp-weighted loom had been available for centuries. This loom was vertical, but probably not freestand-
ing. It was leaned against a wall or tied to a building or tree for support.
On this loom, the warp (vertical threads) were held in place by weights
("loom weights") attached at the bottom. The simple mechanism of attaching weights to yarn sustained the tension in the yarn that allowed
a weaver to move the woof thread in and out in various combinations.

During the Roman period, the warp-weighted loom was slowly replaced by a loom without weights. This latter loom—the two-beam
loom—stretched the warp threads from the top bar down to a station-
ary beam at the bottom of the loom. The weights that hung at the bottom of the early loom were replaced by a beam across the loom's bot-

tom. This innovation held the warp threads in place more tightly, and without the bulk and unwieldiness of the attached loom weights.[13]

Generally speaking, this shift from the warp-weighted to the two-beam loom can be dated to the first century C.E., although the specific times of change would have differed from region to region. The evidence comes from various places. By the mid-first century, Seneca (died 65 C.E.) contrasted Poseidonius's reference (ca. 50 B.C.E.) to the warp-weighted loom with the newer and more complicated weaving arts (*subtillius genus*) of Seneca's own time. Written in the first decade of the first century C.E., Ovid's description of the contest between Pallas and Arachne places both weavers at the two-beam loom. And in the late second century, a text closest in date to the early rabbinic writings, Pollux (floruit 180–192 C.E.) classified the Greek words for loom weights (*agnuthes* and *leiai*) as archaic. In early rabbinic texts, only the newer two-beam loom is described in full. In fact these texts contain no term for "loom weights," a significant absence given that rabbis refer in great detail to many other loom parts and textile production tools.[14]

The technical innovation made it easier to produce tightly woven cloth that became more highly valued. Furthermore, the new two-beam loom was more comfortable for weavers to use. On the older warp-weighted loom, the weaver wove the fabric upward, pushing each new line of woof thread upward into the already woven web. Working at this loom meant standing with arms raised for long periods of time, and constantly pushing one's arms upward against the warp.[15] In contrast, on the new two-beam loom, cloth is woven from the middle of the loom into the bottom, and the already woven web is wrapped around a rotating bottom beam. The weaver does not have to stand with arms constantly raised. Weaving could be done either standing or sitting on a bench or stool, a much more comfortable position to endure for the long hours necessary to produce even a small piece of woven cloth. And rather than expending one's energy pushing the web upward and away from one's body, the new thread is pulled toward the body, down into the already woven web, a far easier motion. At the two-beam loom a weaver works with arms more comfortably stretched in front of the body.[16] The weaver had more consistent control over the tension in the warp threads, and hence, had greater control over the quality of the woven product. By most ancient accounts, the new loom enabled weavers to produce better quality cloth more efficiently and more comfortably.

In Palestine, the end of this technological shift can be dated quite specifically to the mid-second century.[17] The wood that comprised the side and horizontal bars of the Roman-period looms deteriorates with time. As a result, the two-beam looms leave no remains. Archaeologically speaking, only warp-weighted looms are visible. Clay was an important material used to make loom weights. These nondisintegrating clay weights show up both as sets (a warp-weighted loom might use twenty or so weights) and individually. Records of excavations at Palestinian sites with levels that date to the middle and late Roman periods—roughly the second through fourth centuries C.E.—show a nearly total absence of loom weights. This suggests that the technological change from warp-weighted loom to two-beam loom was complete by that time. The two looms had coexisted during the first century. The archaeological evidence shows that this coexistence ended by the mid-second century when the evidence of loom weights disappears. This information about loom technology and the completed change from one form to another by the mid-second century forms the starting point for evaluating three rabbinic passages that refer to these looms and the weavers who used them.

EVIDENCE

All three passages come from the Mishnah or Tosefta, rabbinic writings that were completed and promulgated after this technological shift, at a time when the warp-weighted loom was no longer used in Palestine. The first passage—mNegaim 2.4—sketches the procedure for examining leprous spots (*něgā'îm*) in places on male and female bodies that were deemed by this rabbinic passage to be private and hidden. In this exam, both women and men are asked to position their bodies as if they were doing common work tasks. Men's poses are related to outdoor agricultural production. A man should stand as if hoeing, with his legs spread somewhat apart, to provide visual access to the area around his genitals. And, so that the examiner may view his underarm, a man should stand as if harvesting olives, with both arms raised and extended as if he were picking fruit off the tree. A woman is inspected in different positions and more of them. Standing as if she were kneading dough for bread or cakes allows the examiner to inspect between her legs. Positioned as if she were nursing a child, her breasts are lifted so that the inspector can see their underneath sides. To look for leprous spots in her armpits, she is positioned as if she were weaving at a loom (*běʿômdîn*). To look for spots in her left armpit, she is to mime spinning flax.

She poses with her left arm held high, as if holding the distaff, from which fibers are pulled as the spindle drops to the floor.[18]

The loom that guides the woman's body position for the physical exam can be inferred from the term *bĕʿômdîn*. Built from the root "to stand," the term refers to the position of the weaver, who stands. A weaver who typically stands is at work at the warp-weighted loom. Hence the term *ʿômdîn* refers to a weaver using this loom. This is the older loom that was replaced historically by the two-beam loom. At the warp-weighted loom, the weavers stood with their arms raised, as they pushed new cloth upward into the web. This introduces a curiosity. This passage likely refers to a traditional exam much older than the second century. The positions are common and familiar labors. But this tradition is rewritten in a text that was promulgated and distributed in the early third century. If the exam was to function actively as halakah, then these instructions required both the inspector and the woman being examined to remember a technology that was not only antiquated, but in all likelihood, extinct. In this rabbinic vision of the examination, the woman is made to represent a certain nostalgia and recollection of a past. Posing as if weaving on an antiquated loom, the examined woman simultaneously conveys a manufactured memory of an earlier time.

This first passage links women weavers to the warp-weighted loom. Through the physical positions assumed to accomplish the exam, fantasies of work are inscribed onto Jewish bodies that are the subject of the exam. *Negaʿim* (leprosy) is associated with "sexual" organs—genitalia and breasts—and the examination for this disease makes use of work-related positions. These work positions provide the vantage point for access to parts of the body that are not usually seen, parts that were deemed private, sexual, and hidden from view. Different positions are assigned to men and to women. Specific tasks are associated exclusively with one of two gendered bodies: agricultural hoeing and olive gathering for men; and bread making, nursing, weaving and spinning for women. Although they may seem like natural divisions of work done by women and men, the gendering of these tasks are in fact quite peculiar. The peculiarity becomes evident by considering other possible ways that rabbinic writers could have described this inspection, as they recast it from the domain of Temple priests to their own.

These tasks and their gender associations may seem familiar and natural to some. But they are understood better as rabbinic fantasies of what Jewish men and women should do. The realities (or even the representations of realities) of the labors of men and women were much more complicated. The rabbis knew well that men could bake bread, and that women could harvest olives, because they wrote about them doing so in their own texts. They knew that men worked as weavers and would be familiar with how to position one's arms at the loom. They also knew that most bread was bought at market, especially in towns and cities, and that many households—and women—did not prepare bread at home. They probably knew that wet nurses were used widely, and not just by upper-class women, and that this limited the degree to which mothers might nurse their own children.[19] Despite their knowledge of a variety of overlapping tasks done by women and men, the passage marks out a clear distinction of tasks and their locations. Men are outdoors doing agricultural tasks, and women are in domestic settings where they nurse children, knead bread, weave, and spin.

Writing about the leprosy exam became another site at which to make notions of gender and work seem ordinary and natural. The passage could have listed a single set of common positions for both women and men, and then supplied additional positions where necessary, say for the examination of women's breasts. Furthermore, rabbinic writers did not need to describe the exam through the language of labor. That they did should be our primary curiosity. Gender divisions of labor are exacted in a passage that seemingly has nothing to do with labor. The inspection is precisely a time when a worker has stopped working in order to be examined. Instead, description of this exam became an opportunity to make distinctions of gender and to represent them as part of daily life and its labors.

A second passage, from tractate Zabim, lists situations in which *zav* (*zāb*) impurity might be transmitted from one man to another.[20] Each example sports two men. One—the *zav*—is in the impure state caused by a genital discharge. The second—the *tahor* (*ṭāhôr*)—is in a state of purity but is in danger of receiving the impurity through contact with the *zav*. The text imagines these two men together in positions where, at the moment, they are near each other but not touching. However, their support is unsteady, perhaps a bridge, board, or bed frame, and at any moment they might slip and slide, thus transmitting a secondary (or derivative) impurity from the *zav* to the *tahor*. In the list of these situations in mZabim 3.2, two men are near each other, but only one is in a state of purity. They close or open doors, lift one another out of a pit, and knot ropes together. Two weavers work together. They use either one kind of loom—the *ʿômdîn*—or another—the *yôšbîn*. And according to the halakah, no matter which loom is used, the impurity will not be transmitted.

The passage imagines the men working at both the newer loom and at the older loom. The ʿômdîn is the older, warp-weighted loom associated with female weavers in mNegaim 2.4; a second loom, the yôšbîn, can be identified as the newer two-beam loom. The name derives from the weaver's position while working at the loom. As already described, instead of weaving up toward the top, on this new loom the web is woven down near the bottom. The weaver sits rather than stands. The terminology coincides with the loom's own form of physical support. Unlike warp-weighted looms that lean against walls, the two-beam loom rests on its own base.[21] The significant piece of information for our inquiry is that the passage considers that men might work at both the newer and the older type of loom.

In the third passage, tKelim Baba Batra 1.2, one woman has been weaving with another woman. While they were weaving, the first woman was in a state of purity. She also knew that the cloth on the loom had not contracted any impurities. This toseftan passage expands upon mKelim 21.1, which had already placed the loom into a matrix of impurity and its transmission, and asserted the principle that only loom parts that are directly connected to the woven cloth can transmit impurities to the weaver. To make this point, the mishnaic passage mentions various loom parts. The loom's beams—upper or lower, its heddle bars, and its shed bars do not transmit impurity. Nor are impurities transmitted by touching the unspun yarn on the distaff or on the weighing tray. Impurities can be transmitted by touching the already woven web, the unwoven warp threads that hang vertically, or the yarn spool that is thrown back and forth through the shed. Impurities are also transmitted by the spindle's spun yarn (which had not yet been rewound into a skein or onto a shuttle), yarn that is in the process of being rewound onto a spool or into a skein, or impure yarn that is already woven into the cloth.

The passage considers loom parts, spindle, and other accouterments in great detail, and demonstrates rabbinic knowledge of these minutiae. The loom described by mKelim 21.1 has an upper beam and a lower beam. Thus, the transmission of impurities is illustrated with example of the two-beam loom. To this illustration the Tosefta adds another kind of loom. In further contrast to the Mishnah's description, the Tosefta locates its loom next to the bodies of women. In tKelim Baba Batra 1.2, the first woman approaches Rabbi Ishmael for a purity inspection. Although initially both she and the cloth on the loom had been in a state of purity, she had not been very particular about guarding it. Ishmael presses her on this point, and the woman reports that while the cloth was on the loom, another woman who was menstruating—a *niddah*—had come to help her weave and had "pulled the rope" on the loom with her (*maškāh ʿimi ba-ḥevel*).

For Rabbi Ishmael and the Tosefta this contact becomes the crucial information for assessing whether the loom, cloth, and woman are now in a condition of impurity. For us, it provides additional information about gender and technology. A loom in which a second weaver would "pull the rope" provides the key. The pulled rope identifies the loom as the warp-weighted loom. The rope maneuvers the shed that separates the vertical warp threads so that the shuttle of woof yarn can be passed through to form another row of web. The pulled rope refers most likely to the rope used to keep the weights steady as the shed was moved back and forth, and secondarily, the rope refers to the woof yarn attached to the shuttle, which would be thrown and pulled through the hanging warp threads. While the two-beam loom also had warp threads, they were tightly secured by the bottom beam and thus did not require someone to "pull the rope" to keep the weighted warp threads roughly in place. Accounts of more recent warp-weighted weaving show that two weavers greatly facilitated weaving on this type of loom.[22] Attending to the warp-weighted loom is the Tosefta's contribution to the mishnaic text. Since mKelim 21.1 had located the two-beam loom on a map of ritual purity, tKelim Baba Batra 1.2 enacts a similar mapping, but of another type of loom. In these two passages, the loom that is not explicitly linked with men or with women is the two-beam loom. The mishnaic version presented the two-beam loom without any reference to a human weaver and without directly invoking gender. In tKelim Baba Batra 1.2, the warp-weighted loom is described vividly with female weavers—and with a (male) rabbinic authority. The loom associated with women is the older technology, the more difficult to use warp-weighted loom.

There were many different ways to form gender and display its details in everyday life. Sometimes gender is established as an absolute difference, sometimes as a segregation in which one group has access to a full range of possibilities, while access for another group is more limited. These passages about weavers and looms illustrate the latter attempt at gender formation. This strategy does not demand a total difference and separation. Thus, men and women need not always use distinct looms with no overlap. Rather, these three passages confer a segregation or sequestering of technology. Men are pictured with both the new and the old technology. Women are represented using the warp-weighted loom alone. In these rabbinic representations of weavers at their looms, men have the freedom to move from technology to technology. Women are restricted to one. This is not merely a separation (with its suggestion that the differences are equal), but a segregation that imparts unequal values and hierarchy. The loom to which women are restricted is the old-fashioned loom, the one that produced cloth more slowly and with less ease. Placing women at this older loom marks their lower status in the economy of production, just as it marks men's higher station. If these representations were true depictions of how weavers worked, then women would be placed at a technical disadvantage, making it more difficult for them to compete with male weavers in the production of cloth.

Setting these early rabbinic passages into conversation with other, material texts about looms make another element of gender immediately visible. These rabbinic passages were promulgated from the beginning of the third century and onward. They represent a segregation of technology that would have been historically impossible. In most instances where technology changes, there is a period of overlap in which old and new technologies coexist. But for those who heard and read them from the early third century on, these rabbinic texts present a warp-weighted loom that had disappeared in Palestine by the mid-second century. The evidence for the end of the overlap and the end of warp-weighted weaving in Palestine is archaeological. The telltale sign of the warp-weighted loom is its weights. Loom weights are the only loom parts that are archaeologically visible.[23] For example, excavations from Masada included large amounts of loom weights that can be dated to the mid to late first century.[24]

Beginning in the second century excavation reports show an absence of loom weights in places where they should have been found. For example, despite evidence of human habitation and although all sorts of textiles and tools were found there—including masses of unspun yarn, spindle whorls, skeins of spun yarn, and a hooked needle with a wooden handle used as a weaving shuttle—the excavated caves from the Dead Sea region, just south of Palestine, contain no loom weights.

This suggests that by the mid-130s another loom was in use, one that left no archaeological traces.[25] To the north, reports from Galilean sites with both workshop and domestic buildings used during the second to fourth centuries either show no loom weights, or list an occasional single loom weight. Since objects that look like loom weights must be found in sets or in rows in order to ascertain their function as loom weights, these single artifacts cannot attest to the use of warp-weighted looms past the mid-second century. My surveys of archaeological archives buttress the argument that the warp-weighted loom disappeared from use by the mid-second century. The Rockefeller Museum in East Jerusalem holds materials excavated before the Israeli state's existence. It lists no loom weights from the first century or later in its collections. The Romema storeroom of the Israel Antiquities Authority holds the materials excavated after 1948 from certain regions of Israel and Palestine. Its files for published and unpublished minor objects show vividly the dwindling of loom weights, and hence, warp-weighted looms, by the second century.[26]

Rabbinic descriptions of realia seem so real, but this equation is precisely what needs to be interrogated. The warp-weighted loom vanished from Palestine by the mid-second century. The Mishnah was promulgated in the early third century, the Tosefta a few decades later.[27] The distance between the technology and the text places us readers into the realm of rabbinic fantasy, even when the tools of its imagination are the mundanities of how looms worked and how weavers wove. The disjuncture that disallows the equation of rabbinic realia to reality is that early rabbinic texts from the third century associate with women a loom that had been extinct since the mid-second century. Almost a century after the warp-weighted loom's disappearance, these texts present for their posterity the picture of a woman positioned to work at an antiquated loom. Thus, calling this situation a sequestering or a segregation allows us to believe in some ways that all this was real, that it was lived out, or seen. It lets us analyze these representations as if they were transparent and unmediated comments on daily life, mere details on the way to discussions of more "substantive" halakic topics of the transmission of bodily impurities of genital discharges and menstrual blood.

But in rabbinic texts details matter. Consider how this disjuncture between realia and reality enables rabbinic texts to embed gender into something as ordinary and ubiquitous as weaving. In the passage from tractate Negaim, the pose for women to assume at a purity examination was a mode of weaving that was no longer practiced and no longer available. Nonetheless it will be remembered by examined women, by the examining inspectors, and most of all by the rabbis and students who in their academies—far from female bodies and lesions—will learn and repeat the text. That rabbinic texts should refer to something extinct or ancient is not in itself surprising. The Mishnah and Tosefta refer constantly to things that no longer exist. References to the ritual of the destroyed Temple and the priesthood fill tractate upon tractate. Yet, rabbis had reasons for narrating details of Temple life and priestly practice as they did. What then were the reasons, or better, what were the cultural effects of these legal stories of technology and gender? What did rabbis gain by entangling working bodies, gendered tasks, and concerns for ritual purity? First, this was not a separation on equal terms. Men could use and were represented using both looms. Women were linked with only one. The loom with which women were linked was older, less efficient, and less physically comfortable to use. It did not produce textiles of the quality and at the pace that was possible with the newer two-beam loom.

A second effect was to invest gender into specific technologies. Through vivid passages that place the warp-weighted loom near the bodies of women, the warp-weighted loom itself is feminized and technology itself becomes gendered. As the newer technology was associated with men, the concepts of newness and innovation were masculinized. And, third, apart from the association of a specific technology with a specific gender, weaving technology became another of many sites for the performance and reiteration of gender. Through this reiteration the very idea of gender as a significant difference starts to seem like a natural way for the world to be, as if gender were a matter of course and not a practice whose outlines and details and divisions needed to be carefully tended. Fourth, that the "women's" loom was not just outmoded but obsolete suggests another mundane economic violence. If the material effects of such representations can no longer be proven directly from the fragments that remain from Jewish life in Roman Palestine, they can be imagined without much historical contradiction. In effect, women were separated from viable and profitable technology. Women were removed from realms where their labors could become a viable part of production, trade, and profit. And this removal yields another effect, one that becomes clear when we see how the material and the metaphoric combine. As time progresses and technology changes, a small slice of the past is presented in gendered terms. These passages use women and femininity to represent the old, the antique, the nostalgic. Women are linked with the past.

SIGNS OF DIFFERENCE

Our critical attention seems to fall on smaller and smaller signs of difference. And this only emphasizes one of the strategies through which early rabbinic writings configured gender as an eventually nearly unnoticeable feature of the everyday. Whether with images of a warp-weighted or two-beam loom, wool fibers or flax, in these microdifferences work and gender were embedded into the ordinary, into what was repetitive, mundane and unthought, and into what was ritualized. The familiar and often unnoticed quotidian became a powerful mechanism for the reproduction of gender and other differences.

Pliny, Apuleius, the rabbis, and others who wrote about or listened for or lived or knew or saw these signs of difference can be thought about from another frame of reference. Already by the period of the Roman Empire and the production of early rabbinic texts, spinning, weaving, and other ordinary types of work had long histories as ways to express cultural differences. More than five centuries before, Herodotus (born 484 B.C.E.) had tendered the notion that labors are naturally divided and assigned to either men or women, and that such divisions are a necessary part of a society. He then used his distinctions to express cultural differences between "Greeks" and "Egyptians":

> As the Egyptians have a climate peculiar to themselves, and their river is different in its nature from all other rivers, so they have made all their customs and laws of a kind contrary for the most part to those of all other men. Among them, the women buy and sell, the men abide at home and weave; and whereas in weaving all others push the woof upwards, the Egyptians push it downwards.[28]

Herodotus invoked difference through a series of references, first to climate and rivers, then to the divided labors of women and men. Each of these was a site of ordinary, repeated activity. Thus, differences between Greeks and Egyptians are found in nature. Their Egyptian climate is peculiar, their northern-flowing river is as different from Greek rivers as it is unique. The differences of river and climate set up the next two examples—gendered labors and technologies of weaving—to be understood as similarly "natural." Technology and gender-based divisions of labor are used to show essential cultural differences. If Greek men belong in public places and Greek women stay at home, by doing so they demonstrate their very Greekness. In contrast and opposition, Egyptian men stay indoors and weave, while Egyptian women navigate the worlds of commerce, and the Greek Herodotus clearly devalues this anomaly from his own culture.

And finally, if Greek weavers wove woof thread into warp from the bottom of the loom, and then pushed the new woof upward into the already woven web, Herodotus used variations in these technologies of weaving to describe the cultural differences of Egyptians. Weavers in Egypt, he claims, enter woof threads into warp from the top of the looms, and push the new woof down, adding it to the web that sits below it on the loom.

At issue, of course, is not whether these claims were "true," that is, whether or not Herodotus's comparison of the weaving techniques of Greeks and Egyptians is accurate. In any case, several formats for weaving were available in both Greece and Egypt. Rather, at issue is how Herodotus—and his readers in the Roman period and later—used ordinary motions and movements to write about differences between people, and how they used these differences to forge people into distinct and regionally-based "peoples." Within this standard, one demonstrates the correctness of one's society through the ways in which work and space are allotted to women and to men. One's identity and place among the world's regions are indicated through the mundane, even thoughtless repetitions that interlace woof threads in and out of an already strung warp thread stretched vertically on a loom.[29]

This instance would be just one of many in the Mediterranean of antiquity. That various writers, workers, groups, and collections of texts found different resolutions to the problems and possibilities of gender, labor, tools, and techniques is not surprising. That they used these resolutions to effect different kinds of cultural distinctions is, similarly, unsurprising, although these arrangements were neither essentially necessary, nor were they inevitable.

These attempts, then, would be unremarkable, pertinent only to their times and neighbors. Except, Herodotus had a Roman-period readership. The images he used were learned repeatedly by young men, generation after generation. Similarly, early rabbinic texts were read and studied and commented upon for generations that include the present. Centuries later, the use of loom technology and weaving techniques remained a small but potent way to express difference and its values. The twelfth-century Jewish commentator Rashi used loom technology once again to distinguish men from women, remarking that men weave with their feet, while women use a cane that moves up and down.[30] An eleventh-century Christian commentary on the New Testament Gospel of John sought to explain how Jesus' seamless cloak was produced. One Theophylactus, a bishop in Bulgaria, writes, "Others say that in Palestine they weave their fabrics not as with us, having the warp threads above and weaving below with the bobbin and thus mounting; but on the contrary, the warp threads are below and the web is woven from above."[31] As expressions of difference, these technologies, tools, and labors remained familiar, for centuries.

CHAPTER FOUR

Domesticity

The rabbinic visions for Jewish life that developed after the fall of the Jerusalem Temple contained markedly new formulations of family life. New possibilities and new proprieties were imagined. Many of these new formulations were expressed in the language of property, ex changes of labor and support, and other kinds of economic relations. To the extent that early rabbinic Judaism was persuasive to Jews or, to the extent that it was already embedded in a broader Jewish and Roman culture, these economic innovations touched the intimacy of lives that married women and men spent together. As wives and husbands, they inhabited houses where foods and drink were continually prepared and consumed, where beds were made, slept in and remade, and where a myriad of tasks were carried out, in close relation and close proximity, repeatedly, day in and day out. The familiarity of family relations makes it remarkably easy to think that concepts such as "femininity," "fatherhood," "family," and "domesticity" are natural categories. Their repetition makes it easy to believe that although these concepts change, they have an underlying essence that remains relatively stable. It would seem almost oxymoronic, then, to speak of their histories.

But what happens when we do? Most popular and current renditions of Jewish female domesticity—the relations of women, labor, and home—turn at some point to the image of the "worthy woman" from Proverbs 31.10–31: "A woman of valor, who can find her?"[1] In this biblical text, a married woman transforms wool and flax into high quality and useful clothing for her household, her husband, and herself.

In addition to her unpaid labor of overseeing the management of the household and distributing charity, this woman is economically active. While her husband performs his civic role at the city gates, she weaves linen and sells it to merchants. With the profits she acquires land and plants a vineyard. Her textile work results in products for market. Spinning and weaving are not primarily demonstrations of her sexual fidelity and wifely devotion to her husband, as they would later become. Her work brings wages that can be used to buy land and increase the holdings of the woman and her family, and for this the biblical passage praises her.

Eventually, Proverbs 31 would become central to the gender consciousness of much later Jewish religious culture. It will be recited, for example, as part of a weekly Shabbat home service that pays tribute to wives. However, despite its later popularity, this biblical portrait of domesticity was not central to the gender culture of early rabbinic and Roman-period Judaism. The Targum, a set of Aramaic bible translations that date from this period, often gloss and expand the biblical verses they are supposedly translating. But the woman of valor from Proverbs 31.10–31 receives surprisingly little elaboration in the Targum, suggesting that the image evoked little active interest.[2] This is noteworthy, because in the Roman period, Jewish writers were not at all uninterested in domesticity and the formation of women into wives; far from it. It was just that the possibilities offered by this particular inherited text were of little use to them. A look at how conceptions of what a wife should be changed between the writing of the biblical book of Proverbs and the mishnaic tractate Ketubot explains their lack of interest. It also shows the fallacy of imagining domesticity as natural, essential, or unchanging.

LABORING FOR ONE'S HUSBAND

One reason why the passage from Proverbs was not attractive to rabbinic writers was that this biblical conception of the relations of women, labor, and property differed greatly from that of the rabbis. Proverbs' portrait of an industrious wife ran counter to the new character of the rabbinic wife. The proverbial woman labored by her own command. When her work yielded products and profits and property, she owned and controlled these. She is depicted with a degree of autonomy and independence.[3] In contrast, early rabbinic writings move aspects of the ownership and control of a married woman's labors and work to her husband.[4] The husband would own his wife's work (the completed products and the wages she garnered), and he held authority over his wife's labors (the repetitive daily tasks she would do).[5] As the new rabbinic Judaism emerged, female industry and thrift still matter — as they did in Proverbs — but the control of her labor becomes part of the definition of being female in rabbinic society. Domesticity not only changes from the vision in Proverbs, it becomes a discipline.

Early rabbinic law proposed two categories of labor for Jewish wives. In the first, "labors that a woman does for her husband," wives performed unpaid domestic labors. In the second, a married woman produced commodities or sold her services, and in turn, she received wages, money, objects in kind, or other kinds of profit and recompense. The Mishnah considers these profits to be "new property," and a wife's new property must be turned over to her husband, to whom it will belong.[6] I turn first to the issue of unpaid labor, articulated in the household code of mKetubot 5.5.[7] From one perspective, the passage classifies and clarifies household work for married women. But describing it this way assumes that a prior connection exists between married women and domesticity, and then asks about the details. What happens when we shift perspective and question the proposition that women and domesticity are inherently linked? From another perspective, one that does not assume an essential connection between a married woman and domesticity, it becomes clear that the passage must first constitute the wife as a household worker. This is done as part of and prior to listing the terms for what her work will mean and naming the husband as the owner of her labors.

As part of a discussion about the relation of wives, home, and labor, mKetubot 5.5 enumerates the possibilities for a wife to discharge her labors to any household slaves or servants she brought with her to the marriage. This discussion is followed by several comments, respectively attributed to Rabbi Eliezer and Rabban Shimon ben Gamliel. These comments no longer define female domesticity in terms of actual labor but in terms of sexuality and leisure. The passage mKetubot 5.5. translates as follows:

> These are the labors that the wife does for her husband: she grinds, and she bakes and she launders; she cooks, and she nurses her child; she tends the bedding and she works in wool.
>
> If [the wife] brought [to the husband, when they married] one household slave, then she does not grind and she does not bake and she does not launder.

[If she brought to him] two [household slaves] she does not cook and she does not nurse her child.

[If she brought to him] three [household slaves], she does not tend to the bedding and she does not work in wool.

[If she brought to him] four [household slaves], she may sit upon a chair of leisure.

Rabbi Eliezer says: Even if she brought to him a hundred household slaves, he forces her to work in wool, because leisure brings about sexual temptations and suspicions.
Rabban Shimon ben Gamliel says: If through a vow [her husband] forbid his wife from doing work tasks, he must divorce [her] and give the ketubbah to her, because leisure brings lifelessness upon her.

Ancient references to everyday life seem factual and real, but in this passage, we are deeply immersed in the realm of rabbinic fantasies about domesticity. Under the principle of labors that a wife must do for her husband, the passage lists seven tasks: grinding grain, baking bread, laundering clothing and other textiles, cooking, nursing children, tending the bedding, and working in wool. Following this, it moves immediately to consider how a woman's economic status might affect domesticity. Her economic position is established by the number of servants or slaves she brings with her into the marriage. For households in which wives have servants or slaves, the passage begins to reverse the association of wives with domestic labor. The labor of servants or slaves can replace her own. If through a dowry or inheritance, the wife brings to the marriage one slave, she does not have to grind, bake, or wash. Two slaves will release her from cooking and nursing children. With three slaves, she can refrain from tending to the beds and from working in wool. With four servants or slaves, a married Jewish woman can pursue a life free from domestic labor. Through these exchanges, task after task is removed from her set of responsibilities until none remain.

Reading only this far into the passage, it seems as if mKetubot 5.5 uses distinctions of economic status to create a variety of wives. Just as "woman" is always women, and "femininity" always femininities, "wife" can be construed as various performances of wifery—the acts and activities of being a wife. Depending on her wealth, the contents of a woman's domesticity might differ. Eventually, if a woman were sufficiently wealthy, her wifery could be constructed on terms in which her husband was not the recipient of her labor. For some women, being a wife could be separated from the performance of domesticity.[8]

Reading further, however, it becomes clear that the passage's argument moves away from allowing wives to have varying relations to household labor and domesticity. Instead, the passage removes the possibility of the final, freeing exchange. Following the calculus of traded labors, the position attributed to Rabbi Eliezer reneges the possibility that a wealthy wife could trade away her domestic labors. Even with economic privilege, a woman can never entirely remove domestic duties from her performance of being a wife. All married women are linked with domestic labor. Eliezer's position links wifely labors with concerns about female sexuality: Even if the wife brought a hundred household slaves to the husband when they married, the husband can force her to work in wool. His reasoning is that leisure brings about sexual temptations and suspicions. The link between domesticity and wifery must be retained, and the link is signified by wool work. Echoing other Roman writing, from Livy to Dionysius of Halicarnassus to Apuleius, the passage invokes the familiar notion that labor—and especially wool work—protects women (and the men who claim them) from the sexual temptations associated with leisure. The metaphor of wool work reassures husbands that the sexual temptations of their female relatives and wives are tightly under control.[9]

Echoing these patterns for representing Roman women and wives, wool work becomes the symbol of marital piety for Jewish women. Because of this association, it becomes the only task that a wife cannot trade away. The earlier part of the passage had envisioned *almost all* married women, from poor to affluent, engaged in wool work. Eliezer expands this continuum: *all* women, including the most affluent, must work in wool. Wool work insures sexual loyalties that, like labors, are owed to the husband. If a woman forsakes her labor, she risks also forsaking her sexual morality. Wool work signals both her resistance to sexual temptations and her laboring debts. A wife's household labors belong to her husband's domain and are under his control. Her labors are not imagined as forms of religious piety, or of devotion to family, but as piety to the husband. Jewish wifery includes domestic labor to protect a husband from his wife's sexual betrayal. Of course, including domestic labor in the definition of Jewish wifery also protects his privileges to her household labors and to her laboring body. Releasing a wife—even and especially a wealthy wife—from household work effectively removes her laboring body from her husband's domain. Eliezer's position refuses to diminish so completely this element of a husband's authority.

Eliezer's position is followed by one attributed to Rabban Shimon ben Gamliel. A husband cannot make a vow that forbids his wife from performing her domestic tasks. If the husband makes this kind of vow, he must divorce his wife and give her the ketubbah payment. The reason given: Jewish women must not lead lives of leisure, because the result of leisure for women is "lifelessness." Leisure yields lifelessness, but if we show some skepticism at the logical ease of this equation, some important features become clear. The point that domesticity must always be part of Jewish wifery is made a second time, but in a different way and with another set of ramifications. Shimon ben Gamliel's position effectively prohibits individual husbands and wives from undoing the rabbinic binding of wifery to domesticity. In Roman-period Judaism, vows functioned as a kind of anarchic folk religion, in which certain acts or goods were renounced or set aside in exchange for a wish, promise, or other result. For example, through a vow, a husband could reorganize the distribution of labor in his household. He could release his wife from her domestic labors. Shimon ben Gamliel's position would prohibit these individual attempts to separate domesticity and wifery, and in so doing, to construct wifery on alternate terms.

The rationale given for this prohibition is the protection of women. Wives perform household labors for their own good, and individual husbands must not undermine wifely domesticity, because it benefits the woman by preventing a slide into a condition of lifelessness. The logic of protection is a bit tricky and needs to be unraveled. As a whole, mKetubot 5.5 places wives into an economy of female domesticity, slavery, servitude, and household labors. Structurally, the entire economy is organized around the husband, who is present only as the recipient and owner of labors. To recall, the entire passage explicates the general principle of "labors that the wife performs for her husband." This organization of household life underscores the husband's privileges. Unlike the others, he is not a domestic laborer but the recipient of labors performed by his wife, by servants, or by slaves. The first named position—Rabbi Eliezer's—had deciphered that economy in sexual terms: domestic labor is a discipline that composes and displays a wife's sexual fidelity. The second position—Shimon ben Gamliel's—provides a very different explanation: a wife's labor is for her own benefit. It protects her from the perceived negative effects of (something imagined as) leisure. Whereas in Eliezer's position wool work controls women's sexuality, according to Shimon ben Gamliel, household labor is necessary because it protects the quality of women's lives.

Thus, mKetubot 5.5 concludes with an argument about the protection of women. The discourse of protection is almost always difficult to unravel, since declarations of care, kindness, and benevolence mask the fact that people have unequal relations to power. Shimon ben Gamliel's comment envisions a gendered world in which women are imagined to need rabbinic protection.[10] Included in this is the notion that rabbinic law protects women from the whims of their (Jewish) husbands. From this rabbinic perspective, if an individual Jewish husband releases his wife from domestic labor, this release hastens her downfall into lifelessness. To counter the husband's potential vows, Shimon ben Gamliel claims that the demand that wives engage in domestic labor in fact protects the quality of Jewish women's lives.

Of course, on some level, it is impossible for us to judge how a Jewish woman living in Roman Palestine might have evaluated these options. Since either "choice" limits her considerably, and since both choices construct her as controlled by men, it might be the case that she would have preferred other kinds of options; we can never know. However, for us to side either with Shimon ben Gamliel or with the imagined husband is to think within, and not against, rabbinic logic. If the comment constructs the question of wives' domestic labors as a battle between rabbinic halakah and Jewish husbands, we need not follow the rabbinic text into the logic of its argument. Reading from elsewhere, in this scenario neither husbands nor rabbis protect wives. Shimon ben Gamliel's position would restrict a husband from compromising the economy that the Mishnah sets up as a crucial part of marriage. His claim to protect women (from husbands, from lifelessness) masks the passage's real protection of men. By focusing, as mKetubot 5.5 does, on what women do, the passage effectively hides from view the very men whom it privileges and whose advantages it will extend. This position hides both the husband who controls and owns the wife's labors, and the rabbis who imagine themselves as legislators, but who were, simultaneously, husbands themselves. It makes an economy of discipline and control seem benevolent, and for a woman's own good.

THE WORK OF HER HANDS

Discourses of gender are almost always contradictory, internally riven, and at odds. Mishnah Ketubot 5.5 imagines a wife's daily life as devoted either to domesticity or to leisure. Simultaneously, a second category for women's labor attends to other possibilities, in which a wife works and receives wages and earns a profit. The legalities of mKetubot

5.5 had established women's "nonwaged work" (*melākot*) at home and constituted these as labors she owed to her husband. A second category of female labor was the "work of her hands" (*maʿaśēh yādêhā*). This category includes work through which a wife or daughter brings new property—money, products, and such—into the family economy. It was an innovation of early rabbinic Judaism to remand the profits of a woman's labor to her husband or father, and in doing so, to control women's wages, products, profits, and properties so extensively. This form of economic control affected not just wives, but all women and girls who were part of families and family economies. The general principle was formulated in mKetubot 6.1: "[The] finds of the woman and [the] work of her hands [belong] to her husband, and [concerning] her inheritance, he [owns] fruits [of the inheritance] during her lifetime."[11] Anything of value which a woman gained through her own activity belongs to her husband. That which became hers less actively (such as the "old property" of dowry, inheritance, or gifts, for example) belongs to her, but the husband controls the property and owns the profits.[12] Other passages—discussed in chapter 5—detail a similar relationship between daughter and father, the point being that for any woman under a man's authority, whether husband or father, her laboring body and the profits of her work were to be controlled and owned by that man.

These historic innovations of early rabbinic Judaism remanded the work of wives and daughters to their husband or father. The legal innovation of the work of her hands was paired—at least for wives—with another, that of *mezônôt*, a husband's legal responsibility to maintain and support his wife. (This linking of privilege and responsibility did not extend to daughters, whose fathers were not obligated to support them.) As innovations whose details and goals were still somewhat uncertain, the question of how a man's ownership of female labors and profits was related to his legal obligation to support members of his family was the subject of ongoing debate and contestation. But before veering off into these intricacies—the subject of chapter 5—I return to the differences between biblical and mishnaic versions of domesticity's gendered labors.

THE SPINDLE'S SURPLUS VALUE

The spindle appears repeatedly, a stable sign of unstable and changing notions of femininity. It is present at the climax of mKetubot 5.5, in which Rabbi Eliezer invokes it as the unremovable marker of female

domesticity, the task that cannot be traded away.[13] The icon recurs in
early rabbinic discussions of the work of her hands, that is, in discussions of women's waged labor. The passage mKetubot 5.9 discusses the
special case of a husband who maintains his wife through a guardian
or agent (*i.e.*, through a third person). Such a case might result because
the husband lives in a different locale, because he is looking for employment or travels for business, or because he has several wives and does
not live with all of them. The details of a husband's responsibility to
maintain his wife are narrated vividly, for the first and only time. If a
husband supports his wife through an agent he must provide her with
a bed, mattress and mat, shoes and clothing, and assorted amounts and
types of food. In addition to these material goods and foods, the husband, through his agent, must provide the wife with a silver coin for
what the passage describes as "her needs."[14] Introducing this last aspect
of maintenance—and still discussing the specific case of a woman provided for by a guardian—mKetubot 5.9 translates: "He gives her a silver *māʿāh* for her needs, and she eats with him from one Sabbath to the
next."

But the passage then yields to an instance of conflict. What if the
husband's agent does not provide his part of the bargain? What if he
reneges on the silver coin? What can the wife do? If this happens,
the wife's legal recourse is to withhold the profits from the work of her
hands. The text continues: "And if he does not give a silver *māʿāh*, the
work of her hands is hers." What is striking is that the passage measures the amount of her earned wages that would equal the silver coin
by using the metaphor and weight of spun yarn: "What must [the wife]
do for him? [Her work] must weigh five *selaim* of warp thread, in
Judea, which equals to ten *selaim* in the Galilee. Or, [her work] must
weigh ten *selaim* of woof thread in Judea, which equals twenty *selaim*
in Galilee."[15]

Despite the many kinds of work that women in Roman Palestine
might have done to earn wages or other kinds of profit, the passage
measures the work of her hands in terms of quantities of spun yarn.
Furthermore, this spun yarn is described in weights and thicknesses
necessary for weaving at the loom. The framework of the web is established by the heavier warp yarn, and the thinner woof yarn is woven in
between. By measuring her labor as yarn and not as money, the passage
narrows the range of female labors into the more singular icon of wool
work. By describing a woman's profit-bearing labor through a symbol
of domesticity, the rabbinic passage shortens the range of services and

labors it will represent, and imagine, women doing. And, it prefers to portray a woman's life in terms of barter and exchange that must be mediated through her husband and his agent, rather than to describe her as participating more directly in the economy of marketplace exchange.

How does the early rabbinic spindle work? The spindle combines women's domestic and unpaid labor with women's paid labor. It links a woman's unpaid household labor with the waged fruits of her labor that she also owed to her husband. The spindle flattens out and effaces the major difference between them: namely, that in one of these categories of labor, a woman's work potentially takes place outside of her relation to domesticity and her place within her husband's domain. Discursively, the spindle marks the impossibility of an economic existence for married women that is not controlled by her husband, an existence in which the husband is not the ultimate recipient of her body's labors. Through the recurring figure of the spindle, the work that would place her, even temporarily, outside the realm of domesticity is reconfigured as a domestic task.[16] Writing about these things through the spindle facilitates this kind of discursive and legal control. If a woman's domestic labor is symbolized as wool work, using this figure to regulate her waged labors makes it seem more familiar and "natural" to place these labors on a continuum with her domestic labor. Connecting nonwaged labor to waged, even a wife's waged labor is placed—legally and conceptually—into the domain of her husband's control.

For the real and unknowable families of Roman Palestine, the material results of wives' labors probably mattered greatly. The resources and services made available through the interrelated labor of various household members—wives, husbands, children, servants, or slaves—contributed to making the household run. In the most immediate sense, the surplus value of a woman's paid labor produced resources, either wages or other kinds of reward, that made a positive difference. But the rabbinic text is not concerned with things so prosaic. Consider what is absent from rabbinic possibilities of what wives might do: they express no desires for well-kept houses, nor for the property and resources that a woman's wages might bring. The surplus value of women's labor was not conceived in terms of actual products and services. Through the spindle's shadow, the surplus value of economic resources slides into something else, into the spindle's other value: feminine domesticity, loyalty to husbands, and appropriate practices of wifery for Jewish women. The surplus value of wifely labors was the reproduction of gender, and the performance of appropriate female sexual roles. In mKetubot 5.5, even if a wife had slaves or servants to do the actual tasks, and even if the family could afford to buy all the cloth, clothing, and other textile products it wanted or needed, still her wool work is necessary to display her fidelity to her husband. If the woman and her family were wealthy, the material products of her body's labors were economically unnecessary, but in this fantasy of Jewish wives, she still must spin. The surplus value of the spindle is a declaration that her laboring body belongs to her husband. Through the spindle, the work of her hands is constituted within an economy of sexualized labors, gendered sexuality, and labors that produce gender.

BACK TO PROVERBS

There is a radical economic difference between the wife portrayed in Proverbs 31 and the wife being developed in early rabbinic literature. The wife in Proverbs had economic agency. She wove her linen cloth. She sold it to merchants. With her profits she bought land, and she planted the land with a vineyard. Her initial work at the spindle was transformed into an investment in grapes that would ideally yield continuous profits as new grapes grew, were harvested, sold, or made into wine, year after year. The profits would be her own. Her textile work corresponded with her market activity. She produces, she sells, she makes decisions, she buys, she prospers.

This is what separates the ancient expression of domesticity in Proverbs 31 from the newer rabbinic version. In the Roman period, rabbinic law began to extend the privileges of Jewish husbands by giving them greater control over family economy and over their wives. Chapter 1, above, analyzed the debate in mKetubot 8.1 over two such innovations. The first innovation was the husband's relation to a wife's (or betrothed's) old property, which he controlled and whose profits he owned through his right to usufruct. This new arrangement of control over the woman's old property was accompanied by the legal innovation that granted the husband ownership and control of the wife's new property: everything she found or collected, everything produced by the work of her hands, as well as the profits from inherited property she owned. These innovations clarify the difference between Proverbs 31 and early rabbinic economies of gender, labor, and property.

If the woman of Proverbs 31 had lived instead in the rabbinic imaginary, the profits she made by selling her linen would belong to her husband, the land she bought would be owned by her husband, and the fruit produced in the vineyard would belong to him as well.[17] Proverbs 31 assumes that a wife owns her earnings. In contrast, early rabbinic law remands a wife's earnings to her husband. As compared to this much earlier Israelite text that was a privileged legacy for Jews, the religio-legal texts of Mishnah and Tosefta define women and women's work through very different sets of social, sexual, economic, and family relations.

Interpreters of biblical and rabbinic texts often point to the spindle as a marker of continuity in Israelite and Jewish notions of wives. But this derives from the cultural habit of making the spindle into an icon of an "essential" womanhood, one which remains the same despite apparent differences and change. But in a critical gesture that upsets the idea that gender or sex or labor are essential characters of anything, the dissimilarities will suddenly be highlighted and more easily seen. The spindle changes. In Proverbs 31 and biblical texts more generally, the woman's spindle is a general marker of sexual difference. It refers to femininity as masculinity's difference. It marks a boundary that delineates femininity as what men should not be and what men should not do.[18] The difference between the biblical spindle and the spindle as an icon in Roman, rabbinic, and Roman-period Jewish culture is this: whereas the biblical spindle signifies the desired difference between women and men, it does not include the lessons of sexual containment that the Roman-period spindle conveyed. In Proverbs, wool work and the spindle are signs of female productive labor. In mKetubot 5.5—and especially in the specific context of Rabbi Eliezer's statement—the products that result from wool work are economically unnecessary. Productivity in material terms is not what matters. In tractate Ketubot, wool work is not what facilitates the acquisition of land and vineyards; it is an antidote to what rabbis imagined as always potentially present and dangerous—a wife's sexual desires for someone other than her husband.

Metaphorically, this early rabbinic imbrication of wool work, domesticity, and female sexuality is dramatically different from the similar concerns in Proverbs 31. Unlike the Roman-period text, Proverbs 31 does not always frame its representation of female labor with concerns about sex and promiscuity. Female sexuality and female labor are not joined in the same ways that they will be in early rabbinic writing. Proverbs, too, has its fears of unrestrained female sexuality, but it does not incorporate these into its representation of the wife. Tractate Ketubot recasts women's economic participation into a repetitive situation in which husbands control their wives. Labor becomes a wife's display of sexual loyalty and fidelity. In other words, her domestic labors demonstrate her commitment to containment.

There is something jarring about the cultural history of this sign of women's work. One and the same, the spindle captured the wealthy princess, the protected upper-class daughter, and the matron.[19] It idealized the deceased and now perfect woman.[20] It signified the lower-status freeborn or freed working woman.[21] It evoked female figures that were imagined as divine or semidivine,[22] and it represented the despised work of enslaved women, who were explicitly owned and controlled.[23] It erased the differences between a woman's domestic labor and her market labors, and thus reduced the possibility for imagining a link between "women's work" and economic profit. The cultural oddity of linking wool work, women, and femininity formed a continuum of women, from those who were economically the most free to those who were the most controlled. In linking these women, the icon of female wool work flattens out differences between women. The wealthiest *matrona* is made similar to the lowest female slave. The continuum can be easily collapsed to construct a more singular, manipulable "woman."

Palestinian rabbis proffered their own variations on these discourses, and on issues of wifery, domesticity, and gender more generally, but their results are not categorically different from elements of Roman culture. If the spindle separates early rabbinic Judaism from an aspect of its biblical inheritance, it links rabbis with Roman culture. Attaching the spindle as the sign of women's laboring bodies, rabbis use their representations of Jewish women to show their similarity with something they imagined as "Rome." But since the possibilities of cultural engagement are never limited to either similarity or difference, mimicry or rejection, the following must be noted. In Latin and Greek writings, the spindle grasps at both the promise and the impossibility of female sexual fidelity. In the end, the spindle cannot assure that women were safe for society. Nor could it ensure that society was safe for women. On the other hand, as an offering to Roman culture and an indirect boast of the appropriateness of their families and their matrons by Roman standards, the early rabbinic spindle contains none of this ambiguity. It contains the promise of control and seems to harbor no element of the impossibility of total discipline. If rabbis were ever concerned that even wool work and the spindle might not fully control their women, they never committed this fear to writing.

Domesticity was a specific discipline of gender, one that was neither essential nor historically unchanging, although at times it has been believed to be. Unraveling the rabbinic binding of domesticity with wifeliness complicates our stories about women, men, and rabbis in this period of Jewish history. If this unraveling is a complicated task for us, it must be admitted that the process of constructing these definitions for families was also complicated for them. The kind of attention that early rabbinic writings gave to these innovations suggests the commitment and conflict that accompanied them. These innovations were made part of halakah, and eventually, came to structure Jewish daily life. In Roman-period Judaism, these innovations were not yet "natural" elements of Jewish life. They were specific and historically made decisions about which different rabbis disagreed, at least for a time. Traces of disagreement and contestation still remain, both within and outside early rabbinic texts. It is to these contests that the next chapter attends.

CHAPTER FIVE

Contestations

Family is not an inevitable social structure. Nor are its forms and varieties arrived at without process, or without disagreement and dissent. Both among rabbis, and between rabbis and Jews, the new rabbinic vision of the family was a contested subject. The halakic innovations that expanded the rights of the husband and father were birthed through conflict. Rabbis and Jews of Roman Palestine and its environs did not settle all the details for the changing ideas about families. Nor did they reach consensus on the desires and assumptions that were the foundations for these changes. Amid the details and facts of these early rabbinic innovations, their writings launched a series of polemics, arguments, and ideals. In this chapter I consider a set of passages from early rabbinic writing that is significant for examining the polemic around some of the new changes in family economy: I read the set for traces of contestation and conflict about family and gender. As rabbis debated among themselves the details of women's lives and the privileges of men, marriage documents used by Jews in the new Roman province of Arabia, near the Dead Sea, during the early second century provide another angle into these debates. These marriage documents especially show the discontent of some Jews with the rabbinic reluctance to legislate that fathers maintain their children.

On the way to thinking about contestations within early rabbinic Judaism stand the later traditions that have tried to make these innovations seamless. After the fact, many commentators have wished to connect these changes with prior notions of family within Jewish life and

law. They have claimed that these new ideas about families solved inherent problems, that thus they were necessary and good for all Jews.
One result of this is that the history of contestation and internal critique
has been lost, in favor of a more singular and flattened account. Second,
many traces of the production of these new versions and visions of family have been lost. Deprived of its history of change, the family is then
claimed to be a fount of continuity within Judaism.

These early rabbinic innovations were attempts to restructure the relations of power among family members. On the way to interpreting
Roman and Jewish antiquity stand the formulas that have been used
most frequently to assess power and gender in these texts. Immediately,
two such formulas from modern scholarship come to mind, which I
will call, respectively, "mutual exchange" and "inversion." Whereas the
early rabbis did not explain for us the rationale of their innovations,
as indeed they most often gave few such explanations for much of
what they proposed, the talmudic commentaries offered interpretation.
These talmudic explanations are the basis for scholarly accounts offered much more recently. Both formulas echo talmudic ideology, and
both suggest the extent to which critical scholarship of Jewish antiquity
is still reading within the Talmud's guidelines.

MUTUAL EXCHANGE

One mode for explaining power and gender flattens out any possibility
for seeing inequities against women. In early rabbinic Judaism, husbands gained ownership over their wives' labors and wages, wives lost
control of their labor to their husbands, and wives were to be maintained by their husbands. There has been a tradition that explains this
economy as a relation of mutual, or equivalent exchange. In this explanation, the equivalency of the exchange has been used to argue that
the new vision of marriage was built on a rabbinic ideal of marital mutuality.

A recent scholarly analysis illustrates this formula and provides
an example of its problems. In her 1988 analysis, Wegner refers to
mKetubot 5.9 (discussed in chapter 4), in which a husband supports his
wife through an agent or guardian. This passage contained a provision
whereby a wife may withhold a portion of her earned wages if she
has not received an element of her maintenance, the silver coin for her
needs. After listing the contents of her support, the passage raised the
question of what recourse the wife would have if the husband and his

agent withheld the money for her needs. The answer was that she could withhold the profits of her work, which were measured by amounts of spun yarn.

The passage mKetubot 5.9 refers specifically to the case of a wife whose husband supports her through a third party or guardian. In the following analysis the passage has been interpreted much more broadly and is used to describe the normative system of maintenance provided by a husband who supports his wife directly. Based on mKetubot 5.9, Wegner argues that these arrangements are built on a notion of "mutual exchange" between husband and wife, one that is equivalent, if not equal: "This rule [mKetubot 5.9] demonstrates the perceived reciprocity of the wife's duty to work for her husband and his duty to maintain her—the more so as the sages (as we shall see) spell out precisely how much cloth she must produce. This mutual arrangement, by highlighting the interdependence of the spouses, explicitly recognizes husband and wife as persons of an equivalent order though not of equal status."[1]

This scholarly argument paraphrases a position found more widely in rabbinic interpretation. The exchanges between husbands and wives provide the cornerstone of the family economy. Their positions are described with words like reciprocity, mutual arrangement, interdependence, and equivalence. Each term brings to mind pictures of related people whose roles are complementary to each other and to the welfare of a larger institution, the family. These terms suggest that the losses and gains of the husband and wife are—if we were to be so crass as to want to measure such things—commensurate. Bound together in a reciprocal relation, husband and wife are equivalent. If they occupy roles "of an equivalent order though not of equal status," the meaning of equivalency is, in this analysis, given higher value. "Equal" is disregarded as a desirable term for justice. Equality tends to be equated with sameness, and hence, equal is an untenable description of gender in early rabbinic law because of the ways that this law demands structural differences between women and men. In this logic, "equivalency" is a term of approval.

The formula of mutual exchange works by ignoring any differences of power and influence between family members. In this analysis, the "interdependence" of husband and wife (or wives) is used as a synonym for "mutuality." But the equation of interdependence and mutuality is a false one. Interdependence is a statement about social interrelation, and mutuality is a statement about relations of power. To equate the two flattens out the relations of power. "Interdependence" can mean mutuality, reciprocity, or equivalency, but these are not by definition part of interdependence. A husband (or male head-of-household) can be interdependent with his wife, with his slaves and servants, or with the donkey that he rides to market. But his relations with that donkey, and with those slaves and servants are not mutual. These relations are essentially no more mutual than a legal relationship in which a husband takes his wife's earnings and with these, supports her in return. In this analytic formula, all words are stripped of their power to explain relations of hierarchy and inequality. The de facto equation of interrelationship and mutuality decides in advance that the economic relation between husband and wife are equivalent exchanges.

The tradition of analyzing these marital economic relations as mutual exchange has its origins in talmudic commentary. For instance, consider the explanation from the Babylonian Talmud that "the rabbis taught that her right to support was exchanged in return for the work of her hands."[2] The talmudic position proposes the notion of exchange. It does not necessarily include the notion of mutuality. In the modern scholarly analysis, "exchange" is defined as mutual and reciprocal. With a basis in talmudic traditions, this modern analysis builds on the most positive type of exchange—those that are fair and equivalent in some way. However, exchanges are not by definition fair; exchanges can as easily be biased and exhibit prejudice. The recent emphasis on mutual exchange functions as an apologetic reading of rabbis, one that recuperates the rabbis as useful for modern women and men. "Mutuality" has a positive currency for many in our own times. Asserting that talmudic visions for the economic relations of husbands and wives are based on mutuality makes rabbinic notions of marriage sound desirable and useful for those who wish to retain their rabbinic ancestors within the terms of their modern lives.

The problem with the notion of mutual exchange, whether talmudic or twentieth century, is that it ignores the many ways that early rabbinic Judaism extended the husband's control over his wife and other female family members (although not over his son). The formula of mutual exchange disregards the ongoing concern in these writings to forge through halakah a Jewish wife who will complement a Jewish husband with extensive powers. Conceptually, within the frame of "mutual exchange" the possibility of equivalency and mutuality can be imagined because that frame brackets the legal and social inequities inherent to early rabbinic Judaism. These inequities are present in any economy of marriage, power, and control; but they are easily neglected by analyses that attend mostly to details taken out of this context.

The formula of mutual exchange flattens out relations of power, and makes claims for equivalence by ignoring more complicated evidence. By refusing to flatten and overlook discourses and structures of power, these marital arrangements can be explained quite differently. Married women's labors and property provide the funds for at least part of her support. In turn, her unpaid domestic labors support the daily lives of her husband as well as any children they raise. All funds from the wife's labor or property are always channeled through her husband's hands. Her husband is assigned the responsibility and power to provide for a woman's daily needs of food, clothing, and other things. In both talmudic and twentieth-century forms, the notion of mutual exchange leaves out these and other layers of the family economy. At best, this arrangement makes the wife into her husband's ward, and between two persons of unequal legal and social stature, there can never be equal, equivalent, or mutual exchange. Instead of insisting upon notions of mutuality in Roman-period rabbinic Judaism, these relations of controlling a wife's labors and property in exchange for supporting her daily needs for food, clothing, shelter, and sleep should be seen as another site for controlling Jewish women, as another kind of abstract economic violence.[3]

INVERSION

The talmudic comments on these economic relations of marriage offer several, often contradictory rationales. The following supplements mutual exchange with another explanation, the prevention of marital strife: "[Rav Huna in the name of Rav] established support of the wife as the primary obligation, and the husband was given the right to the work of her hands to prevent enmity."[4] The talmudic notion of "preventing enmity" reappears in Boaz Cohen's *Jewish and Roman Law* (1966). Cohen considers the restriction of a married woman's control of her earned property in light of other early rabbinic regulations of the property rights of slaves and (female) minors. He writes: "The reasons for the curtailment of the *subjecti* were different for each case. The wife suffered a diminution of her rights in order *to assure and insure more domestic concord* [emphasis added], the minor to show more respect and gratitude, and the slave because of his notorious dishonesty and moral turpitude."[5] This example continues talmudic logic. It illustrates a second mode for conceptualizing how relations of gender and power work in families.

This formula is based on what I will call "inversion." This type of explanation interchanges positions of power. In these interchanges, a figure who seems to have power is cast as less powerful or powerless, and a figure who would seem to be less powerful is recast as powerful. However, whereas in explanatory accounts these figures are switched, the actual positions, advantages, and rights do not change. The power-less do not really become powerful and those with power do not really lose it. Paradoxically, this formula both discusses power and keeps its workings invisible.

One ramification of this strategy is that the privileges of powerful people are protected or expanded. In the example from Boaz Cohen's *Jewish and Roman Law*, family members must work together to insure household harmony. However, the person with apparently no role to play in assuring and insuring domestic concord is the male head of the household: the father, husband, slave owner. Other household members—wives, servants and slaves, children—are portrayed as the ones with power in the household, and hence the ones with power to insure peace in the house. Once posited as powerful, they suffer a diminution of rights. But the person with arguably the most power over household members does not similarly suffer a diminution of any rights. This is possible because the analytic formulation has already effectively conceptualized the husband/father as powerless. In this switch, others have the power to insure concord, and accordingly, they must sacrifice their rights to do so. In this narrative the male head of the household has no power; thus, he makes no sacrifices and his rights are protected while others lose theirs. Cohen's story about ancient Jewish households positions this man as powerless. But this is only a transitory position and a temporary rhetorical strategy, with no permanent diminutions of power and privileges for the male husband and father.

Both formulas for conceptualizing gender and power relations are problematic. The first flattens out real differences in favor of writing about a rabbinic potential for mutuality. The second flips around and obscures questions of how rights and privileges are distributed so that these people are made even more powerless. Instead of making gender and power relations visible, both formulas obscure power relations between ancient men and women, and make them more difficult to see. Neither mode examines how power worked with gender. In an odd way, in both formulas gender does not matter. This lack means that both formulas are particularly inappropriate for studying an ancient society in which gender was a significant way to express all sorts of things. It makes no sense to use a conception of power that ignores gender as a tool for explaining a society in which gender mattered very much in the distribution of power. This is especially the case if we are interested in how they made gender make sense.[6] The remainder of this chapter reaches beyond these traditions and talmudically based explanations. Instead of relying on fictions of mutuality and beneficence, I look for traces of argument, conflict, and strife among rabbis and Jews as they tried to sort through the conflicts that marriage posed.

CONTESTING MUTUAL EXCHANGE

When early rabbis addressed the relation between a husband's duty to maintain his wife or wives, and the ownership of a married woman's wages, their debate followed these contours. Did the exchange primarily compensate the husband for the particular costs of keeping his wife fed, clothed and sheltered, and attending to her other needs? Or did the exchange primarily imply a husband's rights of ownership over his wife's new property? The following set of passages get at this debate. They provide two answers to the question, If a married woman earned more than it cost her husband to maintain her, who owned the surplus? If the economic relationship was one of equivalent exchange, then the wife would give her husband the amount necessary for her support. Any surplus would belong to her. On the other hand, if the arrangement was based upon the husband's ownership of his wife's total earnings, then the husband would take the amount necessary to maintain her, and he would also retain the remainder. He would have total control of the wife's new property, to the extent that he would own all that she produced and earned.

In some passages (such as mKetubot 5.9), the connection between wages demanded and maintenance due is clear. In others, the correlation is enigmatic and uncertain. The Mishnah and Tosefta record several conflicting opinions and their resolution. In the first passage, mKetubot 5.4, a husband has made a vow to consecrate the profits of his wife's work. The sages debate whether this consecration is halakically acceptable. In order to vow, the vower must legally own the object vowed. Thus, the issue at hand is whether the husband owns the surplus of his wife's new property; mKetubot 5.4 reads:

One who consecrates [by vow] the work of the hands of his wife: in this case, she works and she eats. [Concerning] the remainder, Rabbi Meir says, it is consecrated. Rabbi Yoḥanan ha-Sandlar says, it is ordinary [*i.e.*, not appropriate for consecration].

The sages agree that the amount necessary to support the wife be used to support her (*i.e.*, "she works and she eats"). Even if the husband has vowed to consecrate her wages, he cannot take her wages and then relieve himself of his duty to maintain her. He must still uphold this obligation. Thus far, the passage holds to a notion of exchange: work wages are traded directly for maintenance. It assumes that the wife's earnings could equal or exceed what it costs her husband to maintain her. In itself, this is a fascinating instance in which rabbis agree that a woman can earn enough to support herself. Upon establishing the trade of wages for support, the passage questions what to do with "the remainder." Once the trade has been effected, do the husband's rights of ownership extend to the surplus, to the remaining amount of the wife's earned wages?

To this question the text circulates different opinions. Rabbi Meir maintains that the excess wages belong to the husband and may be consecrated. The husband owns and controls the entire amount of his wife's profits from work. According to this position, the work of her hands and maintenance are not part of an economy of equivalent exchange. Rather, they are part of a situation in which the husband has full ownership of his wife's earned property. The counteropinion is assigned to Rabbi Yoḥanan ha-Sandlar. According to this counteropinion, the surplus profits from her work must remain ordinary, and thus are inappropriate for consecration. The husband may not consecrate the surplus because the excess wages belong to the wife, and he cannot make a vow using property that does not belong to him. In this position, the relation constitutes equivalent exchange only so far as the wages equal the cost of maintenance.

This passage from the Mishnah clearly displays a lack of consensus. The heart of the disagreement between Rabbis Meir and Yoḥanan ha-Sandlar revolves around the exact extent of the husband's property rights. The disagreement suggests the tensions and uncertainties about the details of marriage and gender in the period of the Mishnah's production and promulgation in the early third century. The rabbis do not yet hold a unified position on all the economic relations of husbands and wives, nor do they share a unified stance on the extent of a husband's power. In short, they had not yet decided whether to give legal sanction to the husband's full extent of ownership of his wife's new property. They had not fully agreed to organize the family economy in this way.

But this uncertainty did not last for long. When the sages of the Tosefta presented their version of the same issue several decades later, this debate was no longer significant. Restating and reinterpreting a line from mKetubot 5.4 (italics below), tKetubot 5.3 records a resolution of the mishnaic debate into a new consensus:

> *One who consecrates the work of the hands of his wife [mKetubot 5.4]:*
> In this case he takes her support (*parnasah*) from it
> And the remainder, he consecrates.

In this commentary the husband owns the total amount of his wife's wages. After providing for her support[7] he may consecrate the remainder. Since he is consecrating property that belongs to him, his vow will be ritually and halakically legitimate. The toseftan passage settles the Mishnah's question: the relation of the work of her hands and maintenance is not an exchange of equivalent amounts, but a demonstration of husbandly ownership and control. Furthermore, in the Tosefta, all traces of the earlier contestation and disagreement have been dropped. Rabbi Yoḥanan's dissent is nowhere to be found. Instead, Rabbi Meir's opinion is restated with the authority of the anonymous voice. The tension has been resolved. The husband controls his wife's wages, in toto, over and beyond what is necessary to support and maintain her.

The early rabbis were undecided about this question for some time; when they did decide, the resolution was not in favor of mutual exchange. Rather, they preferred to extend the husband's control over the wife's earnings. On the evidence of this set of passages, the later analysis that the laws of the work of her hands and of maintenance were characterized by formal and equal exchange cannot be upheld. These passages do not conclude that the exchanges are equivalent. The desire among later interpreters of these texts to see this family economy as mutual and equivalent exonerated ancient rabbis by giving them positions that were not theirs, but which were more acceptable in talmudic and in modern terms. It also masks the struggle among early rabbis over how gender functions in concepts that we might translate as mutuality and fairness. If mutuality was not part of the early rabbinic conception of the family economy, I turn now to the question of fairness. Several passages impart a rabbinic polemic against the economic relations of family members, and often, this polemic is based in assumptions and arguments about fairness. However, fairness is never simply fair; usually it is a choice made among competing claims. Reading rabbinic passages about fairness, not at face value but more critically, the first question must be fairness for whom—fathers, daughters, sons, and/or wives?

THE MAINTENANCE OF DAUGHTERS

In the debate over a husband's control of his wife's earnings, dissent eventually disappeared. The possibility of exchange—a woman's profits in return for a man's material protection—was supplanted, and the husband's ownership and control was extended to cover all his wife's new property. As a father, a man had similarly extensive powers over his daughter's earnings, and mKetubot 4.4 remanded a daughter's work and profits to her father. Comparing the halakah for wives with that of daughters, one major difference is that whereas as a husband a man was obligated to maintain his wife, as a father he was not legally obligated to maintain his daughter. When I teach this set of passages, my students and I usually struggle over the implication of carelessness, heartlessness, and neglect. Yet, law is not life. These are, once again, not descriptions of what Jews of Roman Palestine did, nor do they necessarily represent statements whose effects were carefully considered. These are specific fantasies about the relations between members of a family. The intention was not to starve Jewish children, but to protect Jewish fathers from undue *legal* requirements. Nonetheless, in the process of privileging the father mKetubot 4.4 sacrifices the daughter:

> The father possesses authority over his daughter [with regard to the following]: her betrothal, whether by money, by document, or by sexual intercourse; and he possesses claims regarding what she finds and regarding the work of her hands, and regarding the annulment of her vows and regarding the reception of her *get* (document of divorce). And he does not eat fruits [*i.e.*, own the usufruct of her property] during her lifetime.[8]

In this fantasy of fathers and daughters, the father controls his daughter's betrothal (whether her betrothal is initiated through money, through the ketubbah document, or through intercourse). Until the daughter marries or becomes adult, or in another way leaves her father's household, anything valuable she finds, as well as her profits and earnings, belong to him. In this conception of fatherhood, the father can annul any religious vows that his daughter makes. If she marries and divorces (presumably while still a minor), the father receives the divorce document (*get*) from the husband. However, if the daughter inherits property, the father does not have the right of usufruct; unlike in the case of the wife, the profits from that property belong to the daughter.

If a man were married and had daughters, he owned the wages and profits from the labors of all of these women. But his ownership of their labors and profits takes place within different kinds of economies. Continuing on, mKetubot 4.4 compares the economic relations of a husband to his wife and a father to his daughter. It concludes that husbands have greater privileges over wives than fathers have over daughters. Husbands receive usufruct of their wives' property during her lifetime, whereas fathers do not have this right over their daughters. In return for these greater privileges, the husband is obligated to maintain his wife, to ransom her if she is taken captive, and to attend to her proper burial. The husband has more privileges and more responsibilities and economic burdens.[9]

As husband and father, a man owns the earnings from his wife (or wives) and his daughters. In return, he must maintain his wife. There is no similar demand that he maintain his daughter during his lifetime. In early rabbinic law, neither mothers nor fathers had the legal responsibility to support their children. Mothers had no legal rights to the children, and hence no legal obligations to provide support to them. The children were not under her authority, but under the father's. The father can exact personal services from the children—things like serving him food and drink, washing and dressing him, and so forth. The mother has no right to such filial services. Although fathers had no responsibility to maintain either sons or daughters, they could claim whatever the children found, sons and daughters both. But the father had different relations to sons and daughters. Over the daughter alone, the father had the authority to own and control the wages and other results of her labor. In contrast, sons retained ownership and control of their products and wages.[10]

A further distinction between sons and daughters gave a Jewish son an economic privilege denied to a Jewish daughter: inheritance. Building on biblical law, early rabbinic law mapped out the relations of inheritance. In the normal situation, the father's estate was divided among his sons. If there were no sons, the estate was to be divided among the daughters.[11] The issue of sons' inheritance of their father's estate was linked with the maintenance of daughters, since both issues were part of the question of how a father's property would be distributed. The issues of inheritance and maintenance are especially linked in the situation of a father who died and left behind minor children. Reverting to biblical law, the sons will inherit, and their inheritance money will support them. But there was no such biblical solution for daughters. The early rabbinic solution was that since sons can support themselves through their inheritance, daughters would be maintained from the father's estate until they marry or reach the age of adulthood. But this solution was not without its discontents. What pits sons against daughters in the rabbinic imagination is the fact that both the inheritances of sons and the money for daughter's maintenance will come from the same fund. Whatever the daughters receive will directly lessen the fortune of their brothers.

Questions about how and whether to maintain daughters, both during the father's lifetime and after his death, were hotly debated. Rabbis presented polemics of gender as they argued for what they considered to be equal and fair. Through fragments of remains, it is possible to trace some stances on this issue and to analyze the polemic that emerged. I present one rabbinic expression, mKetubot 4.6, followed by two alternative positions—one slightly later, tKetubot 4.8, and the second, a nonrabbinic Jewish marriage document that appealed to Greek law to assure the maintenance of living children, from slightly earlier.

EQUALITY AND FAIRNESS

The early rabbis struggled over gendered concepts of equality and fairness. The passage mKetubot 4.6 presents a general statement: a father is not obligated to maintain his daughter during his lifetime. The statement is followed by an explanation of sorts, placed in the voice of Rabbi Elazar ben Azaryah, who speaks to the other sages assembled at Yavneh. In rabbinic chronology, this was the first gathering after the destruction of the Jerusalem Temple of the men who would launch the rabbinic movement. Thus, the Mishnah locates this enactment at a crucial moment in the rabbis' own history:

> The father is not obligated (hā-ʾāb ʾênô ḥayāb) concerning the maintenance of his daughter (while he is alive).

> This is the interpretation of Rabbi Elʿazar ben ʿAzaryah [that was pronounced] before the sages at the vineyards (Assembly) at Yavneh:

> [As the situation stands] the sons inherit and the daughters receive maintenance.

Just as the sons only inherit after the father's death, so too the daughters should only receive maintenance after the father's death.[12]

In the passage, Rabbi Elazar ben Azaryah reviews the position that a father is not obligated to support the daughter and provides an explanation for it. If girls receive support (in the form of maintenance) both before and after the death of their father, and sons receive support (in the form of inheritance) only after their father has died, then, he argues, girls and boys have been treated differently. The difference, furthermore, is unfair. It would lead to an inequity against boys, an inequity that would need rectification. The solution presented here is that during their lifetimes, fathers are not halakically obligated to maintain either their daughters or their sons. This solution equalizes the paternal support received by minor sons and daughters (both receive only after the father's death), and renders the situation fair to boys.

Since this solution was offered in the name of fairness and equal treatment, it is worth examining the assumptions that undergird these notions. Elazar ben Azaryah argues that the relation of both sons and daughters to their father must structurally be the same. Elazar seems to use a simple "balance scale" notion of fairness. He weighs the relative gains of the daughters on one side and the relative gains of the sons on the other. In the end, the two sides must balance out. If sons receive property from the father only after his death, so too the daughters. Since sons do not (regularly) receive property while the father is alive, neither should the daughters. To a large degree, this notion of balance is based on denying meaningful social differences between sons and daughters. For the overt purposes of the argument, gender does not matter as a difference. Minor sons and daughters are "the same" and must be treated accordingly.

In reading for gender in rabbinic texts, we must always ask when gender and its distinctions are deemed necessary and important, and when they are deemed not to matter. In other words, what must be questioned are the specific deployments of gender. This means that while the potential effects of different rulings are significant, what is critically important is how gender is made to function as a category, and how this category is used to maintain—or to assimilate—difference. Once this question is posed, the texture of Elazar's argument becomes more complicated. To find his argument persuasive, one must agree to follow Elazar's decision to construct gender as "difference" in certain situations and to construct gender as "similarity" or "sameness" in other situations, and then, all in the course of one argument, we must agree with the way he mixes the two practices together. In this sense, how gender is constructed (as difference or as sameness) is a different question from whether or not these rulings result in positive or negative outcomes for sons and daughters. How gender is constructed is a prior issue to its outcome. But of course, choices about how to construct gender are part of what makes a specific outcome seem obvious and persuasive. To repeat, then: to find Elazar's positions persuasive is to agree with the specific ways that gender is variously constructed (as difference or sameness) in his argument. At the very least, to find his position persuasive means that a reader has agreed not to question the way he constructs gender as a category.

When we stop reading as if we were rabbis and start reading from elsewhere, the passage looks like this. Elazar ben Azaryah avows and averts a possible inequity against orphaned sons through an argument that sons and daughters should be treated "the same." Here, gender is not construed as a difference, but a sameness; differences of sex do not matter. However, the argument for gender-as-sameness is built by excluding precisely the places that gender and its differences do matter. The argument that deploys a notion of fairness and gender neutrality starts to seem more partisan and less gender neutral when one makes several refusals. The first is to refuse to go along with Elazar's exclusions. The argument for rectification makes sense only within a narrow frame of reference. When one starts to admit other elements of the family economy as evidence, the effacements in Elazar's argument become more apparent. Here are some of the missing elements. Arguing that relations between children and their father must be structurally equivalent, Elazar removes from view the fact that the relation of fathers to sons and daughters is already structurally *in*equivalent. Casting the argument narrowly, this legal story ignores the fact that relations of property between fathers, sons, and daughters are already built on a foundation in which gender is a difference that matters: unlike sons, daughters owe their earnings to the father. The confines of Elazar's argument remove from consideration the evidence that a father possessed property rights to his daughter's wages but not his son's. Elazar's argument also ignores another instance where gender is constructed as a difference that matters: inheritance. The entire discussion of posthumous maintenance for daughters is derived from a biblically based inequity of inheritance. Sons inherited from their father, whereas daughters (if they had brothers) did not. Inequities such as these were already part of the structure of family economy, and they were built precisely on the assumption that gender was a difference that mattered greatly.

Absent from Elazar's argument are the complexities of places where gender did matter, and especially, places where gender mattered because it resulted in inequities against girls. Removing inequities against daughters from an explanation that averts a possible inequity against sons could be explained as ingenuous. However, the sophistication displayed by casting an argument that constructs gender so precisely suggests that the producers of this rabbinic text knew how to manipulate and deploy notions of gender, and that they did so with some degree of skill. Their move could be explained as less than conscious if it were not part of a broader rabbinic pattern that constructed men as humans with expanding rights and women as humans whose legal rights will be increasingly restricted.

Reading classical texts that have certain kinds of modern authority, it can become difficult to break down the air of inevitability that seems to accompany them. On the way to explaining early rabbinic Judaism, it is always necessary to stress the quality of "evitability"—the sense that things did not have to turn out the way they did—and in doing so, to consider the solutions they did not choose. So what happens if, as a critical practice, we imagine alternatives that the writers of the Mishnah could have posed, had they not been so committed to a certain formulation of gender. They could have reminded themselves of a daughter's contributions to the family economy. Since a father owns his daughter's earnings (but not the son's), the daughter deserves his maintenance and support. The writers of the Mishnah could have argued that both sons and daughters be allowed to inherit. They could have obligated living fathers to maintain both daughters and sons. They could have recognized gender-based structural differences between son and daughter, and moved to undo this gap. They could have not remanded a daughter's earnings to her father, or, they could have expanded the halakah to remand to the father the son's earnings as well. The mishnaic rabbis and writers could have considered the inequity that if a father died leaving minor sons and adult (or married) daughters, the daughters (since they were adults) would receive nothing from the father's estate. Instead of these or other approaches to questions of fairness, the solution offered by mKetubot 4.6 rescinded any obligation for a living father to maintain his daughters.

The notion of gender implicit in Elazar's argument about fairness is specific and strategic. The result is that a gender-based difference—and an unfairness—is made an integral part of the concept of fairness. Gender is excluded as a factor in the discussion of orphaned sons and daughters. This exclusion is strategic, and it is by excluding considerations of inequities to girls that Elazar's argument for fairness to boys is evoked. Fairness—the differential treatment between sons and daughters—is at issue when males might not be properly privileged. Based on excluding the evidence of inequities against girls, Elazar ben Azaryah can argue that daughters have no claim to maintenance (while their father is alive) not because they are "girls," but because the sages must be fair. He removes himself rhetorically from arguing about gender when in fact he is very precisely building on assumptions about how sexual difference matters. This notion of fairness is gendered because what matters primarily is the potential inequity against boys alone. Thus, gender is built right into the category of fairness—it is operative but invisible.

This is not the last word on the subject of maintenance and inheritance. Elazar's enactment at Yavneh will itself be challenged on the grounds that it does not sufficiently protect sons. Revisiting the question of orphans, this next passage—mKetubot 13.3, repeated with slight variation as mBaba Batra 9.1—places sons and daughters onto a battlefield of gender-based privilege. In mKetubot 13.3 the halakah according to Elazar ben Azaryah stands, but a complaint is lodged against it; in this complaint, the plights of fatherless daughters and sons are narrated in such a way that brothers and sisters are pitted against each other in another gendered construction of fairness:

> [Suppose the case of a man] who died and left sons and daughters:
>
> When the estate is large, the sons inherit and the daughters receive support.
>
> But when the estate is small, the daughters receive maintenance and the sons go around at the doors [the sons go begging for charity].
>
> ʾAdmon says: Because I am male, should I be disadvantaged?
>
> Rabban Gamliel said: I approve [I agree with the reasoning] of the words of ʾAdmon.

Appearing several times as a figure in early rabbinic writing, Admon was a judge during the Second Temple period. Tractates Ketubot and Baba Batra list his opinions, and adjoin two (including this one) with Rabban Gamliel's approval. Admon's argument is that in certain economic situations, the law for maintaining minor daughters after the father dies is unfair to the sons. So long as the estate is wealthy enough to support both girls and boys, the law is fair. But if the father is poor and the estate small, there will not be enough funds to furnish the sons' inheritances after the girls have been maintained and married. For poorer families, Admon argues, the law is unfair to boys, whose inheritance will effectively be given over to their sisters. Rabban Gamliel's approval adds additional weight to Admon's reasoning. This passage does not contribute to early rabbinic law per se. The law to which it refers, stands. But reading Mishnah solely for law ignores all the other kinds of cultural work that the religio-legal text might accomplish. Legal writing narrates stories and presents ways of seeing the world. Even a position that is not the majority opinion becomes part of an ethos, part of what will be repeated and studied, part of what will continue to be imaginable. Mishnaic writers valued this position enough to include it, not once, but twice. They not only gave it voice through Admon, they seconded it with the authority of Rabban Gamliel. If the law stands, nonetheless, the inclusion of Admon's argument allows the Mishnah to proffer a powerful set of assumptions for thinking about gender and for judging fairness.

The question attributed to Admon—"Because I am male, should I be disadvantaged?"—is remarkably multifaceted. Admon's rhetoric creates a gender-based unity. The phrase is not "because *they* are male" but is personalized in the singular: "because *I* am male." This phrasing elides the boys who might "go begging" with himself. Their potential disadvantage becomes his own, and by extension, Gamliel's own, and the rabbis' own. As a construction of masculine unity, it allows Admon to create connections among men. Admon employs language that is broader than the specific group of males under discussion, namely, minor sons of poor dead fathers who also have minor sisters. Doing so, he asserts a disadvantaged status for *all men*. Through the claim that all men are being deprivileged, he sets the stage for the strategy of inversion. His broad claim to the disadvantaged status of men evokes a sense of masculine powerlessness and deprivation. He attends to a social group—men—who nearly entirely controlled the production of religious texts, places of worship, families, courts, and businesses, who were the primary inheritors of property, and who had demonstrated their power, influence, and dominance in Jewish society. Instead of accounting for why men had these powers, the story that the Mishnah's Admon tells about boys repositions men as powerless and as victims.

But their position as victims is only textual and only temporary. The victimhood of boys was only one way to narrate the situation of poor families with small estates. Admon's narration should be understood as a strategy to gain recompense. By articulating a situation of inequity, it becomes "logical" to "restore" the economic privileges for all kinds of men. Admon's argument defines masculinity (at least in part) through the economic privileges of inheritance. He will not allow poor orphaned minor sons to be defined as "not men," as outside the circle of masculine economic privileges. When Admon tells this story about sons who are disadvantaged, he does so in defense of men and the privileges they deserve. The legal story about deprivileged sons whose inheritances have gone to support their sisters assumes, simultaneously, that males deserve cultural, legal, and financial advantage. If males are disempowered, this is an unnatural state of affairs in need of rectification.

Admon's argument is richer still. The brief narrative vividly portrays inequity. It pictures orphaned girls who procure comfortable lives while orphaned boys obtain only the harshness of begging and a life dependent upon charity. This narrowly drawn picture bolsters the argument that boys are being treated unfairly. Yet, the depiction of possibilities is highly selective. Other early rabbinic passages both assume and explicitly discuss sons (and daughters) who work and earn wages. Papyrus documents from Roman Egypt confirm the extensive participation of children, particularly boys, in the work force.[13] However, to argue its point, mKetubot 13.3 disregards these social possibilities. For the sake of an argument, its sons cannot work, nor be taken care of by relatives, but must beg from door to door. This narrative favors a particular view of the plight of the sons, one that restricts other scenarios to make its point. And what might other options have been? Admon and Gamliel did not consider any corollary situations: If maintenance to girls was to be discontinued and boys were to receive their inheritance directly, then what would be the fate of the girls? Would they be raised by other families? Receive charity? Would the girls "go begging"? And if so, would this be as problematic to the rabbis as the boys' mendicancy and reliance on the charity of others? Once again, even a brief foray into social options that could have been part of the text's stories and assumptions about gender, inheritance, and the care of children, had the rabbinic text held other commitments, shows the specificity of the stories told.

As we know them from the Mishnah, the rabbis possessed obvious skills as educated legal rhetoricians.[14] Their skill extended to polemics of gender and to the nuances of the construction of gender itself. The desperate plight of orphaned boys going begging prepares the imagination to be persuaded by Admon's conclusion. Like the enactment of Elazar ben Azaryah, Admon's argument appeals to the strategy of inversion, and the particular and peculiar story of orphaned sons and daughters that would justify the conclusion of male disadvantage. The argument for disadvantage works by depicting a situation in which power and privilege are inverted from the usual.[15]

These rabbinic arguments were one way to conceptualize men and to construct fatherhood and the relative privileges of sons and daughters. Other Jewish texts show alternatives, also expressed through the legal issue of the maintenance and support of children. I turn now to these contestations and alternatives.

ALTERNATIVES

How do we move beyond the confines of these early rabbinic arguments, to see these positions for what they were: very specific conceptions of law and stories about life that were part of a more multivalent and divided discourse? One way is to imagine alternate possibilities that place rabbinic decisions into relief. Another way is to find more direct evidence for alternate routes taken by other Jews.

Debates by Jews about the priority, legality, and practical urgency of maintaining children were not limited to rabbinic disputes narrated in their own texts. Early rabbinic law provided maintenance for daughters after the father's death, but this remained controversial. A Jewish marriage contract that dates to the earlier part of the second century shows part of the insufficiency of the rabbinic position. A different alternative was selected by a Jewish family who lived near the Dead Sea in the newly created Roman province of Provincia Arabia. The contract (catalogued as Papyrus Yadin 18, or PY18) illustrates another Jewish alternative for obligating a living father to maintain his children. The document comes from the excavated archive of Babatha, an archive that included several marriage documents from the early second century. The marriage of one Shelamzion was contracted by two Jews: her father, Judah son of Eleazar, and her husband-to-be, Judah Cimber son of Ananias son of Somolas. Judah son of Eleazar is transferring his daughter Shelamzion to Judah, surnamed Cimber, so that Shelamzion may become this wife. The document contains a clause about Judah Cimber's obligation to support his minor children. The clause's terminology refers to this obligation as "Greek custom."[16] This marriage document and another[17] indicate that when some Jews in the regions adjacent to

Palestine wished to use the power of legal contract to assure paternal support of children—sons and daughters both, they did so through recourse not to Jewish law or to any form of developing rabbinic law, but to what they knew as Greek legal custom. The document, itself written in Greek, translates as follows:

> In the consulship of Publius Metilius Nepos for the second time and Marcus Annius Libo on the nones of April, and by the compute of the new province of Arabia year twenty-third on the fifteenth of month Xandikos, in Maoza, Zoara district, Judah son of Eleazar also known as Khtusion, gave over Shelamzion, his very own daughter, a virgin, to Judah surnamed Cimber son of Ananias son of Somalas, both of the village of En-gedi in Judea residing here, for Shelamzion to be a wedded wife to Judah Cimber for the partnership of marriage according to the laws, she bringing to him on account of bridal gift feminine adornment in silver and gold and clothing appraised by mutual agreement, as they both say, to be worth two hundred denarii of silver, which appraised value the bridegroom Judah called Cimber acknowledged that he has received from her by hand forthwith from Judah her father and that he owes to the said Shelamzion his wife together with another three hundred denarii which he promised to give to her in addition to the sum of her aforesaid bridal gift, all accounted toward her dowry, *pursuant to his undertaking of feeding and clothing both her and the children to come in accordance with Greek legal custom (hellēnikō nomō)* [emphasis added] upon the said Judah Cimber's good faith and peril and [the security] of all his possessions, both those which he now possesses in his said home village and here and all those which he may in addition validly acquire everywhere, in whatever manner his wife Shelamzion may choose, or whoever acts through her or for her may choose, to carry out the execution. Judah called Cimber shall redeem this contract for his wife Shelamzion, whenever she may demand it of him, in silver secured in due form, at his own expense interposing no objection. If not, he shall pay to her all the aforesaid denarii twofold, she having the right of execution, both from Judah Cimber her husband and upon the possessions validly his, in whatever manner Shelamzion or whoever acts through her or for her may choose to carry out the execution. In good faith the formal question was asked and it was acknowledged in reply that this is thus rightly done.[18]

In the eastern regions of Syria-Palestine, Arabia, and Egypt there were several overlapping legal systems to which people could appeal. Each region contained varying combinations of Roman and local legal traditions. Representing one of these traditions for Syria-Palestine, the early rabbis were ambivalent about obligating a father to maintain his children, whether female or male. If a Jew—a bride's father such as Judah son of Eleazar—wanted assurance that his son-in-law (the father of his future grandchildren) would be legally obliged to maintain the children, he could turn to the authority of Greek law, rather than a version of Jewish law.[19] In this marriage document, Jews seeking to insure a type of maintenance for children turn to what they see as Greek law, in which the practice of legally obligating fathers to support their children was more culturally familiar and more highly valued. To place this marriage contract into another context, Greek papyri from the adjacent region of Egypt show that paternal maintenance of children was not an ambivalent value, but was among a father's most prominent obligations.[20]

Looking to the italicized middle of the marriage contract, the phrase *hellēnikō nomō*, "in accordance with Greek legal custom," refers grammatically to what precedes it directly: the feeding and clothing of wife and children. The scholarly debate about this clause has interpreted the reference to Greek legal custom in terms of the husband's maintenance of the wife.[21] I disagree with this reading. The emphasis on the maintenance of the wife would be surprising because it is superfluous. A wife's maintenance is guaranteed by developing rabbinic law. Another document from the same place and time, the ketubbah of Babatha is a Jewish marriage document that adheres more formally to the conventions of the Jewish ketubbah. As fragmented as it is, it clearly relies on Jewish law to provide for the maintenance of the wife.[22] Ranon Katzoff argues that the phrase *hellēnikō nomō* refers "to an economic standard, namely to such things as quantities of food, clothing, and household help. . . . It is reasonable to suppose that this is an economically higher standard than the minima required by mKetubot 5.8–9 and related texts."[23] Yet, his argument for a "higher standard" appeals to a passage (mKetubot 5.9, discussed above) that refers specifically to the case of a wife maintained through a third party, not to the relatively more normal situation of a wife and husband living together.[24] The rabbinic text he cites cannot support his claim.

Greek documents from nearby Egypt understood fatherhood to include the support of children. They marked this vision of fatherhood in terms of legal obligation. This explains why Greek law was invoked in this marriage document used by Jews. At issue is not providing the wife with a higher standard of maintenance. Rather, the effect is to supply what was not available in Jewish law: the paternal maintenance of children. Reference was made to *hellēnikō nomō* as a way to assure Shelamzion's father that her new husband Judah Cimber would support and maintain Shelamzion's children.

The example of Jews taking recourse to Greek legal customs becomes even more significant when it is considered alongside the slightly later rabbinic debates about whether fathers have legal responsibility to support their children. Early rabbinic law allows a special clause that obligates the father to maintain daughters to be written into the ketubbah. But this use of contractual arrangement to change the practice of fatherhood was not an assumed part of rabbinic law, nor did it become a normative part of the rabbinic ketubbah.[25] As a contrast to early rabbinic writings, this marriage contract from Provincia Arabia shows another second-century conception of what Jewish fatherhood might mean.

The desire by these Arabian Jews to contract and construct a notion of Jewish fatherhood in which children were maintained during the father's lifetime finds a parallel in a passage from the third-century Tosefta. For rabbis in Roman Palestine, the issue of whether or not fathers should be legally responsible for supporting their children after death continued to be divisive. In contrast to the position articulated through Elazar ben Azaryah (mKetubot 4.6, above), tKetubot 4.8 strikes a different rabbinic position. In contrast to the prior passage's decision and explanation that the living father is not obligated to maintain his daughter, tKetubot 4.8 recounts, arranges, and concludes the mishnaic debate quite differently. According to this passage, living fathers must support both female and male minor children. At issue is where the authority for this responsibility can be located. According to the text's anonymous voice, the origin is biblical: "It is a commandment (mitzvah) to maintain the daughter, and it is not necessary to say, [to maintain as well] the son." The counteropinion is that of Rabbi Yoḥanan ben Beroqah, who argues that the responsibility is of rabbinic origin: "It is an obligation (ḥôbāh) to support the daughter." In ruling that living fathers should maintain their daughters (and sons), Yoḥanan ben Beroqah reverses mKetubot 4.6, which had argued that a father was not obligated to maintain his daughter.[26] The Arabian Jewish marriage document, and this passage from the Tosefta, provided alternative ways to obligate fathers to support their children. Both of these considered it desirable that fatherhood include legal obligations to children. Dating from both before and after the Mishnah's writing, both positions highlight the tenacity with which the Mishnah held to its particular view of the maintenance of daughters and sons. Both highlight the extent to which its visions extended the privilege of male family members.

CHAPTER SIX

Gossip

In a story from a corner of the Mishnah, women meet under the moonlight. Spindles in hand, they twist fibers into yarn and gossip all the while. So begins the sixth chapter of Mishnah tractate Sotah. This tractate contains the early rabbinic discussion of the exposure and punishment of a woman whose husband suspects her of extramarital sexuality. A group of Jewish women make judicious use of the nighttime light. And they fill the tedium of spinning thread with conversations about local people and events. The rabbinic narrators of this scene are concerned with the problem of finding evidence that backs up the husband's suspicions and hence allows him to end the marriage. The Bible-based rite of bitter waters, the *mê ha-mārîm,* was to have adjudicated the wife's innocence or guilt through an imbibed potion prepared by the priests. However, this possibility of ascertaining truth had vanished with the destruction of the Jerusalem Temple and with the end of an officiating priesthood.[1]

In post-Temple Judaism, confirming the husband's suspicions would rely on more mundane modes of finding the truth about the sotah, the accused wife. In mSotah 6.1, Rabbi Eliezer considers any transient source—or in the Mishnah's euphemism, the flying bird—sufficient evidence for the husband to divorce his suspected wife. With this kind of information, he may end the marriage but must supply her the ketubbah (marriage settlement). But the flying bird is an unaccountable source of truth, and to counter this, the Mishnah proposes another more embodied source. The passage imagines that the talk of women as they spin

will include rumors of other women. It imagines that the content of
these rumors will be transmitted to the husband, that somehow, from a
distance, he too will participate in the gossip by receiving its contents.
If tales of a woman's sexual transgressions reach these women and,
through them, reach her husband, on this evidence the husband must
divorce the wife he has accused of infidelity and give her the ketubbah.
Whereas in many instances of early rabbinic law, the witness of women
does not count as such, reports from women who gossip while they spin
will count as evidence that testifies to a wife's adultery.

Upon reflection, this brief story of some women's testimony about
another woman's vice signals a paradox in early rabbinic Judaism. Despite the apparent confidence of early rabbinic legal texts, rabbis in Roman Palestine had few formal powers of enforcement over other Jews.
They had no governing apparatus to speak of. They had limited juridical authority, no police force, and no military. They controlled no educational system, and as yet had limited influence and interest in the developing synagogue. Rabbis were not granted the authority to mint
coins, and thus had no access to the most popular media of Roman antiquity, the official power to circulate slogans and symbols on the front
and back of money. Rather, Jews traded and circulated coins minted by
Rome and by local cities. The paradox is that when the Mishnah was
produced, and in the early years of its promulgation, early rabbinic law
did not yet have the bureaucratic means to enforce its legalities. There
were few formal mechanisms for transforming a specifically rabbinic
version of Judaism into a more generally practiced Judaism, a Judaism
in which the adjective "rabbinic" would be unnecessary because its
presence would always be assumed.

The lack of formal mechanisms has particular ramifications when
we consider rabbinic writings about women, gender, and sexuality.
Lee Levine observes that in third-century Palestine, "the sages had neither the economic means, independent political base, nor unequivo-
cal social support that would have allowed them to function autono-
mously within the [Jewish] community." Furthermore, the rabbis were
a "small, closely knit coterie of savants, whose very numbers allowed
for a high degree of social and religious cohesiveness."[2] The closely knit
coterie that Levine correctly observes was, of course, a coterie of men.
Rabbis were an all-male social group, who focused a good deal of attention upon the regulation and control of women, but lacked formal modes of social control to enact their visions. How then can we
start to think about how rabbinic notions of women, gender, and sexu-

ality might have circulated outside of these all-male groups, and how these visions were made persuasive to other Jewish men, and to Jewish women?

In other words, how might aspects of the ritualized, legalized society that were articulated as fantasy in early rabbinic texts have become the culture of Jews? Clearly, mine is not a question about formal education, nor about the spread of careful knowledge of rabbinic texts and their exact contents. It is not about how rabbis taught each other, nor about how they taught successive generations of students. After all, most Jewish men and the vast majority of Jewish women were not literate in any language, and certainly not in the Hebrew favored as the written language of rabbis. Rather, at issue is an inquiry into the informalities of social control, and the production of that vague sense of the everyday known as "ethos," an everyday in which halakah comes to seem natural and comes to be nearly self-enforced. In its broadest terms, the inquiry is about how halakah and its suppositions might have become part of "the way things were," a naturalized set of (rabbinic) Jewish assumptions about the world, whether we call this society, culture, discourse, or everyday life.

Left with few and fragmentary traces of Roman-period Judaism and Jewish life in Palestine, it is nearly impossible to detail the historic and practical means through which rabbinic ideas and ideals became an ethos of everyday Jewish life. What remains are clues within rabbinic texts for how they imagined their regulation of gender and sexuality into a discipline practiced in everyday life. Since we cannot know this story from any other perspective, we are left asking how rabbis wrote about enforcing their social fantasies upon others, including and especially, Jewish women. Women were not part of the all-male system of study and collegiality rabbis envisioned for themselves, but women's adherence to rabbinic halakah, and to a (rabbinic) Jewish ethos was necessary for the support and continuation of that very system.

(WO)MEN POLICING WOMEN

Now, gossip is not among the topics or sources that scholars are supposed to take seriously, and herein lies a problem.[3] In narrating Jewish life, early rabbinic texts themselves make use of gossip, those informal repetitions of information about people and events. In mKetubot 7.3, for example, the sages respond to Rabbi Meir's position regarding how a man who betrothed a woman might go about gaining recompense if, later, he found that her body had defects. The sages argue that the man can only complain validly about defects on parts of the woman's body that are normally hidden from view. Furthermore, they add, if there were a local bathhouse, he cannot complain about her at all, since he could have asked his female relatives to observe her beforehand, that is, before the betrothal. He could have asked his aunts, sisters, mother, or female cousins to inspect her nude body as they all bathed, naked in the supposedly female privacy of the single-sex bathhouse. These female relatives could have served as the extension of his own eyes. The passage imagines that women gaze upon each others' naked bodies and presumes that their gazes will become information available to men. Through women's reports about one another, men become voyeurs of women's naked bodies. In discussing these texts, I hasten to add that my concern is not whether the results of such cross-gender spying were temporarily positive or negative for individual women; in this case, for example, the bathhouse gazes would prevent the betrothed woman from being summarily released from the marriage plans. Rather than argue about arguable results, I am interested in how this story of (fe)male gazes and reports became part of a series of rabbinic mechanisms for informal power and control over Jewish women.

The strategy that uses women to aid the enforcement of rabbinic marriage prescriptions also underwrites the story of the women who spin thread beneath the moonlight. Mishnah tractate Sotah builds upon Numbers 5.11–31 for the detailed procedure that a husband may implement when he suspects his wife of adultery. The Mishnah schematizes the process in the following way. Once the husband suspects his wife of adultery, he must first warn her of his suspicions, and this warning must take place in front of two male witnesses. He must warn her to stay away from the suspected partner and to refrain even from talking with this person. After this initial instruction, if the husband still suspects that his wife is having a sexual affair, he may formally accuse her of adultery. Once he voices this accusation, any of several things might happen. If neither witnesses nor other evidence exist to prove her transgression, the wife must either admit her guilt or claim her innocence. If she admits guilt, the husband must divorce her. When divorced this way, the wife loses her ketubbah, the property settlement promised to her as part of the contract of marriage. If the wife claims innocence, then, in the absence of witnesses or other convicting evidence, the husband must bring her to the Temple in Jerusalem to drink the *mê hamārîm*, the potion of bitter waters. The husband will bring his wife to the Temple and hand her over to the priests. The priests will dishevel her clothing and hair, bind her with ropes, and put her on public display.

Describing a ritual that was last practiced over a hundred years before, tractate Sotah presents this fantasy of the bound and controlled female body with greater detail than is found almost anywhere else in Mishnah or Tosefta.[4] After the public display of her shamed body, the priests administer the ritual of bitter waters. According to biblical and rabbinic traditions, the potion will uphold the wife's innocence by causing no ill effects on her body.[5] In this case, the woman returns to her status as her husband's wife. Alternately, the potion will distort and maim her body, and thus establish the truth of her sexual transgression. Her body's memory is transformed into proof as her transfigured body demonstrates her guilt. The marriage ends, the wife forfeits her ketubbah payment, and the husband is free to remarry.

Rabbinic discussions of the sotah are set within the physical impossibility of enacting the rite. Situated in a third-century text, tractate Sotah is a legal fiction about an acknowledgedly archaic ritual.[6] Without the magic of the priestly potion, suspecting husbands must find other kinds of evidence. This is where the spinners enter. Under the moonlight, women spin fibers into thread. Simultaneously, they spin their own identities as trustworthy and reliable women, and spin tales about women who have flaunted and shown disdain for the conditions of rabbinic marriage. That they gossip while they spin at night, rather than while they cook, or gather water, or meet at market, or share a meal, or perform any number of daytime activities is not incidental. Spinning shows the quality of their own characters. They are out under the moonlight, taking advantage of every last drop of light to be productive workers. Spinning displays their loyalty and respectability, their domesticity and thrift. It establishes them as reliable witnesses against another woman's transgression.

Unlike these women, the sotah embodies illicit female sexuality. The accused woman has not been fully contained by the constraints of marriage. She is the opposite of the gathered women: a rabbinic Other and their Other as well. In the scene, the women are depicted en masse; the sotah is singled out. They are trusted; she is suspect. The massed women's voices not only are heard, but count as evidence; the sotah is voiceless, except at the end of her trial, when she must repeat the consenting phrase "amen, amen." Thus, not all women are the same. Tractate Sotah divides women into at least two groups, and the distinction is made according to how women adhere to rabbinic sexual codes. The spinning women of mSotah 6.1 are the good women. They become part of a mechanism that enforces the regulation of women's sexual behavior by punishing any transgressors. The sotah—the accused wife—is their opposite. In making these distinctions, the rabbinic text makes sure to separate the sotah entirely from other women. Absent from the gathering, the sotah is qualitatively outside their group. She shares neither their activity, nor their respectable character. In short, the accused wife does not spin.

In imagining the sotah's punishment, the rabbinic passage groups the women spinners with male enforcers: priests, rabbis, and husbands. The rabbinic passage imagines that women themselves will take on policing and punishing powers over other women. Of course, the women's policing power is limited by the rabbinic bias that would generally limit witness to men. Based on the evidence offered by these women, the husband may divorce his wife, but still he must give her the ketubbah; the women's witness is not considered sufficiently strong testimony to allow the husband to send the woman away ketubbah-less. Still, the report of positive rumors about the accused woman will end her marriage. Incorrect or false information passed on by the spinners, too, will end the woman's marriage. If the accused woman were innocent and if the rumors were untrue or mean-spirited, still the spinners' talk would deny her the opportunity to defend herself, to prevail against their accusations with claims to her innocence. In the world of tractate Sotah respectable women are not in solidarity with other women, but with the male rabbinic elite. The halakic vignette engages women in the defense and protection of the rabbinic social order: women help men punish women who transgress.

The theme that women will police women recurs in the rabbinic accounts of Queen Helene of Adiabene. Stories about Queen Helene are found in many places in ancient literature, from the Mishnah and Tosefta, to Josephus's *Jewish Antiquities,* to Pausanias's account of Helene's monumental grave in Jerusalem. In Josephus's account, Helene converts to Judaism along with her son Izates and other members of the royal family. As he tells it, "a Jewish merchant named Amanias visited the king's wives and taught them to worship God after the manner of the Jewish tradition. It was through their agency that Amanias was brought to the notice of Izates, whom he similarly won over, with the co-operation of the women." Josephus depicts Helene as a woman who loves and is loyal to Judaism, that is, as a woman who cooperates.

Confirming her new allegiance to the Jewish God, Queen Helene makes a pilgrimage to Jerusalem to give thanks-offerings at the Temple. Arriving in Jerusalem during a famine, she distributes money, arranges for massive imports of grain from Alexandria and dried figs from Cyprus, and performs other good deeds for the city and those who live there. As Josephus's modern commentators have long noted, the historian promises at a later date to tell his readers the details of these deeds, but never does.[7]

The Mishnah recounts details of Helene's good deeds and gifts. One present they recall was a golden candlestick placed over the door of the Sanctuary in the Jerusalem Temple. The second gift was a golden tablet on which was written the biblical paragraph of the sotah.[8] In this report, Helene supports and enables the public shaming of the suspected wife. With her gift, the Mishnah's Helene helps the masculinist social order to police and punish women. The Tosefta offers its own detail: the tablet with the sotah's refrain is so golden that "at the time that the sun rises, golden rays shine forth, so they know the sun is rising."[9] The plaque for the sotah ritual indicates the glimmer and newness of the emerging day. The usefulness of Helene's plaque is not limited to one rite. Rather, it is a timepiece helpful to Jews every day. The mechanism for the social control of transgressive women doubles as a helpful reminder of ordinary time and the ritualized repetition of prayer.[10]

Passages such as these borrow women to police other women's sexuality. As imagined figures, women such as Helene or the spinners both mask the power of men and pay tribute to it. Through these representations of women, rabbinic texts depict female support for a masculinist social order. On the one hand, men carried out these rites, men authorized the law upon which they were based, and men filled the ranks of the priesthood that officiated and the rabbinate that continued to discuss these trials against women's bodies in detail for centuries after the ritual's demise. Yet in passages such as these, rabbinic writers craft women—the female objects of rabbinic codes of female sexuality—into that code's enforcers. In this analysis, I must raise a larger point about the suppositions generally at work in studying rabbinic Judaism, gender, and Jewish women in antiquity. Because of the relative invisibility of women in rabbinic and other ancient Jewish texts, there has been a tendency among both feminist and nonfeminist scholars to celebrate any inclusion of women and to make these inclusions into happy stories. This celebration of women's presence is linked to an apologetic presumption that as Jewish elites, rabbis were benevolent, that their engagements with power were benign and deployed sincerely for the good of all Jews (as opposed to the more malevolent quality of law and power attributed to nearly every other group imaginable).

Consider the following recent account of Helene's gift to the Second Temple: "It is noteworthy that Helene contributed something that would be clearly identified with women. By providing the words of an oath on a plaque, Queen Helene shortened the woman's humiliating ordeal, because the priest would not have to find the words of the oath in a Torah scroll."[11] This kind of analysis ignores the presence of masculinist control over women, whether priestly or rabbinic. Before reaching the moment in which the biblical text is recited and the potion drunk, this ritual has already included a public display of the sotah in tattered clothes and loose hair, which other women were encouraged to see. The accused woman has already been carefully transferred from her husband to the priests through the hands of several male officials. She has already been demeaned in nearly the worst ways that biblical, Jewish, and rabbinic texts imagine for women. This account proposes that Helene's gift shows a solidarity with other women, and especially with accused women, because it shortens the time it would otherwise take for a priest to find the proper text in a scroll. But this argument is only possible if one plucks a brief moment away from the broader context of Jewish male fantasies about the bondage and domination of women. On the one hand, the knowledge of the spinning women is admitted to the canon of rabbinic evidence. But on the other, in one of the few places where women's observations count, the terms are that they must witness against other women. Neither Helene nor the spinning women are examples of rabbinic benevolence. The inclusion of women in these rabbinic passages is integrally linked with rabbinic narrations of their own power to discipline.

Furthermore, this account of Helene and the rabbis ignores the specific potency of rabbinic narration. This is not a pristine or unmediated Helene who tells us of her gift (and even such a first-hand telling would not escape the conventions of narration). In her appearances in early rabbinic writing, Helene works for them. Through the well-known trope of the beneficent public gift, the Queen's conversion and her gifts to Jerusalem demonstrate the importance of Judaism in the Roman world. Portraits of a Temple which foreign kings and queens fill with gold treasures would be a suitable—even understandable—image for rabbinic writers who wished for Judaism a somewhat greater stature than the post-Temple version had. Rabbinic writing uses these vignettes about Queen Helene to speak to issues of women and gender. Serving as a rabbinic example, Helene embodies the desire for Judaism. She is a woman who chooses Judaism and adheres to it piously. In one portrayal, Helene builds an extravagantly tall sukkah; in another, she becomes a Nazirite. She supports Judaism's rites, rituals and codes; she is a woman who loves and does not dissent. Helene donates a golden plaque that helps husbands control and punish their wives. She cooperates, implicitly endorses this control of transgressive women, and helps to enforce it. Thus, rabbis use Helene as an exemplar of female obedience, an illustration of a woman who leads the way in aiding and abetting their version of Judaism.

In these passages, early rabbinic law should not be understood exclusively in the juridical sense, as a series of cultural practices that punish violations, or as a set of laws imposed "from outside" upon women's bodies. Instead, these rabbinic men's laws for women's sexuality are envisioned as something that women themselves desire. Women become the law, through the law. Rabbinic law is something that respectable women themselves will uphold. In the case of Helene's gift and the women who spin, women police other women. Certain women model for others a fidelity to early rabbinic law. Rabbinic stories such as these lessen the gap between men's legal texts and women's bodies. Instead, they demonstrate examples in which Jewish women's bodies articulate adherence to mitzvot and halakah. From another angle, Jewish women do not precede the law, but become (rabbinic) Jewish women through embodying the law.

THE LAW OF THE JEWS

The repertoire of informal mechanisms for (imagining) the control of women continues. The next passage, from mishnah Ketubot, details the legal consequences for women who transgress the norms of rabbinic marriage. These consequences rely on the formal authorities of courts and contracts. But more intriguing are the passage's claims about the sources for its laws for women. An innovation of the Roman period, Jewish marriage with ketubbah worked as a contractual pledge.[12] Rather than exchanging money at the start of the marriage, ketubbah was a promise that if and when the marriage ended, the wife would receive property valued at a specific amount. Thus, if the husband died, or if the marriage ended in divorce, the wife would receive her ketubbah. Modern interpreters of Judaism commonly describe this innovation as positive for women. They argue that it increased Jewish women's status and offered them unparalleled protection. In a remarkable refraction of the notion that women's desire to marry exceeds that of men, it is often claimed that this legal innovation was an economic encouragement for men to marry, since they would not have to pay first, so to speak, but merely promise the funds for a later date.[13]

To say that marriage with ketubbah is positive for women is to ignore the relations of power that early rabbinic writings afforded to this arrangement. For instance, marriage with ketubbah contained the repeated threat that a wife might be divorced *without* ketubbah. That is to say, the promise of the ketubbah payment as "protection" for a woman coexisted with the control of women within marriage; it can be reduced if she resists and is rebellious against marriage's demands. In mKetubot 5.7, the ketubbah of the rebellious wife will be reduced by seven denarii each week of her rebellion. At the same time, if a husband is deemed to rebel against his wife, her ketubbah is increased, but only by three (or in an alternate opinion, one and a half) denarii per week. Ketubbah, the withholding of ketubbah, and the threat of penurious divorce are another means of persuading women to follow halakah and its notions of appropriate marital behavior.[14]

Early rabbinic deliberations contain examples in which a husband might divorce his wife and *not* pay her the ketubbah. The early rabbis seem caught within several desires. On the one hand, they wish to assure a divorced woman about her ketubbah payment. On the other, they wish to find ways for individual men to resist this, and to allow these men to end their marriages without the cost of paying ketubbah. Listing reasons why a husband may divorce his wife and not pay ketubbah, mKetubot 7.6 appeals to two specific authorities, Torah, and the law of Jews.

> And these [women] leave [their marriage, *i.e.*, are divorced] without [receiving their] ketubbah:
>
> One who transgresses the Law of Moses and [the law of] Jews.
>
> And what are [the transgressions of the] Law of Moses (*dat mōšeh*)? She causes [her husband] to eat [food] that was not tithed [properly]; Or, she has sexual intercourse with him [while in a state of] menstrual impurity; Or, she does not separate the portion of dough for the priests; Or, she vows, but does not fulfill the vow.
>
> And what are [the transgressions of the] law of Jews (*dat yĕhûdît*)? She goes out and her hair is uncovered; Or, she spins in the marketplace; Or, she speaks with all men (or, with anyone);

Abba Shaul says: Also, one who curses his (*i.e.,* her husband's) ancestors to his face (*i.e.,* within his hearing).

Rabbi Tarfon says: Also, one who shouts. What does "one who shouts" mean? When she speaks inside her house and her neighbors hear her voice.

The passage begins with the statement that "These women are divorced without receiving their ketubbah." The initial list appeals to the Law of Moses, or Torah, and includes transgressions of four types of ritual mitzvot. First among these are wives who prepare food, but do not put aside the appropriate amount to be taken and consecrated to the Temple and its priesthood; thus, they cause their husbands to eat food that has not been properly tithed. Also listed are women who have sexual intercourse with their husbands while in *niddah,* thus disobeying the prohibition on sex during this time; women who prepare dough but do not separate the portion set aside for priests; and last, women who make vows, but then do not fulfill the vow's promises.[15] For violations of these commandments, women may be divorced without ketubbah. It is not at all surprising that an early rabbinic text would appeal to Torah as an arbiter of law, even though they made selective use of Scripture. On the other hand, the fact that rabbinic law would punish wives so severely for violations of mitzvot is somewhat surprising. Indeed, why violations of these mitzvot and not others? Why is the punishment related so closely to the economy of marriage and divorce?

Even more intriguing is the second list of transgressions against what the Mishnah calls the *dat yĕhûdît,* or "law of Jews."[16] Invoking this "law of Jews," the passage lists additional acts that violate rabbinic Jewish codes of marriage, violations for which the wife can be punished by divorce without ketubbah. Compared to the first list, these acts of feminine transgression are more specifically social. In the first two examples, the wife goes out with her hair uncovered, and she spins in the marketplace.[17] Both scenes place women outside the bounds of their own homes, courtyards, and alleys. Each punishes a woman for taking what she does "at home" and doing it in other places, or with other people. Thus, a woman need not cover her hair at home, but this version of the *dat yĕhûdît* demands that she do so when she goes out.[18] Domestic spinning is allowed, and in some opinions it is necessary, but it cannot be done in the marketplace.[19] Location is crucial. The next three transgressions focus on a woman's voice: her partners in conversation, the content of her speech, and the strength of her voice's sound. Thus, the passage appeals to the "law of Jews" to punish a wife who

speaks with many men.[20] The interjection accorded to Abba Shaul adds
the detail of a woman who curses her husband's parents in his hearing.
And last, Rabbi Tarfon attends to the timbre of a wife's voice; he disallows "shouts" and restricts her volume and noise. In this restriction, a
wife may use her voice to speak, but only so loudly as will fit the architectural and social borders of her "house." The sound of her voice
should not leave the interior of her home to reach her neighbors' ears.
Neighbors become intimate and informal police, brought in to judge
the moments when a wife's speech and sounds are too loud for propriety. All these things are invoked as *dat yĕhûdît,* the law of Jews.

Multiple layers of the construction of gender and legal authority are
at work in this passage. Much of early rabbinic law does not note the
sources of its own authority. In this instance, the text claims the authority of the law of Jews to prescribe legal punishment for wives who transgress femininity. In rabbinic writing, the phrase *dat yĕhûdît* is used almost exclusively to refer to the authority that underpins marriage
customs; the phrase appears both in legal writing and in marriage documents. "*Yĕhûdît*" invokes a broad sense of "Jewish" consensus for these
social proprieties for married women. Appearing in this passage about
a wife's transgressions, the phrase also allows a slippage between rabbinic halakah and the law of Jews. The slippage links the two authorities. Just as Torah became an assumed part of halakah, so too a conception of Jewish legal custom (outside Torah) is used here as a parallel
source for rabbinic law.

The link is significant because it places "rabbinicness" on a continuum with "Jewishness." Early rabbinic Judaism attempted to figure out
the relations of rabbis and Jews in various ways, and always for various
reasons. In many passages, early rabbinic writers preferred to see distinctions between rabbis and Jews, particularly those they called "*amei
ha-aretz*" (people of the land). Furthermore, as the last chapter demonstrated, there certainly were differences and conflicts between rabbinic
culture and Jewish culture, especially regarding the various terms of
marriage. Thus, a passage that represents a continuity between Bible-
based rabbinic law and the law of Jews is noteworthy. Since rabbis do
not always seek this kind of consensual relation with other Jews, why
do they depict consensus and continuity in the case of marriage and the
punishment of transgressive women?

In mKetubot 7.6, this strategic flattening of distinctions between
Rabbis and Jews is accompanied by another powerful flattening. The
passage constructs a unitary law of Jews. Yet, Roman Palestine con-

tained many communities of Jews with differing laws and customs and sensibilities, some of which were in conflict and disagreement. In post-Temple Judaism in Roman Palestine, social conflict was not limited to a monolithic set of Rabbis versus a monolithic set of Jews.[21] The Mishnah refers to all this as the law of Jews, as if there were just one. In this instance, the rabbinic passage resists imagining differences among and between Jews and their legal customs. Instead, it crafts a sense of unified Jewish opinion of what married women should and should not do. And, regarding these norms and proprieties of women's behavior, it forms an alliance between Jewish and rabbinic legal custom.

The existence of a Jewish communal law is one kind of community that this passage evokes. As such, it is an abstraction, a community whose contours and place are never made clear. The second type of community is closer at hand, more embodied. The description of each transgression contains someone other than the woman herself: someone else sees, someone watches, someone listens, and someone hears. These people are just beyond the text's actual words, but they are implied. The husband eats the untithed food, or touches his wife's menstruating (or postmenstrual) body. Other people observe the woman's uncovered hair and fill the marketplace. When the wife speaks to "all men," presumably the men hear, and speak back. The curses she utters are heard by the husband. And neighbors are ever present, listening for too-loud noises. Thus, the unspecified, unobservable, nonempirical community evoked by the abstraction, the law of the Jews, appears alongside this second (and simultaneous) community, the marketplace Jews, husbands, passing men, and neighbors. Other people's eyes and ears are fashioned into a community of watchers. Other Jews' senses form a society of impending visual and aural awareness of Jewish women's acts.

LOVE/WORK

To different degrees and in different ways, early rabbinic texts were carefully and skillfully crafted. Early rabbinic Judaism imagined many kinds of social pressures upon women. These rabbinic fantasies included the formal punishments of halakah. They invoked the authority of community and its informal networks of talk and gossip. They relied upon real and imagined gazes at clothed women in the marketplace and naked (or near naked) women in the bathhouse. These fantasies of everyday culture may seem vividly real. But they are analyzed better as mechanisms that move legal fantasies from the legal text to the human body, mechanisms that allay the difference between the two. We tend to think of law as something written in law books—or scrolls—or papyrus codices—and enforced by judges, courts, police and military forces. Yet, each of the Mishnah's mechanisms imagine rabbinic law as part of the everyday. In the informal repetitions of everyday life, law becomes effective as internalized social control. Michel de Certeau's articulation is apropos: "In order for the law to be written on bodies an apparatus is required that can mediate the relation between the former and the latter."[22] Although written formally as deliberation and code, law works most powerfully in its informality, when it crafts human nature itself. With this transformation of law to the body, there is, to quote Michel Foucault, "no need for arms, physical violence, material constraints. Just a gaze. An inspecting gaze, a gaze which each individual under its weight will end by interiorising to the point that he is his own overseer, each individual thus exercising this surveillance over, and against, himself."[23] In such a process, law is written on the body, and the body—here, the Jewish woman's body—both enacts the law, and in doing so, becomes the law.

Feeling intellectually comfortable with the theoretical formulation of "writing law on the body" (or its variant, law "inscribed on the body") may seem difficult to readers who are unfamiliar with this way of thinking about how law and culture form human bodies. It may seem odd to readers who conceptualize the human body as something "natural," as something that predates "culture," and as an entity that exists "before the law." The modern western imagination tends to imagine human beings that are transcultural, whose bodies precede the law, and hence, do not depend on the specificities of different cultures and societies. Bodies are imagined as separate from law, and thus imagined as coherent selves with agency, able to resist law or agree to it, whichever the case may be.[24]

To begin making a conceptual shift from the notion of subjects that precede the law, to the notion of subjects constructed by the law, consider the illustration offered by a passage from Avot de Rabbi Natan about workers and their bodies:

> Rabbi Elazar ben Azaryah says: Work is great because every kind of craftsman goes out and is proud of his occupation (or: praises himself for his craft). How? The weaver (ṭarsis) goes out with the whorl (karkār) on his ear and is proud of his occupation. The dyer goes out with some undyed wool on his ear and is proud of his occupation. The scribe goes out with the pen on his ear and is proud of his occupation.[25]

In the scene, proud workers wear symbols of their trades on their bodies. The weaver wears a spindle whorl, the dyer wears undyed wool, and the scribe wears a pen. Each implement is placed on the side of the head, tucked behind the ear where it can be felt by the worker and seen by all others. Wearing the symbol of one's work conveys pride. This passage emphasizes the moral and social necessities of labor. The passage shows overtly how labor is marked on the body. It vividly demonstrates the power of the body to display. These specific marks are removable, certainly, but they are present and visible emblems. These bodies are culturally inscribed as workers' bodies through the accessories and signs of their trade. And since a symbol rarely has a singular meaning, the marks that show workers' pride also convey other things. For instance, would the whorl behind the ear remind those who encountered the weaver on the street of the stereotypes of weavers as feminized men? Would the mark of a scribe's pen convey various notions of the scribe's social station to those who saw him? Would those who saw the dyer's earful of wool look to his hands to see the stains, would they compare the dyer with the ill-reputed tanner, accused of dirty hands and stinking odors? This illustration does not parallel exactly the inscription of law upon the human body; the passage is not about halakah after all, and a man's pride in his occupation is not law. But it shows very well how an abstract notion such as pride can be marked on the body, and how as a result, a human being can be constituted as a laboring body.

If this is not precisely the inscription of halakah on the human body, it is something equally powerful; the inscription on the body of an ethos, in which the relation of artisans to labor will be one of pride. The issue of how rabbinic law is written into human bodies that then reenact law raises the question of ethos—the creation and perpetuation and modification of naturalized assumptions about the world. Thinking about ethos means considering the process by which certain things will seem natural and normal, usually through the power of repetition and reiteration, while other things become less easily imagined, if at all. The idea to consider, then, is that the construction and rabbinic narration of an ethos for halakah might be just as important as the actual details of halakah.

Thinking about ethos and halakah, I turn to another passage from Avot de Rabbi Natan (B). This passage is significant. In it, both ethos and gossip are powerfully endorsed as intertwined modes of social control. Thus, the question of informal and extralegal discipline has another angle, from which women and men create, become part of, and are affected by networks of public talk and truth. This passage comments on the phrase "love work" that appears in Pirke Avot (Chapters of the Fathers): "Shemaiah and Avtalyon took over from them. Shemaiah says: Love work, hate lordship, and seek no intimacy with the ruling powers." In the genealogy of rabbis and their ancestry that Pirke Avot presents, Shemaiah and Avtalyon were one of the five pairs of rulers who transferred the Oral Law from Ezra and the men of the Great Assembly to the Pharisees and on to the rabbis themselves.[26] In Avot de Rabbi Natan, the statement from Pirke Avot is expanded and its meanings are derived.

The commentary on the phrase "love work" begins with a tumbling run through biblical text. Prooftexts secure scriptural origins for the statement that one should love work. God created the world with a word (Psalms 33.6) and this was work, "as Scripture says: His work which he had done" (Genesis 2.2). Since God did work, all the more so should the sons of men work. Adam (the first human) tasted nothing until he had worked,[27] and God placed Adam into the Garden of Eden to work it and to keep it (Genesis 2.15). "Work is great because as Israel was commanded concerning the Sabbath, so too were they commanded concerning work." And as proof for this, "Six days you will labor and do all your work; but the seventh is a Sabbath to the Lord your God" (Exodus 20.9–10).

Following the plethora of prooftexts, the timbre of the passage changes and the explanation of the phrase "love work" follows a different tact:

> Rabbi [Yehudah ha-Nasi] says: Great is work because anyone who does not engage in work, the sons of men (*běnê ʾādām*)[28] talk about him: How does so and so get anything to eat? How does he get anything to drink?
> A parable (*mašal*): To what may this be compared? To a woman who does not have a husband, and yet adorns herself and goes out in the marketplace. People talk about her in the same way people talk about anyone who does not engage in work.

The passage moves from the authority of Scripture to the panopticon of public prattle. A man should work because if not, others will ask how he gains food to eat and drinks to quench his thirst. In contrast to the abstract community, or the authority of a communally shared Scripture, this particular and peculiar community is nearby and attentive. At its forefront are the observing eyes, listening ears, and speaking mouths of embodied neighbors and villagers. The sons of men gossip. The reputation of the nonworker will be sullied by their speculation. The passage defines work through the public consequences of not working. Work does not automatically bring respectability. But not working allows others to inquire into one's sources of sustenance. To set and sustain an ethos in which work is necessary, the passage invokes the power of observation and conversation. People might raise questions: How does so and so get anything to eat? How does he get anything to drink? One must work because if not, this will be observed, and people will talk.[29]

This scene elides rabbinic scrutiny with these public gazes. The formality of biblical prooftexts joins with the informality of gossip (and the textuality of rabbinic representations of gossip). But note the differences: gossip is powerful precisely because one has little recourse to a commonly held knowledge. Unlike scrolls of Scripture and authoritative text, gossip is unregulated. It creates multiple truths, with no recourse for judging which "truth" is more "true." In gossip, there is no learned partner to argue with, no text to consult, only the circulation of oral and aural judgment. The persons talked about have little if any control, as others craft and fashion their character. And public talk soon is removed from the temporary (and contingent) authority of witness and observation. The fact of being observed and then spoken about is quickly replaced as gossip becomes a series of oral repetitions: "so-and-so saw such-and-such." Observation is replaced by the reiteration and repetition of what one has heard.

As tools for social control, talk, gossip, and the realm of rumor are informal but powerful. Public talk creates informal networks of truth. It sets up certain standards of judgment. This passage from Avot de Rabbi Natan makes its readers aware of the power of public talk. It invokes the fear of public talk as a justification for why one should work and love work. Then, to explain further the scenario of gossip and the working man, the passage introduces a parable. The man's situation (his gender has been made clear through pronouns and verb forms) is compared to that of an unmarried woman who adorns herself and goes out into the marketplace. As a result of her venture, people will gossip. The parable explains the position of the male nonworker through the persona of the ornamented woman who ventures into the marketplace. It assumes that the ornamented and unbounded woman will be a familiar topic of conversation. Presumably, the cultural commonplace of noticing and gossiping about such a woman would make transparently clear the earlier point about villagers who gossip about a lazy man.

But in the process of clarification, the passage makes another layer of

points. The "woman in the marketplace" was a familiar trope in rabbinic, Jewish, and other cultures in the Roman Empire. Marketplaces
and other well-traveled areas were (imagined as) sites where female
sexuality was particularly problematic. The easy movement and sexual
availability of women in the marketplace was a recurring theme. Instances abound, as rabbis retell a story of the marketplace of Alexandria, where women are grabbed into marriage against their will; or
when they decree that a woman who does her spinning in the marketplace may be divorced without her ketubbah payment.[30] The market
abounds with unrestricted sexual gazes. These gazes are masculine.
They originate from the bodies of men and focus on the bodies of
women. Rabbis imagine the marketplace as a site filled with multiple
masculine bodies and ocular desires. One of their responses is to cover
women's heads and to contain the female body through clothing.[31] But
clothing—even head covering—is not enough. In this parable, the
woman adorns herself. She is clothed, but she subverts the propriety of
clothing through extra acts of ornamentation. Adorning herself, she
defies the ideal of feminine simplicity and pays special attention to her
body's attractiveness. Furthermore, she is unmarried. As yet unclaimed
by a male husband, she either disregards her status as her father's concern, or she is legally autonomous, unbeholden to any particular man.

So, breaking the rules and conventions that would define a woman's
body, the unmarried woman adorns herself and ventures into the marketplace. However, the passage makes clear that she is still beholden to
the abstract voyeur whose gaze is imagined as an inherent part of the
marketplace. Again, as with the male nonworker, people talk. The passage likens the gossip about the unmarried woman's (presumed) promiscuity to the questions asked about the nonworking man: How does he
eat? How does he drink? One ramification is clear. If men work and
women stay at home, both will be guaranteed anonymity and freedom from village gazes and tongues. Except, in the woman's case, the
specific details and questions of their talk are unimportant, or at least
absent from the passage's concern: People talk about her *in the same
way* people talk about anyone who does not engage in work. For
the adorned woman, particular content does not matter so much as the
specter of gossip itself.

The specter of people talking can be added to the list of mechanisms
of enforcement in rabbinic writing. In this fantasy, public talk creates
an ethos that supports halakah. Just as the specter of neighborly gazes

and gossip is aroused for the social control of women, the specter of gender is provoked to create a set of social meanings for working men. To discipline the male nonlaborer the passage summons gossip—the same mechanism that disciplines women into appropriate practices of gender and sexual behavior. It should be no longer be surprising to find sexuality, gender, and work tangled together. The reasons why men should love work are cast within the language of transgressive female sexuality. The suspicions about a woman's promiscuity parallel a man's refusal to work. She suspends the proprieties of sexual virtue, he refrains from labor. Her licentious immodesty is active. She adorns herself and moves into the marketplace, but ideally, she should be more passive. His act of nonwork is linked to his passivity. As the focus of spoken commentary, his disreputability rests on inertness, immobility, and abstinence. The passage links immobility with women; thus, the man's passivity feminizes him, and this is not seen as a tribute. The watchful attentions and tones he receives—How does he eat? How does he drink?—are ones focused more appropriately (within this expression of rabbinic culture) upon women.[32]

GOSSIP

In the absence of more formal modes for enforcing rabbinic visions of culture, law, and society, the informalities of public gazes and chatter are not to be underrated.[33] Gossip and public talk were important mechanisms for a religious movement that in its initial years had no systematic, bureaucratic forms of enforcement for most aspects of its law. Public talk created and distributed everyday stories that were exchanged between family members, between people who lived in the same village, alleyway, courtyard, who worked near each other in the marketplace, who tilled the same fields, processed grapes and olives, or who met to draw water and fill buckets from shared cisterns and wells. These everyday stories forge an ethos in which human action and understanding take place. In exceedingly informal ways, they create, modify, and perpetuate an everyday and commonplace reality.

The rabbinic passages discussed here proffered several simultaneous strategies for disseminating a culture of gender: gossip and community gazes, whether nearby or abstract; women who police women; and women who share with men information derived in women-only spaces. This repertoire of strategies included the naturalized habits that

women themselves will assume, especially as they interiorized a rabbinic Jewish ethos. Through these and other strategies, early rabbinic
literature suggested informal ways that their prescriptions for gender
might become an everyday Jewish "commonsense." Living amid strong
notions of what is appropriate, approved, and rewarded, women and
men will internalize these gazes, restrictions, and codes. In this way, a
rabbinic ethos will become an integral part of the ordinary and invisible. Or so early rabbinic literature will have us agree, with images of
Helene's golden sotah plaque that simultaneously and repetitively re-
flects each morning's rising sun and enables the telling of time. Or with
the portrayal of dispersed eyes and ears whose reports can invoke punishment. These passages become a pattern. A series of representations
emerge that display how rabbinic notions might become part of the
Jewish everyday, and that show the "marking or shaping [of] bodies in
the name of a law."[34]

Gossip and other kinds of voyeuristic talk were ways that ancient
rabbis wrote and read about women, gender, work, and sexuality. At
the same time, gossip and acts of seeing are also ways that we can start
to account for the complexities of an ethos of gender and halakah. The
following anecdote comes from the volume *Engendering Archaeology*.
The archaeologist R. E. Tringham is recounting the process of setting
aside some inherited scholarly frameworks that had ceased to explain
that which needed explanation. Tringham had been presenting new research on household organization in prehistoric southeast Europe to a
seminar of colleagues. The anthropologist Henrietta Moore interrupted
and asked Tringham how she envisaged the households she analyzed.
Tringham responded, and narrates the conversation that ensued:

> "You mean how do I imagine their composition?" thinking: Oh, heavens,
> she wants me to imagine their kinship structure, but I am interested in what
> households did, not what they comprised . . .
>
> Henrietta said, "No, how do you envisage them going about their daily
> actions?"
>
> You can imagine, I felt quite defensive. "Archaeologists don't do that. We
> don't go around envisaging people leading cows to pasture and gossiping
> around the household chores."
>
> "Yes, but what if you were allowed to do it; just relax; no one will tell.
> Now, just tell us how you see them. What do they look like?"
>
> "Well, there's a house, and cows, and pigs, and garbage . . . "
>
> "Yes, but the people, tell us about the people."

"Well . . . ," I said. And then I realized what I saw. "I see," I said, " . . . a lot of faceless blobs."

And then it dawned on me what she wanted me to see. That until, as an archaeologist, you can learn to give your imagined societies faces, you cannot envisage gender.[35]

When I first read this exchange, I was impressed by its punch line, by the vivid account of moving from "faceless blobs" toward seeing faces when we make (hi)stories of ancient societies, or, better, when we write about ancient people. The punch line remains an important critique and challenge. Tringham's embarrassment is poignant, and hers is an accurate statement of what we archaeologists and historians resist: "We don't go around envisaging people leading cows to pasture and gossiping around the household chores." But using this vignette now as a critical tool, what I find most helpful are its reminders to look painstakingly at what it is that we historians and archaeologists already do—or don't do. "How do you imagine? "How do you envisage?" These questions point to the prior and ongoing necessity of articulating that which structures what we see or don't see when we look at the past. "Imagining faces" means coming to terms with the imaginedness of the societies we study, as well as with the consequences of these imaginations.

Gossip prompts these reflections on rabbinic fantasies of women, gender, and social control. In thinking and writing about early rabbinic Judaism and Jewish practice, we miss the chatter, the gossip, the language and words and sensibilities that filled in time. Categorically, we annul from history the conversation and small talk, the tattles, the comments and commentary that give sound and meaning to ordinary acts such as cooking, walking from place to place, eating midday meals, placing olives into a press, draining wine from fermented grape skins, hammering and retting flax, and much, much more. Deleting bodies, faces and voices, we imagine antiquity as somehow silent, as soundless as the current reconstruction of the Parthenon in Athens with its ancient paints effaced in favor of a pristine white.[36] Clearly, we don't have records of gossip by Jews in Roman Palestine; we barely have inscriptional remnants of their graffiti. Circulations of information and judgment, networks of story and sound—the effect was ethos, naturalized ways of making sense of the world. It is here that the most fascinating—and irretrievable—parts of antiquity are contained: acts of collaboration, resistance, boredom, mundanity, creativity, imagination, monotony, and other nearly unknowable things. Still, the category of unrecorded talk, the words and conversations that were not among the infinitesimal fraction that remain for us, crafted into rabbinic and other written texts, these need to be imagined—historically and critically— back into tales of Jews and Judaism in the past.[37]

Finally, gossip is not just about what was part of Roman and Jewish antiquity but absent in our historical accounts. It is not just about what needs to be added if we are to consider women's lives and the construction of gender historically. Gossip is about mechanisms of power that were very much present in the way early rabbinic texts narrated their world. Typically, studies of early rabbinic Judaism have focused on the sociology of institutions, asking questions about the numerical strength of the rabbinic movement, its relations with Rome and the imperial bureaucracies, the relation of rabbis with the Patriarchate, the recognition of Palestinian rabbis as a local elite, and rabbinic engagement with educational systems and legal courts. In focusing on these formal questions of early rabbinic authority, the issue of how that influence might have spread in small, ordinary, and informal ways is left to the side.

Yet power that is formal, physical, or which depends on enforcement through law and other governing apparatus is not at the forefront of how early rabbinic writing creates the gendered lives of women and men. To say this is not to ignore rabbinic interest in written contracts, their examples of court decisions about the details of marriage and divorce, or instances of physical punishment. While early rabbinic texts sometimes refer to the physical control of women, the imprisonment of women and the idea of female seclusion were not the preferred rabbinic modes. For instance, when tSotah 5.9 discusses different men's "tastes for women's behavior" they do not favor the model of Pappos ben Judah, who locked the door of his house to keep his wife inside when he went out. They deride this husband as a foolish man who finds a fly in his cup and tosses the fly out and does not drink what is in the cup." His behavior is contrasted with the admired "ordinary man," who sees his wife talking with neighbors and relatives, and lets her be. This ordinary man is one for whom a fly falls into his cup, and he tosses the fly away and drinks what remains. At the same time, although derided, the model of imprisonment is still made real through narration. It is not preferred, but neither is it described as bad (as are some other examples of husbands' treatment of their wives in the same passage) and moved absolutely beyond the pale of rabbinic approval, to the realm of things that are beyond mention.[38] Yet despite examples such as these, neither formal courts nor physical custody were primary ways for rabbis to imagine the control of women.

Through stories about women's bodies, early rabbis narrated how their version of Judaism might become more widely persuasive and practiced. With networks of gazes, gossip, and other community pressures, rabbinic texts depict how a wide array of Jews could enact rabbinic notions as everyday Jewish culture. Despite its modern reputation, rabbinic Judaism was not—once we think about women—a tradition based on written words. Rabbinic Judaism was not expressed solely as the details of carefully composed decisions, nor transmitted through the meticulous handwriting of scribes and the studious repetitions of rabbis. Rather, a rabbinic Jewish ethos of gender was represented as real through the informality of talk, chatter, and other brokered information. Through these informal and in-forming modes, rabbinic law gained "the credibility attached to a discourse articulated by bodies." In an everyday ethos of halakah, Jewish bodies and Jewish subjects were shaped and gendered accordingly. The weaver wears the whorl, and becomes, at least in part, the many things that the whorl signifies. From this angle, the notion of "legal story" expands. It is no longer limited to the stories that appear in legal writing, nor to the unspoken assumptions that undergird legal positions and argument. Legal stories are also what happen when law becomes embodied. In this vision, gendered Jewish bodies become repetitive halakic texts. Rabbinic law becomes living stories that are interiorized into the "natural" body as everyday knowledge.

Epilogue

Burying Spindles with the Dead

High above the western shore of the Dead Sea lives a testament to just how high the human soul can soar. Come experience Masada and hear its ancient heart still beat.
> *Travel ad placed in U.S. magazines*
> *by Israel Ministry of Tourism*

Do we have to see Roman ruins again?
> *Anonymous student*

To make antiquity familiar, minute traces and random fragments are
forged into images, emotions, and stories. Looking for words to describe the desire to turn fragments into something coherent and whole,
I reach for the dictionary. Leafing through, not quite aimlessly, I find
nostalgia: "a wistful desire to return in thought or in fact to a former
time in one's life, to one's home or homeland, or to one's family and
friends; a sentimental yearning for the happiness of a former place or
time." Tracing an antiquity of its own, the English language dictionary
derives *nostalgia* from the Greek *nostos,* "to return home," combined
with *algia,* "pain."

Antiquity is often imagined as if it were some kind of long-lost
home. In this dream, its religions are part of our origins, its men are our
fathers, and its women our mothers. When antiquity is the source for
classical culture, it is imagined to hold an essence—a fundamental continuity—that is transmitted from them to us. Imagined as such, ancient
history is about nostalgia. It yields reunions with ancestors and returns
us to homes we never knew. But what happens when these assumptions
about our relations to antiquity are challenged? What happens when
the starting point for thinking about antiquity is not the ability to re-
construct it and make it live again, but its very demise. Antiquity is
gone. There are no homes awaiting our return. There is no former time

to resurrect. If these are our starting points, what other options for thinking about antiquity become imaginable?

My eyes continue down the dictionary page. I find a word I had not previously known: *nostomania*. Defined as "intense homesickness," nostomania is "an irresistible compulsion to return home." The dictionary entry ends with a caution. Nostomania is "a desire that can never be met." I compare this with nostalgia's certainty that home exists. As a relation to a past time and place, nostomania carries a very different kind of emotion. It provokes alternate questions. What does it mean to create antiquity as a home, to craft a time into a place for which one could be homesick? After all, homes change, as do our relationships with them. Sometimes homes are places of safety and love. Other times they are sites of confinement and danger, locations to leave, places where decisions are made about who may be present, and under what terms.[1] Nostalgia builds identity—for oneself, for one's group— on a deeply felt relation to faraway times, places, and people. Nostomania can provide a critical angle from which to think about this process. It suggests new ways to think about the (ir)resistible compulsion to identify with times and places that no longer exist. Nostomania forces us to consider nostalgia as a compulsion, and it raises questions about whether and how this compulsion can be resisted. Nostalgia yearns for home, for things that belong to us, and for women and men to whom we are related. Nostomania recognizes the impossibility of this venture.

When fragments of antiquity are made into whole stories, they are released from the burdens of ambiguity and uncertainty. Between the nostalgic romance of an accessible and unmediated past, and its nostomanic impossibilities, what complexities are flattened out? Writing as a professional historian and religionist, I am concerned with what happens when the "irresistible compulsion" which can never be fulfilled is combined (usually in unacknowledged ways) with notions of history and identity that only uneasily tolerate difference and complexity and ambiguity.

Much of this book has been overtly about rabbis and gender, and only implicitly about history. Now I turn more directly to the latter. In broadly drawn strokes I wish to pressure the dream of return. I want to think about some of the ways we make the past meaningful. And I want to consider what this has meant for Jews and Jewish feminists. Doing so, I imagine there must be alternatives for how to write about rabbis, gender, and Judaism from a feminist ethos that does not assume any of these things to be essential or stable categories.[2]

To do this I offer a final reading of a Roman-period text plus a look at a cultural practice; both offer different perspectives on gender, everyday life, continuity, and change in Roman Palestine. The text is the apocalyptic tract II Baruch, which dates from the decades following the destruction of the Jerusalem Temple in 70 C.E. The cultural practice is the placing of spindle whorls as grave goods in burials throughout Palestine.

This said, my reading doesn't really begin with these pieces of ancient evidence. Instead, it starts where most of us tend to start, really, with the many ways that we "know" about Jews and Judaism in Roman Palestine. Because on the way to II Baruch and spindles placed in graves stand all sorts of conscious and less than conscious modes for knowing about Jews, Judaism, women, men, and history. Roman Palestine is claimed as an ancestral home for Jews and honored as the birthplace of Jesus, Christianity, and the earliest Christian communities. Its antiquities are both vacation spots for American and European tourists and sites of political and religious turbulence. The most popular and well-known images of rabbinic Judaism are of its men. Histories written about the people and their traditions come wrapped in the terms of European modernity. And as Israel, the modern nation-state that now exists on the province over which the Roman Empire once held sway, the remains of Roman Palestine are the focus of nationalist and Zionist attention. These and more are part of how we know this time and place, these traditions and people. This knowledge is where I start.

BIRTHPLACES

In Jewish religious history, Roman Palestine is often announced as the birthplace of the classic rabbinic tradition. The term is gendered and the women are absent. The mothers of this tradition—and their progeny—are all men. As a birthplace of something important, Roman Palestine is conventionally narrated in grandiose ways. The second century becomes a time in between two major formulations of Judaism. Preceding it was the Jerusalem Temple, with its majestic architecture, its political intrigue, its extensive priesthood, its sacrifices of animals and offerings of meal and incense, and its tents of pilgrims. The century after the temple's destruction flows into rabbinic Judaism, with its synagogues and study houses, its esteem for formal prayer and scriptural readings, its circles of rabbis, its focus on relations between persons, and its articulation of halakah for ordinary and everyday events. The narration is elegant in its simplicity and in its seamlessness. This period of time is made intelligible to us through a reassuring pattern: destruction and devastation followed by gestation and rebirth.

But this narrative and its variations are possible only when we tell Jewish religious history as if we stood with elite Jewish men—whether rabbis, priests, Pharisees, Sadducees, or other male leaders—and used their eyes and their values. Continuing these sympathies and identifications, we risk always looking as (we imagine) they looked. In other words, if we forget where we have positioned ourselves, then theirs become the invisible but powerful eyes we use to look at other people's bodies, even when we consider women's lives, and even if we are women.[3]

Current versions of Jewish religious history are based almost entirely upon the experiences and texts of Jewish men. The relative elegance of these stories about Roman Palestine and the early rabbis is built both upon absences and upon the inclusion of stereotyped figures that are by now all too obvious. The Temple was designed and built by men. It brought glory to male leaders. Spatially, it organized gender so that Jewish women were kept to the outer precincts, while Jewish men were allowed closer to the Holy of Holies. The priesthood was all male, although to be sure it depended upon the labors of women. Sacrifices could be offered by both men and women, but only men could venture near the places in the Temple where sacrifices happened, and husbands would make sacrifices on behalf of their wives and family. The rabbinate was an all-male group. The rituals of prayer and Torah reading were obligations incurred only by men, and only men were rewarded for these disciplines. The highly prized acts of legal commentary and metalegal analysis, as well as the midrashic reading of biblical texts, entirely excluded women. Despite the evidence that some women were leaders in synagogue congregations and Jewish communities (in areas other than Palestine), more generally, men held these influential roles. Eventually, although several centuries later, women who participated in synagogue services were moved to separate rooms or to upper galleries.

Without an active critical engagement, we can never do anything other than repeat these gendered patterns as we write and read about them. In addition to these patterns, Jewish religious history has been a peculiarly modern task. With the Enlightenment's development of new ideas about religion and history and with the emancipations that began in the late eighteenth century, Jewish traditions were reformulated as "religion" and as "history." History was one way to make past time make sense. Tales of Jews and Judaism were made to fit the conceptual forms peculiar to European modernity. After all, history is not natural, but a specifically Western European conception of the relation of time and events. Since emancipation, histories about Jews and Judaism emulated the categories offered by the West. In the nineteenth century, the male intellectuals of the Wissenschaft des Judentums invested the "historyless" Jews with a history of their own. Their adoption of this category meant forming a past for Jews in historical terms. Using these terms, Jewish intellectuals crafted new stories about Jews and Judaism that would fit the standards of respectability proffered by the academy and Western intellectual life.

These histories had very real consequences. Narrating a Jewish history helped to form Jews and Judaism into a "people." In Western European culture, a history was part of what a people had. A people's history linked them to their "nation" as much as it formed that nation. History demonstrated a people's essence. It explained their uniqueness, and it marked what separated them from others. After emancipation, one goal of Jewish history was to demonstrate that despite apparent changes and despite superficial developments, the "Jewish people" too had an unchanging essence. Writing histories about Jews became one way that Jewish intellectuals demonstrated their humanness. History was one of many ways they refashioned themselves as citizens and showed non-Jewish Europeans that Jews, too, were a people and a nation. Jewish history was to show that modern Jews shared a continuous essence with ancestors in distant pasts and places. In this way, a notion of identity—one that presupposes a shared essence between modern people and people of past times—is built right into the writing of history.[4]

These highly personal and nationalist quests for histories about past times were simultaneously stories for and about the present. But the crux is this: the intellectuals of the Wissenschaft des Judentums—and those who have inherited their terms—invoked the authority of academic method to claim that these stories were not about them but about "real Jews" in ancient times. Increasingly, the historian's desires were imagined to influence only negligibly the history told. This resulted in a paradox. The demands of historical objectivity stressed the difference between the present historian and the past being written about. But intrinsically, the definition of history contained the unspoken demand for connection. As this demand becomes less visible and more veiled, and as the demand for the performance of scholarly objectivity becomes more prominent, the fantasy of a scholar's detachment became persuasive. In much of Western culture, history became a naturalized part of what human beings have. The past as a construction of the present was forgotten. Except, when you look closely enough at the stories about Roman-period Judaism (and Rome, more generally) that arise from this paradox, they start to look exceedingly similar to a whole array of modern utopias and dystopias.

With the creation of a Jewish state, Jewish history was put to new uses. It was used to craft a physical sense of belonging to the land that some Jews now occupied. Furthermore, Jewish history was used to promote, in most instances, a sense that Jews exclusively belonged in that land. Geographers mapped the region, linked Hebrew names to places, and associated them with past Jewish occupancy. Historians wrote about Jews who lived in the region throughout the centuries. Archaeologists excavated sites, and in doing so, used the newly excavated landscape as an authority to make vivid a Jewish history in this region, one that emphasized the region's Jewish occupants.[5]

By and large, the historical accounts that have excluded women have excluded other occupants as well. As Nadia Abu El-Haj writes, the history of this region has been constructed as "one's relation not to the past of the territory itself but rather to that of particular groups who resided and ruled therein" (215). Although Abu El-Haj was not speaking about women and the rulership of men, her point is well applied. The exclusion of women takes place when we position ourselves with, and as, those who "ruled therein." But to limit Abu El-Haj's insight to how it highlights the process of excluding women would do unutterable violence to the other exclusions that these tales of Roman Palestine and Jewish history effect. Narrating the history of Roman Palestine as the history solely of Jews contributes to a political ethos in which it has become "natural" for many people to think that only Jews belong in the region of Israel and Palestine.

It is not easy to think about both of these exclusions simultaneously. Indeed, the process and effects of these exclusions have been different. They must not be flattened out, as if all exclusions were somehow the same. However, this book has insistently focused on imbrications—on the necessity of thinking about several things simultaneously. These histories of exclusion were products from and for certain political climates. With the changing of political realities, and with changing notions of where a historian's sympathies might lay, our stories about this place must be revised.[6] Some will wish to continue writing and telling

Jewish religious history within these conventions and with these political loyalties. But others of us will wish to look from elsewhere, with other assumptions and expanded sympathies, to consider what the past looks like without the certainties that have been rendered highly uncertain.

If these claims to significant absences and patterns are true, and they are, then the ways that many of us repeat the history of Judaism have been rendered highly problematic. This problem is the new challenge. How can we study antiquity, Palestine, and Judaism through a feminist practice that is critical of the inherited intellectual traditions that have provided us with authority and credibility and a place to stand, and simultaneously, have limited what we can do with this authority and these stances?[7] To begin an answer, I offer some tentative thoughts about Roman-period Judaism from amid the messiness of modernity's legacy and antiquity's fragments.

ALTERNATE UNDERTAKINGS

In some ways and not others, Jewish life in Roman Palestine was begun anew in the second century. The region became part of a Roman province. Some of its rites, leaders, and sensibilities changed. It all depends on which texts we read, how many texts we read together, how we read, and who we imagine ourselves in sympathy with. One text—II Baruch—makes a major and dramatic break with the past and demands the cessation of the ordinary. This tract is about exile, desecration, and hibernation. It expresses the searing pain felt at the destruction of the Jerusalem Temple and the military loss to Rome. The text is an apocalypse, a genre concerned with the end of a time. Written in the early years of the second century, II Baruch is one of the few remaining Jewish nonrabbinic writings from that time. Most likely written originally in Hebrew, it was translated into Greek and from Greek, into Syriac, the only language in which it is currently available. The Syriac translation was copied and transmitted for centuries by Christian scribes. To communicate the pathos of the newly destroyed Second Temple, the tract uses Baruch, a figure from the biblical accounts of the destruction of the First Temple, roughly six hundred years before. Like many other apocalypses, this one is pseudonymous. Its author or authors hide in Baruch's name, which they invoke as their own voice (although for the sake of convenience I will refer to both the text and the author as "Baruch").

As this apocalypse begins, the Jerusalem Temple is under siege. Baruch watches an angel descend into the Temple's most sacred spot, the Holy of Holies. The angel is on a mission of rescue. From the Temple the angel retrieves a number of items: the woven veil that separated the Holy of Holies from other temple precincts, the holy ephod worn by the High Priest, the mercy seat, the tables for showbread, the priestly clothing, and the incense altar. The angel buries these deep in the earth, to be guarded until the Temple is restored. Once the holy objects are secured, the angel instructs other angels to destroy Jerusalem's walls and to overthrow its foundations.[8]

When Jerusalem is destroyed, a voice announces that God has left and that God will no longer guard the Temple. People start to leave. But Baruch hears God's voice telling him to stay in Jerusalem, and so he does. He sits in front of the Temple's doors and raises a lament at the torture of destruction (II Baruch 10.6–19). Baruch's lament blesses the unborn and the dead who do not have to bear the pain he feels at these afflictions. He calls on the sirens, the *lilin*, the demons and dragons, on all human and extrahuman beings to mourn with him. To show sympathy with the desecration of the extraordinary and sacred Temple, ordinary life must now stop. Farmers should not sow. Fruit trees should not offer harvest. Grapevines should not yield wine. Nature should cease giving, the heavens should hold back their rain and dew. The sun must retract its rays and the moon withdraw its reflected light. All fertility must stop. The land's ecology must mirror the military destruction of the Temple and city. Home has been destroyed. Human life should not reproduce. There should be no more marriages, no more children, no more families. There must be no more sexuality and no more pleasure.

Then Baruch's attention turns to the Temple priests. For them, Baruch has no sympathy. As caretakers who have been careless, they are the villains of his lament. The priests must cast the Sanctuary keys to the heavens, giving them back to God. "Guard your house yourself," Baruch has the priests announce to God, "Because we have been found to be false stewards." While the Temple stood, the priests had offered atonement and purification for Jews. But now the male priests have sinned. They have disgraced themselves and forfeited the Temple for all Jews. Baruch looks elsewhere for sources of purity and renewal. With the priesthood in disgrace and the Temple destroyed, Baruch turns to the margins of the Temple economy.

There, in the female bodies of virgin spinners, Baruch finds an image of redemption for Jews. In the lament's final verse, Baruch uses the virgin spinners to express his hopes for purity, possibility, and the future. The spinners emulate the priests, in a way. Just as the Temple guardians had tossed their keys heavenward, the spinners throw their tools to the fire: "And you, virgins who spin linen, and silk with the gold of Ophir: make haste and take all things and cast them into the fire so that it may carry them to him who made them." Virgins do not reproduce life. They represent the opposite of sexual pleasure, reproduction, and human continuity. Virgins are the type of sexual, that is, nonsexual, being whose presence is appropriate in Baruch's vision of the postdestruction world. In the lament, the virgins are spinning luxury thread. Metaphorically, gold from Ophir is the highest quality gold, procured by Solomon for the Temple and worn as luxury ornaments by women in the royal court.[9] But now the production of these precious things must cease, even when these luxuries are produced by women who do not (re)produce human life. As the priests tossed away their keys, and as the angel buried the Temple's sacred objects deep in the ground, the virgins must toss the linen and silk and gold threads into the fire. They too must return their tools to God for safekeeping. The lament concludes: "And the flame sends them to him who created them, so that the enemies do not take possession of them." The fire that destroys also protects. Casting the fine-spun thread into the fire, the virgins continue the work of the angel who had saved the Temple veil and other sacred goods and placed them into safekeeping for the distant future. The virgins' spun progeny is arrested by fire, held in abeyance, and maintained until an unknown future time.

Baruch's lament expresses an ethos of destruction writ large, a destruction whose effects must be felt everywhere, and by all. The Temple's destruction means that everything must cease. God's home has been destroyed, and human homes must follow suit by ceasing fertility. Both the present and the near future are characterized by hibernation and denial of life. All production is deferred. The sun withdraws, the rain ceases, and the spindle's twirl stops. The people have been exiled and what remains is the singular male voice relating the tale. In II Baruch, the suspension (but not death) of humanity is marked when male priests release the power they have held and misused. Baruch displaces female reproduction onto the bodies of men. Men—rather than women—are directed to cease reproduction. Women's bodies are imaged as the infertile and nonsexual bodies of female virgins, who are not involved in the reproduction of human life, and now must cease their other kinds of production. The tract II Baruch portrays a temporary near-death experience for Jews. The result is isolation, enforced desolation, and mourning through radical change. Baruch's world is suspended somewhere between life and death. Life at the Temple ended in a moment of drama, the everyday ends by slow withdrawal and attrition.

In contrast, consider another account of life, death, and gender. The apocalyptic tract II Baruch features an angel who buries objects underground. The following evidence, from roughly the same period, features a similar act in a more mundane and ordinary context. As part of the rites and practices that ceremonially mark the end of life, grave goods were buried with the dead. Before, after, and during the second century, loved ones and professional buriers placed objects into the graves. Among these goods, the spindle appears once again.[10] People filled graves with all sorts of objects. In a Jerusalem tomb someone placed bracelets, a metal vessel, three clay lamps, four vases, a dark-gray spindle whorl, and a bronze mirror. One group burial at Meiron contained glass bottles and vessels, a bronze spoon, two spindle whorls, and a ceramic inkwell. Family members were buried in a tomb at Philadelphia (Amman) with bone needles, pottery jugs, bowls and flasks, lamps, gold earrings, amulet cases, silver rings, bells, bracelets of bronze, iron and glass, a key, knife fragments, pendants, coins, beads, and glass vases. A tomb near Nablus contained four lamps, a glass bottle, three small glass beads, a spindle whorl, an ivory pin and a ring. And at Naḥf, the dead were buried with bone hairpins, two bone needles, two spindle whorls, bronze bracelets, an iron knife and an iron spearhead, gold earrings, bronze coins, and lamps. In other graves people had placed clay pots, bronze mirrors, kohl sticks, incense burners, a silver cosmetic spatula, along with coins from cities both nearby and far.[11] Graves in which the deceased were buried with spindles and spindle whorls have been excavated at Jerusalem and in the catacombs at Beth Shearim, at sites such as Akko, Nahariya, and Ascalon near the Mediterranean's shores, and inland at places such as Meiron, Silet edh-Dahr, and Beth Shean. Far from being only about the dead, funerary practices are performed by living people for themselves and others. Grave goods were placed in the graves of women, men, children, and in group burials.[12] Materials from homes were gathered by those who survived the dead. This ritual act forged connections between a lived life and its bodily end. These burial goods emphasize the continuity of the ordinary.

I had learned about the habit of placing spindles and spindle whorls with the dead during my search for material culture related to women's lives. These artifacts are usually ignored. Categorized as "small objects" or "minor objects," upon excavation they are usually recorded and stored away without raising much interest. Often they are deemed unworthy of the time of the excavator and team and not published fully in the initial, interim, or final reports of excavated archaeological sites.[13] This lack of interest has been exacerbated in excavations undertaken since 1947 and the beginning of the state of Israel. Grave goods and buried spindle whorls are enmeshed in cultures of gender, in which certain classes of artifacts are deemed masculine and favored while others are devalued as feminine. They are also enmeshed in archaeological nationalism. As archaeology became increasingly part of Israeli/Jewish nationalist discourse, the favored archaeology was big, monumental, and fit into an emerging narrative of Jewish prosperity and importance. Interest in the archaeology of households waned, as did the earlier antiquarian practice of cataloguing small objects.

Spindles were made by placing a circular object with a hole pierced through the center onto a rod.[14] The whorl provided weight and momentum when the spindle was dropped from chest height to the ground as it twirled fiber into yarn. Made mostly of wood, the rods have disintegrated, leaving behind whorls of clay, glass, and stone. Spindles and whorls were not expensive items. The closest information we have is Diocletian's *Price Edict,* a fourth-century document that lists a boxwood spindle with a whorl at 12 denarii, and spindle and whorl sets from other woods at 15 denarii. The price of spindles can be compared to the stabilized prices for, say, second-quality needles at 2 denarii a piece, an Italian pint of wine from the Tiburtine region at 30 denarii, four eggs for 4 denarii, ten large pomegranates for 8 denarii, 50 denarii for one day's work as a stonemason(with maintenance), and 20 denarii in wages for a weaver who could produce one pound of second-quality textiles, either linen or wool.[15] Some of the buried spindle whorls are more decorative and valuable than others, with incised concentric circles or punch-hole designs on ivory, bone, or glass. But most of the whorls are of nondescript gray stone, or serpentine, or local basalt. Many are chipped and scratched from wear.

Since spindles remain barely and poorly published, research took me to Israel's archaeological storerooms. I sat in the dusty archives, day after day, weighing spindle whorls, measuring the lengths of their holes, carefully recording and rechecking the notes of those who excavated and catalogued them. In the tedium of all this, I considered various ways to write about what I was finding, or not finding. I had begun the project hoping to "find women," and the spindle had seemed like a good place to start. But stories about women and gender overlap with others, and these grave goods tell multiple tales. Placing personal goods in graves was not a practice looked upon highly by spokesmen for elite culture. The rabbinic Jewish tractate on mourning, Semaḥot, barely mentions the practice. The Roman jurist Ulpian locates the practice in a class other than his own: "Ornaments should not be buried with corpses, nor anything else of the kind, as happens among the simpler folk."[16] About these once-silent artifacts it turns out there is much to say. They display an ordinary piety at odds with more elite pronouncements. And they show that where some saw death as the alienation of human life, others understood it as an extension of the quotidian and ordinary.

There is more. Burying spindles with the dead was not limited to Palestine but done throughout Europe, and closer by in Amman and Pella, Vasa in Cyprus, and Meroe in Egypt.[17] The practice was not new to Roman Palestine nor unique to its Jews. Nothing in this one ritual of burial emphasizes regional or ethnic or religious distinctions as significant things to announce at the end of a human's life. This offers another sensibility of the period, one that knows little of the discontinuity of the Temple's destruction, the effects of military campaigns throughout the region, the end of the active priesthood, religious conflict, and the changes in the political organization of the region. Although some of these events may have affected those who lived during this time, such things seem not to have disturbed or interrupted or affected the practices of burying things with the dead (although changes can be seen in other rites of burial).

Typically, Roman Palestine and its environs are studied in terms of religious, ethnic, and national differences that are important markers now (differences that were given both similar and different meanings in Roman antiquity). Current national boundaries tend to be used as the boundaries for studying past times, so that Jerusalem/Aelia Capitolina is not considered on a continuum with Amman/Philadelphia. But these tombs and their contents are part of new stories to be told about Roman Palestine. Regional identity is invisible. The practice of burying grave goods does not allow for the distinction of Christians, Jews, or people with other religious and philosophical loyalties. Many of the graves which contain these goods cannot be identified with any specific religious practice, although at least three of these sites can be identified as Jewish with a high degree of certainty (at Meiron, Jerusalem, and Beth

Shearim), and several burials can be linked with self-identifying Christians. Placing grave goods with the dead may not have been a habit for the majority of Jews (but given the politics of excavating graves that are located in what is now Israel and the past practices of excavating and recording the contents of graves, it will be relatively impossible to know) nor for a majority of Christians, Jewish-Christians, or pagans. But these rites of burial were something shared by people associated with Palestine's various religious and ethnic commitments.

The grave goods are a way to see similarities between people who lived in this region. Graves were places where certain kinds of differences did not matter, or were not expressed as such. Taking this into consideration should alter the scholarly and public traditions that take modern categories of peoplehood and religion and use them to find distinct peoples and religions in Roman Palestine. These grave goods show the region to be one whose women and men did not use every available opportunity to imagine and to enact these kinds of differences.[18]

PROMISES TO BURY

For those of us who identify with—or are identified as—women who suffered and survived centuries of erasure and other oppressions, it is tempting to wish to find something solid, and to hold onto it tightly. At burial, the spindle took a human woman and memorialized her into an ideal vision of femininity. The buried spindles and spindle whorls have some written correlates, and these provide a way to link them with specific notions about women. Inscriptions throughout the Roman-influenced world used the image of the spindle to signify the women who were idealized upon their deaths. From the turn of the second century comes this epitaph: "She was strong, good, resolute, honest, a most reliable guardian, neat at home and neat enough abroad, well known to everybody, and the only person who could rise to all occasions. . . . Her yarn was never out of her hands with good reason."[19] From slightly earlier we read about Claudia, who was charming in conversation, her conduct always appropriate, who kept house and made wool.[20] And Amymone: the best and the loveliest, wool working, pious, modest, frugal, chaste, domestic.[21] Funerary monuments commissioned for the wealthy contained bas-reliefs of women holding spindles or distaffs.[22] The tools of spinning and wool work commemorated women's lives, including the lives of Jewish women. A monument at Akmonia marks the place that two women, Makaria and Alexandria, were buried by Aurelios

Phrougianos and his wife Aurelia Juliana. The right side of the monument depicts a distaff and spindle as well as a comb, mirror, and basket.[23] Another burial monument, also from a Jewish family and dated to 255/256, depicts a spindle and distaff.[24] The inscriptions and relief work use the vocabulary of spindles and wool baskets to compliment women whose wealthy families could purchase such expensive carved-stone memorials. Spindles appear in all sorts of burials, from the catacombs of the elite, to well-carved and extensive family graves, to unmarked burials in caves, to secondary burials in ossuaries. The buried spindles and spindle whorls were—at least sometimes—a nonwritten parallel to these more easily deciphered meanings of written epitaphs and artistic reliefs.

The spindle is seductive. Finding this popular icon of womanhood, I had hoped that I was finding something "really" about women's lives. It is easy to reach for the spindle, a tool used by some women, and a metaphor for all women for so many centuries and in so many places, and to confuse it as "women's own." Perhaps the problem is not the tool nor even the metaphor, but the desire to find something from history to own. Our modern habits for making history are built on the promise of essential links between human beings from different times. These claims about essence make it seem almost natural to cling to various versions of people and past time and, despite apparent differences, to conflate "them" with "us." This conflation offers a sense of ancestry. When history-writing is infused this way, it offers a pleasing solution to a widely shared "sentimental yearning for a former home or homeland." It produces family, imagined ancestors: fathers, brothers, mothers, sisters, grandparents, and cousins.

But to satisfy this yearning, which of life's complexities are flattened and erased? These spindles were tools used by women. But they should never be seen as benign souvenirs, mementos of our visits to women in antiquity. Spindles were also used by men. And they were also metaphors that powerfully restricted the imagination of what women could be, shaping them instead into a confining notion of femininity. Along with other mechanisms, the spindle narrowed a broad range of women's acts and experiences into a more singular and manipulable icon. It reified gender and its divisions, and crafted "women's" character into something distinct from "men's." Metaphorically, the spindle was to eliminate the confusion caused by activities and identities that women and men might share. Spindle and loom symbolized the essence of womanhood—even if its demands could not be met by most women.

In one sense, this metaphor from masculinist culture is "really" about women. Women's lives are shaped by the cultures in which we live. If there is no human subject before the law, there is also no woman before the patriarchy, no inner essence waiting to emerge. One goal of women's history has been to find examples of women whose lives were relatively unscathed by various patriarchies, to locate an essence of "woman" that remains continuous and unaffected through the apparent power of masculinism. This dream is part of what makes it tempting to reach for the spindle as a positive image of femininity, women's acts, and feminist religiosity. The desire to find the spindle and cling to it tightly is based in the assumption that individuals and groups have continuous essences, and the conviction that this is a good thing.

But to one feminist claim that the spindle is an image to salvage for women, that it indicates women's resistance within patriarchy, or that it represents a shared experience between women, comes another, also feminist, critique of essentialism in all its forms.[25] If spindles and looms are meaningful images for some women and feminists, it may be because many of us have inherited a world in which these icons are still familiar and powerful, and despite our best intentions, we often replicate its patterns and terms.

So, what's a feminist intellectual with a critique of essentialism to do with the spindle? For starters, she can break the habit of repeating automatically the link between spinning and women. She can refuse the certainty of this association and instead find its complexity. Or she can see it as a trace of a process, evidence of an attempt to construct women and gender on certain terms and not others. For instance, at least some of the time, these spindles buried with the dead can be said to represent ancient women and/or to represent familiar figures used to represent ancient women. But there's more. Buried spindles were not just about the dead. These goods were placed with the dead by those still living, by those who perhaps gathered things from the deceased's home or collected them from neighbors and relatives. In the sight of the living, the site of death was another place to display the ideals and tensions of womanhood. People saw these things being put into the grave, and perhaps registered them or commented upon them. Buried spindles and other kinds of grave goods are about what living people found to be important. Or perhaps not? Spindles were only one item among many. Grave goods were only one rite and one sight in burial rituals that could be quite ornate, with their processions and musicians and performances of mourning and grief. Amid the wailers, the flutists, the chatter of relatives and friends, would these two-centimeter-wide round objects have even been noticed?

As we keep looking at spindles, their meanings shift and expand. They seem less stable. Sometimes the spindle is an overdetermined way to refer to women. Sometimes it refers to men's places in a culture of gender.[26] And sometimes the spindle's relation to gender was nonexistent. Or ambiguous: in a secondary burial at Meiron were placed a ceramic inkwell, glass bottles and vessels, two spindle whorls, a bronze spoon, and more. Seven people were buried. Analysis of the bones reveals that there were three humans of unidentified sex who died before age twelve. The fourth was a girl in her teens who died between thirteen and eighteen. The fifth was a man who lived to age forty. And the age and sex of the sixth and seventh humans buried here remain unidentified. In a case like this, what do the spindle whorls mean? "Whose" are they, and can they be linked to any one member of this group explicitly?[27]

Sometimes the spindle was not evidence of human women and men but of a masculinist culture which powerfully set the terms for the lives of women and men, albeit in different ways and with different effects. The spindle was used to commemorate and compliment women. It also constrained them. Locating traces of women and the construction of gender in antiquity can always be celebrated. But any celebration of the spindle's woman is always entangled with an acceptance of masculinism's web. What is actually found leaves much less reason to celebrate.[28] Refusing to celebrate patriarchy's women does not make ancient women disappear into a morass of theoretical distinction-making. It does record the possibility of a nonessentializing feminist practice for writing about antiquity's women, gender, rabbis, Jews, Romans, and everything else.

In light of a history in which women were present and a historiography in which women have been absent, I can understand the hesitation to let go of the spindle's woman. Letting go might seem ludicrous when history has left so few remains of women. But why be bound to history's leftovers? The nostalgic desire to find oneself in history—and to find friends among history's women—can be challenged. We need not rely on inherited, masculinist, and constricting notions of what women are.

And so, to consider one last time the spinning of fantasies and spinning as a gender fantasy, look at the spindle's appearance in a recent rabbinic responsa that addresses the question of whether women can study Torah (by which it means Talmud, or Oral Law). The rabbinic writer notes that in his Jewish society in Israel, large parts of women's lives take place outside their homes. He contrasts this with the situation of Jews in the time of the rabbis, when "the woman never left the house and did not participate in the affairs of the world; all her concern and wisdom was limited to running the household and raising the children." This ancient utopia draws on a myth of antiquity as simpler and more primitive, with clearer roles for women and men, a vision not entirely different from the elite Roman conception of their past. This rabbinic writer ignores the fact that his claims were largely untrue for ancient Jewish women. Instead, this narration depends upon the nostalgic ideal in which the premodern world is related to the modern world as its opposite and its redemption. Instead, he continues, women today own businesses, they teach at universities, and work in offices. Women have access to all sorts of education. Women should be taught Talmud, this responsa argues, because this will serve as a counterweight to "secular knowledge" and the temptations of leisure. Talmud study will take up time that women would otherwise spend in trivial pursuits, such as travel, swimming, or going to the movies. Women who study Talmud will more conscientiously protect the purities of "the family, the table, and the kitchen."

The paraphrased words of Rabbi Eliezer and Shimon ben Gamliel reemerge. Only now, their positions are so naturalized and familiar that the responsa does not find it necessary to cite its talmudic source: "Were I to know that if we banned women from studying and teaching Torah, they would stay home to use the spindle, I would agree, but to give her the opportunity to be idle from study and deal, God forbid, in trivialities, is not judicious."[29] The words of the ancient rabbis, repeated through centuries, have become common knowledge. They are now habit, part of an ethos. The spindle reappears in a familiar form, as an antidote to the temptations that leisure might hold for Jewish women.

But as usual, the spindle is complicated. After all, the responsa wishes to expand women's rights and the possibilities for their lives. The rabbi who penned this responsa does wish to change centuries of Jewish practice and to reward women for their study of Torah and Talmud. Yet, the argument to expand women's options is built on the still powerful idea that what women should really do is symbolized by the spindle. This is not a utopia, but a concession. Nostalgic visions of whole and wholesome worlds are still in place. Despite the "fallenness" of modernity, proper homes still await a possible return. And as part of this desire, the imagined, essential link between spindles, wool work, and femininity has a powerful place. As the male writer of this responsa would expand women's access to rights and rewards in order to accommodate the conditions of a fallen world, the nostalgic emblem of a woman's feminine essence reappears, still helpful after all these years.

Our modern ways of making the past make meaning offer no salvation and little redemption. Relations with the past are never innocent. They are always gendered, and often with ill effects. Europe's appropriation of the past as "history" was a way to colonize and own that past. It crafted fragments of a Greek and Roman and, increasingly, Aryan antiquity into fictions about peoplehood and national origins. Archaeology as an Israeli and Jewish nationalist discourse crafted a certain region of the world into an almost exclusively Jewish place, with ramifications and limited terms for other people who have lived there and who live there now. All these efforts are consistent and coeval with a masculinist intellectual ethos. In its many versions, this has produced stories which erase and efface women or which include women in ways that range from the hideous to the benign.

What might it mean to replace the romance of nostalgia (with its pretense that "you can be there") with the terror of nostomania, the desire that can never be met? It could mean releasing antiquity and its women from functioning as simplified expressions of our identity. If we insist on narrating the past, we could at least do so in ways that do not efface complexity. Identification with people and times and places need not rely on constrictive notions of essence. It can allow ambiguity, contradiction, and it need not organize relations into sets of oppositional two's.

This does not mean ceasing to know things that happened. Nor does it mean desisting from wanting to explain them. Instead it means a tentative commitment to know these things differently and to restrain from making them work for us in quite the ways that they have. Undoing these kinds of identifications and ceasing the repetition of certain tales, we can let the past be different. We can stop forcing it to be a reflection of "us" (whether we admit this practice or not). We can stop fantasizing the past as a home to return to. We can cease forging ancient people into our ancestors, from claiming them in the various guises of allies, heroes, enemies, villains, or friends. Starting here, and looking from elsewhere for something different, we can study in ways that need not repeat their habits for our futures.

Notes

INTRODUCTION: STORIES ABOUT SPINNERS AND WEAVERS

1. Walter Benjamin, *Illuminations*, 91.

2. Odyssey 2.94–110, 19.137–165. On the Homeric Penelope, see Nancy Felson Rubin, *Regarding Penelope: From Character to Poetics*; Marylin Katz, *Penelope's Renown: Meaning and Indeterminacy in the Odyssey*; and Beth Cohen, ed., *The Distaff Side: Representing the Female in Homer's* Odyssey.

3. See C. Robert, "Die Fusswaschung des Odysseus auf zwei Reliefs des fünften Jahrhunderts"; Frank Brommer, *Vasenlisten zur griechischen Heldensage*, 2: 308, 328; and s.v. "Penelope" in Wilhelm Heinrich Roscher, *Ausfuhrliches Lexikon der griechischen und romischen Mythologie*.

4. Adolf Furtwängler, *Griechische Vasenmalerai*, 3: pl. 142.

5. On bronze mirrors, see Marie-Madeleine Mactoux, *Penelope: Légende et Mythe*. On the Roman-period reliefs and frescoes, see references to the standard collections and museum locations in Mactoux, 143–151.

6. The references are from Pausanias, *Descriptio Graeciae*. These images of Roman Penelopes are selected from a much broader collection. The indeterminacy of Penelope in these Roman readings is compounded by various traditions about her genealogy and her progeny. In one trend, Penelope was related to Artemis, and her name associated with temples.

7. The passivity in artistic representations of Penelope is noted also by Mactoux, *Penelope*, 41–44.

8. For other examples of how Penelope becomes part of the landscape see Plutarch *Greek Questions* 302 and W. R. Halliday, *The Greek Questions of Plutarch*, 144. This example is slightly less genealogically direct than those offered by Pausanias: In Sparta a shrine to Odysseus was built due to his marriage to Penelope and Penelope's relation to Sparta (as daughter of the Spartan Ikarios). The woman Penelope is the link between the two men and allows Sparta to claim Odysseus as their own.

9. In defense of Pausanias, see Christian Habricht, *Pausanias' Guide to Ancient Greece*. On the reputed tomb site today, see Mactoux, *Penelope*, pl. XIII.

10. Propertius *Elegies* 2.9.1–52. The image of Penelope appears throughout Propertius's *Elegies*: 3.12.38, 3.13.24, and 4.5.7. The Roman elegists often used mythic and epic figures to write about their own loves and passions. As will become clear, Roman elegists such as Propertius and Ovid are particularly forthcoming with expansions and redefinitions of gender and sexual roles. Barbara Gold writes, in "Finding the Female in Roman Poetry," in Nancy Sorkin Rabinowitz and Amy Richlin, eds., *Feminist Theory and the Classics*: "In contrast to authors such as Virgil, the elegists are more self-conscious in their treatment of gender reversals. The redefinitions of gender found in elegy were developed in response to both the heavily moralistic patriarchal value system that had existed in Rome for centuries and the breakdown of social values at the end of the first century B.C.E." (85). That the elegists recast certain conceptions of genders and practiced certain kinds of cross-gender identifications is not to exalt them or to equate any change in gender roles with a positive change for women. For a sense of these debates among feminist classicists see Amy Richlin, "Reading Ovid's Rapes," in Amy Richlin, ed., *Pornography and Representation in Greece and Rome,* and Maria Wyke, "Mistress and Metaphor in Augustan Elegy."

11. Ovid *Tristia* 5.5, 5.14. Translations are from David Slavitt, *Ovid's Poetry of Exile.*

12. Ovid *Heroides* 1.

13. Letter translated by R. Hock, "The Epistles of Crates," in Abraham J. Malherbe, *The Cynic Epistles.* Epistle number 9, *To Mnasos:* "Do not abstain from the most beautiful ornament, but adorn yourself every day so that you may stand out. The most beautiful ornament is the one that decorates you most beautifully, but the one that decorates you most nobly is the one that makes you decorous, and it is decorum that makes you most decorous. Both Penelope and Alcestis, I think, adorned themselves with it and even now they are praised and honored for their virtue. In order, then, that you, too, might become like them, try to hold fast to this advice."

14. s.v. "Penelope." Robert E. Bell, *Women of Classical Mythology: A Biographical Dictionary,* 348–351.

15. Juvenal *Satires* 2.36–57. See Edward Courtney, *A Commentary on the Satires of Juvenal,* 130–131.

16. Other heroines had similar long histories in European culture as pliable icons for femininity, figures that (to quote Mary Hamer) were exceptionally able to "generate and sustain fantasy." On Cleopatra, see Mary Hamer, *Signs of Cleopatra: History, Politics, Representation.* On the "color" and whitening of Cleopatra, see the review "Classical Cliches" by Shelley Haley of Elaine Fantham, et al., *Women in the Classical World: Image and Text* in *The Women's Review of Books* 12 (1994): 26–27. On the Homeric Kirke, see Judith Yarnall, *Transformations of Circe: The History of an Enchantress.* From roughly the sixth century, Homeric epics were out of fashion as pedagogy and literature; hence female figures such as Circe and Penelope were excavated and rediscovered through the vision of writers and artists of the European Renaissance.

17. Joan Wallach Scott, *Gender and the Politics of History*, 2 (emphasis added).

18. A. A. Long, "Stoic Readings of Homer," in Lamberton and Keaney, eds., *Homer's Ancient Readers*, 48–49.

19. Feminist history "becomes not just an attempt to correct or supplement an incomplete record of the past but a way of critically understanding how history operates as a site of the production of gender knowledge" (Scott, *Gender and the Politics of History*, 10).

20. Cicero *De Natura Deorum: Academica*.

21. ySotah 3.19a (= bYoma 60b).

22. I leave these references to the first few centuries deliberately vague. These periods are long due for reconsideration, and in fact some of this is already happening, with various degrees of success. The conventions of Jewish history divide time in ways that focus on politics and military endeavor, so that periods conclude with the military defeats of either 70 or 135, the end years for the two Roman-Jewish wars in Palestine. Narration of the next period usually begins with the Mishnah and the patriarchate of Rabbi Judah in the early third century, and tends to concentrate on religion. The move to reconsider historical periods that were named largely in the absence of consideration of women and women's experiences was outlined in Joan Kelly ("Did Women Have a Renaissance?"). For applications of Kelly's concerns to the reperiodization of Jewish history, see Shulamit Magnus, "Out of the Ghetto."

23. To articulate this simultaneous ambivalence and desire in the production of history, I am indebted to Gayatri Chakravorty Spivak in *Outside in the Teaching Machine*. Spivak writes that "persistently to critique a structure that one cannot not (wish to) inhabit is the deconstructive stance" (284). The ambivalence I express here is also related to the historical and ongoing attachments of Jewish Studies (and its predecessor the Wissenschaft des Judentums) to the European category of history, and how this attachment must be reconsidered. Such attachments to and ambivalences with history have yet to be seriously engaged by intellectuals who work on Jewish materials. See Miriam Peskowitz and Laura Levitt, "A Way In," in Peskowitz and Levitt, eds., *Judaism Since Gender*.

24. I thank Maxine Grossman for our discussions about these topics.

25. See Rosalind Shaw and Charles Stewart, "Introduction: Problematizing Syncretism," in Stewart and Shaw, eds., *Syncretism/Anti-syncretism*; syncretism becomes part of "an evolutionary scheme, view[ed] as an intermediate stage prior to Christian monotheism" (4–5).

26. My suggestion is not that the term "talmudic Judaism" never be used. As Daniel Boyarin reminds me, the term is very appropriate when used to refer to the specific articulation of Judaism through talmudic writings.

27. Here, the arguments of David Weiss Halivni for dissent within early rabbinic Judaism add a texture of fractiousness. Halivni argues that there was much opposition to the Mishnah at the time of its appearance, as witnessed by the multiple times that Amoraim sidetracked Rabbi Judah's decisions, the Tosefta's many additions to the Mishnah, and the Tosefta's reversal of many mishnaic decisions. See Halivni, "The Reception Accorded to Rabbi Judah's Mishnah," 204–212.

28. See Kalman Bland, "Medievals Are Not Us." The tactic of defamiliari-

zation reveals the strangeness of the familiar. It is necessary to interrupt the ease with which "pasts" are elided into "presents." My specific argument refers to Judaism, but a similar mechanism is at work elsewhere. Western Europe has imagined its origins through fantasies about antiquity. As David Konstans and Martha Nussbaum in their "Preface to 'Sexuality in Greek and Roman Society'" write: "The appropriation of classical Greece and Rome as origins and models of a so-called 'Western' tradition has helped to obscure some of the deep differences between ancient and modern societies" (iii).

29. I disagree with Ramsay MacMullen's separation of the Jews; he writes in his essay "The Historical Role of the Masses in Late Antiquity": "Culture in the anthropological sense divided the population of the Mediterranean world long before the Romans assembled it all into a single political entity. . . . An exception: still at the end, the Jews, most distinctly themselves, retained a way of life centered in a common religion, and were on that account seen as set apart and inassimilable, at least by Christians" (MacMullen, *Changes in the Roman Empire*, 251).

30. The absence of Jews remains true for almost all treatments of Roman antiquity, including the new scholarship on women and gender. See as examples Pauline Schmitt Pantel, ed., *A History of Women in the West,* vol. 1, *From Ancient Goddesses to Christian Saints* and Gillian Clark, *Women in Antiquity: Pagan and Christian Life-Styles.* An important exception, by virtue of his training and interests in the Roman East, is Fergus Millar, *The Roman Near East 31 B.C.–A.D. 337.* Rabinowitz and Richlin, in *Feminist Theory and the Classics,* do not include among their articles the study of Jewish women who lived throughout the regions of the Roman Empire but do refer to the necessity, by those who study classics, to pay attention to Christians and Jews (as examples of "nonelite culture" with regard to Rome) and promise that "taking the most radical stance of current feminism, we will not only attend to women, we will look for the difference among women of different classes, races, ethnicities, and sexualities" (11).

31. On Europe's creation of its Roman past, and ultimately its Sanskritic and Aryan past, see Maurice Olender, *The Languages of Paradise: Race, Religion and Philology in the Nineteenth Century* and Anthony Grafton, *New Worlds, Ancient Texts: The Power of Tradition and the Shock of Discovery.* I wish to emphasize the double move I am making here: a logic of inclusion (of Jewish minorities, and below, of women) is combined with a narration of the past that recognizes the past as representation, thus effecting its deconstruction as "truth." So long as the ancient past has cultural capital and as long as it is narrated as such, its minorities must be included. I hope that recognizing this double move makes clear that inclusion is not sufficient.

32. Baruch Bokser, "Rabbinic Responses to Catastrophe: From Continuity to Discontinuity." For other ancient and modern scholarly recountings of the destruction of the Second Temple, see II Baruch, Seder Olam, mTaanit 4.1 ff., and Josephus *Wars,* as well as Robert Kirschner, "Apocalyptic and Rabbinic Responses to the Destruction of 70"; Robert Goldenberg, "Early Rabbinic Explanations of the Destruction of Jerusalem"; and Shaye J. D. Cohen, "The Destruction: From Scripture to Midrash."

33. In some ways, this focus on destruction and rebirth can be located more fully in Diaspora interests. In "The Death of Memory and the Memory of Death: Masada and the Holocaust as Historical Metaphors," Yael Zerubavel suggests that the event from the First Jewish Revolt of greatest interest in the formation of Israeli Jewishness is the battle of Masada. Instead of emphasizing a narrative of destruction, devastation, and rebirth, the Israeli/Jewish narrative stresses Masada as a beginning of Jewish rebellion and patriotic defense of land.

34. I take my cue for this question in part from Judith Bennett, who suggests broadly that times of upheaval and social change are also times where women's roles might change and furthermore where it might be less difficult than usual to see traces of changes for women and gender. See Bennett, "Feminism and History," 264. On changes for royal Roman women in the second century, see M. T. Boatwright, "The Imperial Women of the Early Second Century A.C."

35. While in this book I do not attend overtly to the constructed character of such terms and concepts as "religion" and "culture," let me at least call attention to the oddity of using such relatively recent notions of how the world works when we write about antiquity. On religion, see Talal Asad, *Genealogies of Religion* and Robert Baird, *Inventing Religion in the Western Imaginary*. On culture, see Virginia Dominguez, "Invoking Culture: The Messy Side of 'Cultural Politics,' " 237–259. Although his name will appear only rarely in these pages, I am indebted to Howard Eilberg-Schwartz's critical examination in *The Savage in Judaism* of how ancient Judaism came to be studied within the terms, images, and desires of the Christian West.

36. Bernadette Brooten, *Women Leaders in the Ancient Synagogue: Inscriptional Evidence and Background Issues*. See additional sources in Ross Kraemer, *Her Share of the Blessings*, chaps. 8, 9. On medieval evidence for the institution of the separate gallery for women in the synagogue, see Shmuel Safrai, "Was There a Women's Gallery in the Synagogue in Antiquity?" While I do not offer a full review of feminist work in Jewish history and religion of the Roman period, I wish to acknowledge these scholars whose work has been formative for my own, and whose work continues to be important and provocative. Without their early and ongoing research, the questions I pose here could not have been conceptualized or undertaken.

37. See for example, Gildas Hamel, *Poverty and Charity in Roman Palestine;* Martin Goodman, *State and Society in Roman Galilee;* Ze'ev Safrai, *The Economy of Roman Palestine,* and David Fiensy, *The Social History of Palestine in the Herodian Period*. Almost all work in the field shares the problem of masculinizing the category "worker" so that women are always excluded from considerations of work and production, domains which become masculine at their inception. See further, Daniel Sperber, *Roman Palestine 200–400. Money and Prices* and *Roman Palestine 200–400. The Land;* Arye Ben-David, *Talmudische Ökonomie: Die Wirtschaft des Jüdischen Palästina zur Zeit der Mischna und des Talmud;* Douglas Oakman, *Jesus and the Economic Questions of His Day;* J. H. Heinemann, "The Status of the Laborer in Jewish Law and Society in the Tannaitic Period."

38. See Judith Hauptman, "Women's Liberation in the Talmudic Period: An

Assessment" and more recently, "Feminist Perspectives on Rabbinic Texts"; Judith Baskin, "The Separation of Women in Rabbinic Judaism"; Daniel Boyarin, *Carnal Israel: Reading Sex in Talmudic Culture;* and Judith Romney Wegner, *Chattel or Person? The Status of Women in the Mishnah.*

39. mOholot 16.2, tUqsin 2.5, tAhilot 8.8.

40. Return of found objects: mBaba Metzia 2.1–2.

41. Flax and wool combs: mKelim 13.8; gloves of dyers: mKelim 16.6; woven cloth: mKelim 27.7–8; metal spindle whorls: mKelim 11.6 and tKelim Baba Metzia 1.5; spindles from Arbela, Galilee: tParah 12.16; skeins of flax, thread, and loom parts: mNegaim 11.8–11; *niddah:* tTohorot 4.11; weavers: mZavim 3.2.

42. Joan Kelly, "The Doubled Vision of Feminist Theory," 51–64 in her *Women, History, and Theory* (1984); published originally in *Feminist Studies* 5 (1979): 216–227. The history of thought since the early 1970s contains many examples of insights and paths not followed up, as scholars worked out some issues and concerns but left others by the way. On the one hand, her conceptualizing of doubledness seems clumsy, when read from the conceptual sophistication granted by fifteen years of feminist theory. Yet, I return to Kelly because her vision still offers the eloquence of feminist politics to feminist theory, and because her (and other socialist/materialist feminist thinkers') insistence on women's work has been among those issues which have gone relatively unattended as feminist theory has been increasingly interested in construing research on the body in terms of the body's sexualities. On the relatively narrow scope of questions asked about gender and bodies, see Caroline Walker Bynum, "Why All the Fuss about the Body: A Medievalist's Perspective"; Naomi Seidman, "Carnal Knowledge"; Teresa L. Ebert, "Ludic Feminism, the Body, Performance, and Labor" and more recently, her *Ludic Feminism and After;* and Alice Kessler-Harris, *A Woman's Wage: Historical Meanings and Social Consequences.*

43. Henri Lefebvre, "The Everyday and Everydayness," 9.

44. The evidence is fraught with difficulties. Recently, Ze'ev Safrai has argued that "the most important industry in Palestine was the textile industry" (*The Economy of Roman Palestine,* 192). Michael Avi-Yonah, *The Jews of Palestine,* 22, argues that textile production was the most important and widespread industry. Gedaliah Alon, *Toldot ha-Yehudim be-Erets-Yisrael bi-tekufat ha-Mishnah veha-Talmud* (70–640) ranks textiles just behind olive oil and wine. At issue in assessing the relation of these industries is the different kinds of evidence each leaves behind. The remains of olive oil production are large circular stone vats, with grind stones at their center, an artifact with an almost indefinite life span. Similarly, evidence for wine production comes in the form of large stone apparati (drainage bins and the like). The evidence for textile production—such as spindles, dye vats, and looms—is much more environmentally fragile and becomes archaeologically invisible. For comparison: while acknowledging the difficulties of ascertaining the numbers of persons working in any one industry, in "Urban Craftsmen in Roman Egypt," Peter van Minnen estimates that "it would be a reasonable guess that roughly 50 percent of the working population or up till 20 percent of the total population of a town like Oxyrhynchus was engaged in the textile trade" (76).

ONE: PATRIARCHY'S ORDINARINESS

1. On some of these issues, see Amy Richlin, "Hijacking the Palladium: Feminists in Classics," and "The Ethnographer's Dilemma and the Dream of a Lost Golden Age," in Nancy Sorkin Rabinowitz and Amy Richlin, eds., *Feminist Theory and the Classics;* Caroline Walker Bynum, "Introduction: The Complexity of Symbols"; Lynn Davidman and Shelly Tenenbaum, eds., *Feminist Perspectives on Jewish Studies;* and the discussion in Ross Kraemer, *Her Share of the Blessings: Women's Religions Among Pagans, Jews, and Christians in the Greco-Roman World.*

2. On this period see Peter Brown, *The World of Late Antiquity,* A.D. *150–170;* Michael Grant, *The Antonines: The Roman Empire in Transition;* and Fergus Millar, *The Roman Near East, 31* B.C.–A.D. *337,* 99–140.

3. See Lee Levine, *The Rabbinic Class of Roman Palestine in Late Antiquity* and Shaye J. D. Cohen, "The Place of the Rabbi in Jewish Society of the Second Century," 157–173 in L. Levine, ed., *The Galilee in Late Antiquity,* and Cohen's remarks elsewhere.

4. Talmudic texts are alternately normative, binding, hegemonic, meaningful, or ignored by Jews. Still, even this statement does not express the varied meanings of "Talmud" for those who may or may not accept its halakic authority. Reform, secular, and Jews with various relations with Judaism and Jewishness see the Talmud in ways that range from ignorance to disdain to respectful distance to nostalgia to romanticization. These relations and others preserve the text's cultural authority, even if its halakah goes unobserved and unknown. Furthermore, these texts carry symbolic status for Jews and for non-Jews. Apart from devotion expressed by an individual or community, talmudic writing serves to signify a canonical, classical religion, even for those who would associate these texts as part of "the past" or as "what other Jews do." This obtains particularly within the realm of the history of religions, where religious traditions are often associated with the specific texts upon which and from which authority is claimed (hence the equation of "Talmud" with "Judaism"). In thinking through the complicated privilege of talmudic texts, Adi Ophir's discussion has been helpful. In his "From Pharaoh to Saddam Hussein: The Reproduction of the Other in the Passover Haggadah," in *The 'Other' in Jewish History and Thought,* ed. Laurence Silberstein and Robert Cohn, 205–235, he writes: "A privileged text is part of the very process of acculturation that serves to unify a culture over and above its different, particular spheres or fields." Ophir notes insightfully what is also a paradox for me: writing about the Talmud as a privileged text, when in fact it is defamiliarized and less than privileged in most communities in which I live, work, and write.

5. The terseness and implicit cross-referencing within these texts results in a somewhat awkward apparatus. The differentiation between brackets and parentheses is simultaneously necessary and murky; there will be much overlap. As with any language translation, the translation of passages from the Mishnah and Tosefta is implicitly an interpretation. Within a project that interrupts the desire to see the past as familiar, it is as problematic to offer up ancient Hebrew (or, Greek, Latin, and Aramaic texts) in English as it is necessary to do so. Most people are not fluid readers of these ancient languages (especially since access

to these languages is a privilege of class and other statuses, as well as the educations thereby afforded). For those unfamiliar with these languages, I will refer in notes to English translations when these are available and/or reliable.

6. My notion of "legal story" stems not from the talmudist's notion of "legal fictions" but from Vicki Schultz's writings on "judicial story." See her "Telling Stories about Women and Work" and "Women 'Before' the Law." As a critical practice, reading for legal stories means reading legal texts in ways that always note them as representations and as cultural effects. Legal statements are read for how they encode explanations, interpretive frameworks, and characterizations of human beings. These things and more are part of a matrix of assumptions about how the world works, and as such they govern the "sense" and "logic" articulated in early rabbinic legal texts. Locating this matrix of assumptions is the focus of this type of analysis. Reading for legal stories is to emphasize the importance of narration and textuality in these legal writings, to keep in view the fact of the Mishnah's literary crafting. Interpretation of early rabbinic legal texts has been remarkably circumscribed. Typically, passages from early rabbinic law are cited straightforwardly, as if they were unmediated by the fact of their being written. One trend uses long lists of passages as if they were documentary evidence for history and/or society. Often this practice removes passages from their argumentative context. They are decontextualized and treated as if they were univalent and uncomplicated. Another tendency reads these passages as halakah but sees this as an outcome of the human condition and not as a process that constructs human subjects, that imagines realities, and that fashions rabbinic selves. Much work needs to be done to shift the way we conventionally read passages from the Mishnah and Tosefta, to unsettle these inherited modes, even for those of us who don't consider ourselves as subjects of such inheritances. In response, I do not propose one specific theory or strategy for reading these texts. Rather, I experiment with the differences made by this angle in. I leave the theoretical exposition to a later date, or to the interests of someone more prone to expositions of literary and legal theory. In experimenting with reading early rabbinic legal texts in ways different from the inherited practices of talmudic law, I owe a debt particularly to feminist theorists such as Vicki Schultz, Patricia Williams, and Judith Butler.

A survey of published scholarship on the Mishnah and Tosefta finds very little precedent for reading legal texts this way. A fairly powerful distinction between halakic and aggadic material has operated in which certain modes of reading and interpretation are deemed appropriate for midrash and aggada, but these reading modes are not used as either an ethos or a strategy for reading halakic and religio-legal texts. For possibilities of charting alternate modes for reading the Mishnah and Tosefta, see the work of Bernard Jackson, and of Stephen Fraade, who stresses (in *From Tradition to Commentary: Torah and its Interpretation in the Midrash Sifre to Deuteronomy*) the "textual meaning in the complex interplay of the centripetal and centrifugal forces respectively of linguistic-literary signification and social-cultural practice." Having worked extensively with the nonlegal materials in Sifre, he notes that his "next step will be to sharpen my focus even more on the texts of that legal core, asking whether they, too, should be engaged in the dialogical complexity and performative *work* of their discursive rhetoric and not simply for the legal norms, hermeneutics, or justifications they are conventionally thought monologically to contain" (163–64). Fraade refers to a common practice that reads the mostly legal texts of the Mishnah and Tosefta, and the legal texts in early rabbinic midrash, as straightforward accounts of "legal norms, hermeneutics, or justifications." The problem to which Fraade alludes and within which I work, is this: underwriting the current reading of early rabbinic legal texts is a positivist-inspired notion that law is straightforward in the meanings it makes, and that legal writing is not part of the same process of mediation and representation that characterizes other types of writing. These assumptions have their ramifications: a primary question asked of midrashic materials has been, "How do these texts make meaning?" Scholarly assumptions about legal writing have foreclosed all but the most rudimentary of questions about how various meanings were and are made through legal writing.

7. See Louis Epstein, *The Jewish Marriage Contract*, chaps. 6–7, and Baruch Levine, "Mulugu/Melug: The Origins of a Talmudic Legal Institution.". There is a complicated history to these legal terms, and I both mean and do not mean to simplify it here. *Mulug* develops from its status as a wife's private property into something over which the husband has tenancy. Early rabbinic texts do not articulate reasons for these changes, which favor the husband. Talmudic sources (Sanhedrin 71a, Nazir 24b) develop the rationale, "How can a woman own anything; whatever she owns belongs to her husband." As well, the Talmud will reinterpret these extensions of a husband's privilege as mutual obligations between husband and wife; a discourse of "mutuality" effaces the presence of a real imbalance of power relations between husband and wife. Scholarly interpreters are often complicit with this: see Ze'ev Falk, "Mutual Obligation in the Ketubah" and A. S. Kofsky, "A Comparative Analysis of Women's Property Rights in Jewish Law and Anglo-American Law."

8. The problem might be specifically rabbinic. At this point in the development of Jewish law and practice, *kiddushin* and *nesuin* have been unjoined. In earlier periods the legalities of betrothal and marriage had taken place at the same time, and later in Jewish religious history, they would again rejoined. One result of the unjoining was the creation of a new legal period between betrothal and marriage the contours of which were to be imagined and defined by the rabbis.

9. Consider the material benefits by imagining this scenario: a woman's family has given her an orchard of olive trees. If her husband has usufruct, then he owns the olives that are harvested from the trees and sold. If the woman and man are betrothed and not married until eight or ten months later, it becomes clear that the material stakes are the profits from a year's worth of olive growing, and whether these profits belong to the "husband" or to the betrothed woman.

10. See mBaba Qamma 8.1, tBaba Qamma 5.12, mAvot 5.20, and Numbers Rabba 5.15.

11. mKetubot 3.7, 3.9, 4.1. Elsewhere, see mArakin 3.4.

12. It is also possible that the text engages *both* claims of determinacy and of indeterminacy in different ways and at different times; see below, chapter 5, for an example of a rabbinic passage that deploys notions of gender-as-difference as it simultaneously denies gender-as-difference.

13. I have in mind here the work of several scholars. Judith Romney Wegner's *Chattel or Person? The Status of Women in the Mishnah* is of foremost importance. I am indebted to her research and respectfully take issue with a good many of her conclusions and with many of the assumptions that undergird her reading of the Mishnah. Explicating mKetubot 8.1, for example, Wegner writes: "But if a wife retains legal ownership of her property, why limit her power to control it at all? The restriction is all the more surprising as sages themselves note their 'embarrassment' at the lack of authority for this rule. The answer must be that the wife has voluntarily surrendered her right to control the property" (90). Although I would like to feign astonishment that the supposition that women volunteer for their subjugated status passes as an "answer" to a more complicated question, there is an intellectual genealogy to this argument. Wegner's work seems to be committed to classically liberal notions of agency, wherein human subjects exist prior to the law, and hence, consent to the law and its demands. This assumption of liberal legal theory is combined with a protection of the ancient rabbis and a desire to find somewhere to stand as a feminist within rabbinic law. Arguments such as this protect the oppressiveness of certain rabbinic traditions by making claims about women's agency; in other words, rabbinic patriarchy could not have been so bad, since women participated knowingly.

14. Of course, such a possibility can be imagined only by restricting Gamliel to the characterization of him in mKetubot 8.1. In other passages, analyzed in chapter 5, Gamliel comes down decidedly in favor of privileges for men.

15. I have chosen to present composite positions and possibilities for feminist readings rather than engage in one-sided arguments with colleagues who will not in these same pages be able to argue back. I refer readers to work by scholars such as the following: Judith Hauptman, "Feminist Perspectives on Rabbinic Texts," 40–61 in Davidman and Tenenbaum, eds. *Feminist Perspectives on Jewish Studies;* Judith Baskin, "The Separation of Women in Rabbinic Judaism"; Daniel Boyarin, *Carnal Israel: Reading Sex in Rabbinic Culture;* Léonie Archer, *Her Price Is Beyond Rubies: The Jewish Woman in Graeco-Roman Palestine;* the various works of Louis Epstein; Paul V. M. Flesher, "Are Women Property in the System of the Mishnah?"; Gunter Meyer, *Die Jüdische Frau in der Hellenistich-Romischen Antike;* Wegner, *Chattel or Person?;* Tal Ilan, *Jewish Women in Greco-Roman Palestine: An Inquiry into Image and Status;* and Gail Labovitz, "Arguing for Women in Talmud."

16. See for example, tEduyot 1.4.

17. The argument invokes a man's desire for the property and profit he will gain through marriage as his primary rationale for that marriage. Within this reasoning, the desire against changes (to this fiscal attraction) becomes the reason to restrict the woman's control over her property. This overt deployment of a notion of justice for men/husbands stands in contrast to the absence in Gamliel's defense of a notion of justice for women. Here, as elsewhere in early rabbinic writing, gender is made to matter explicitly in some places, and not in others.

18. Calling into question male dominance over women has been the basic insight of feminist acts, Women's Studies, and feminist theory. With the professionalization of these critical practices, male dominance has also become that

which is supposed to go unsaid. I am indebted to conversations with Naomi Seidman about the necessity of reclaiming a critique of patriarchy for academic feminism; see her "Theorizing Jewish Patriarchy *in extremis*," in Miriam Peskowitz and Laura Levitt, eds., *Judaism Since Gender.* I am also grateful to Judith Baskin, Gail Labovitz, Laura Levitt, and Daniel Boyarin, who in different ways pushed me to locate myself more clearly within feminist possibilities for reading rabbinic texts.

TWO: DAILY LABORS

1. della Corte, *Case ed abitanti di Pompei,* 12 ff., nos. 185–187. See also *Corpus Inscriptionum Latinarum* (henceforth CIL) 4:1943, 1495–1498, 1500, 1501, 1503, 1509, 1510. The graffiti was located in a peristyle of a house located at region VII of the Pompeii excavations, insula 8 (entrance 5). The house is that of M. Terentius Eudoxus. Walter Moeller ("The Male Weavers at Pompeii) reports that two of the female names are Jewish—Vebius Tamudianus and Maria—and suggests they were Jewish slaves brought to Pompeii and elsewhere in Italy after the First Jewish Revolt. Moeller has been quite adamant in his revisionist argument that, based on the evidence of Pompeii, weaving was not a domestic production of women, but an organized industry staffed by men. On men as weavers, see Leonard Curchin, "Men of the Cloth: Reflexions on the Roman Linen Trade, Based on a New Document from Bordeaux"; and Wesley Thompson, "Weaving: A Man's Work."

Similar divisions of labor at Pompeii wherein five men are *textores* and two women are *quasillariae* are visible in graffiti at the house of the Minuci (I.x.8); see Moeller, 39.

The Pompeii evidence for professionalized female spinners, and below, the evidence for male spinners, shows as false the still-cited conclusion by A. H. M. Jones in "The Cloth Industry under the Roman Empire" that "[i]t must be presumed that the spinning was done, as today in the Near East, by women in their spare time."

2. The modern myth that textiles were produced privately at home is counteracted by ancient evidence. On clothing sold and purchased see tShabbat 1.9, tMegillah 1.5, mMoed Qatan 2.5, and mBaba Qamma 10.9/tBaba Qamma 11.5 in which women sell wool items in Judaea and flax items in the Galilee. See also inscriptions of a silk merchant from Berytus (CII 873) and a linen merchant from Joffa (CII 93331) in Jean-Baptiste Frey, ed., *Corpus Inscriptionum Iudaicarum* (abbreviated as CII here); and of cloth merchant (no. 189) in B. Mazar, *Beth Shearim,* vol. 1.

3. On reading for gender, see Susan Shapiro, "A Matter of Discipline: Reading for Gender in Jewish Philosophy."

4. Judith Hauptman's work has shown the preliminary fruits of close comparative readings of disagreements between the Mishnah and Tosefta. See her "Maternal Dissent: Women and Procreation in the Mishna" and her broader discussion in "Feminist Perspectives on Rabbinic Texts." See also the comparative work on the Mishnah and Tosefta by Jacob Neusner, and the earlier work by Boaz Cohen, *Mishnah and Tosefta.* As compared to Hauptman, from whom I have learned very much, I am reading these two texts with a different goal in

mind. Hauptman seeks in the Tosefta a rabbinic voice that is more feminist than the Mishnah. She explains the Tosefta as a way not taken by the canonical rabbinic tradition. In "Feminist Perspectives" she writes that "it should be possible, by carefully comparing the two documents . . . to determine whether the Mishnah's approach or attitude can be characterized as more or less feminist than the Tosefta's. . . . If it turns out that the Mishnah's rulings with respect to divorce are consistently more strict than those of the Tosefta, then it may be true that the document that assumed ascendancy and became canon for later generations was more pietistic and less feminist than others that existed roughly at the same time." I disagree with using the modern word "feminist" to describe any aspect of rabbinic documents, and prefer more accurate if awkward phrasings (*i.e.*, these texts are "helpful for certain feminists," "useful for feminists, strategically," and so forth). I find no way to stretch the terms "feminist" or "protofeminist" to incorporate the documents of rabbinic Judaism, and still retain any sense of their descriptive usefulness.

5. Here is a brief coda to this extensive reading of relatively few words. The sages' response is unambiguous, but the passage itself is not unambivalent. If Yehudah's position is not authorized as halakah, by virtue of its presence in the text, these words are authorized writing. To modern eyes, minority positions are those that have lost. But this is not the case in talmudic writing and interpretation. Positions that have lost are simply not included and transmitted in the first place. Inclusion connotes a degree of respect or a lesson to be learned. Minority positions are possibilities, and the inclusion of possibilities contributed to a cultural ethos in which certain things were imaginable, even if they were legally proscribed. The inclusion of these two positions on the category of gender suggests that, in rabbinic texts, using gender to make different types of humans into opposites, and then limiting sexuality to partners of the opposite sex, was not so totally successful, certain, and assured that other possibilities—especially for men—could not be imagined. The very articulation of this fantasy points to rabbinic uncertainty, but it also points to the rabbis' active desire to make these uncertainties more certain. This and other passages that contain minority positions which might be helpful to those who wish to use rabbinic texts as allies for changing current practices of gender and sexuality raise the following paradox. Read one way, at the same time that early rabbinic texts consciously intervene in gender culture and offer varying notions of what women and men are, they present this notion of *yiḥud* as if men and women had essential and unchanging sexual natures, and thus, as if it were impossible to intervene and change sexuality and gender. Read differently, at the same time as the rabbinic text presents *yiḥud* as if it were impossible to intervene in gender culture, as if men and women had essential and unchanging sexual natures, the rabbis undermine this by demonstrating an intervention in gender culture, by offering varying notions of what women and men are, and by offering various articulations of what gender is.

6. Men who work with fibers: mKelim 12.1, mDemai 1.4, tKelim Baba Metzia 2.4.

7. Weavers: tBaba Metzia 7.1, tBaba Metzia 7.15–17, mEduyot 1.3, and tEduyot 1.3. See chapter 3, below.

8. Peddlers: mMaasrot 2.1–3, mKelim 2.4; millstone grinders: mBaba Ba-

tra 2.3m; barbers: mShevuot 8.5, mShabbat 1.2; tailors: mBaba Kamma 10.10, mShabbat 1.3; launderers/fullers: mBaba Kamma 10.10. Few of these statements are vivid characterizations of men. However, since women workers are always mentioned explicitly while male workers are deemed the norm, these references can be assumed to refer to men.

9. John Winkler, *The Constraints of Desire;* Michel Foucault, *The History of Sexuality,* vol. 3; and Amy Richlin, "Zeus and Metis." On a more general note, undoing the distinction between truthful description and imaginative fantasy calls into question all of the existing handbooks and publications on work, labor, and textile production (in Roman Palestine, in the Talmud, etc.), which precede as if these are references to real physical practices. Much of this scholarly writing ignores the cultural uses of these brief rabbinic texts about textile workers, in favor of culling from them as if they were "facts" of a very different kind.

10. The inclusion of goldsmith is based on a different Tosefta manuscript than I have used. I cite the parenthetical comment about women and beauty parlors so that readers unfamiliar with the field of rabbinic studies can see the kind of stereotyped and degrading comments appearing in scholarship.

11. J. H. Heinemann, in the classic article "The Status of the Labourer in Jewish Law and Society in the Tannaitic Period" (1954), explains the various classifications of workers and then inserts a paragraph about "women workers." In this and almost every other treatment of labor and work in Jewish antiquity, the category of "worker" is masculinized and refers to the male who works; women's work is additional, and marked as such. Furthermore, women's work is usually stereotyped and described as indoor labor, domestic tasks, and wool work. Most descriptions take as fact notions of women's work whose cultural function as gender ideology I am demonstrating. In "Spinning Tales and Crafting Identities" I critiqued the portrayal of women's work, based equally in positivist uses of ancient sources and in uncritical replication of modern sexist attitudes, with reference to the classic early twentieth-century work of Samuel Krauss. It is troubling to see these portrayals repeated in the recent spate of books on work and economy in rabbinic thought and in Roman Palestine. In addition to this example from Aberbach's work, note Ze'ev Safrai, *The Economy of Roman Palestine,* who discusses women's labor as if there existed an essential connection between women, wool, and domesticity: "A woman who works outside the house is referred to as 'weaving in the market,' once again demonstrating the female proclivity for this avocation. . . . the involvement of women in the treatment of flax also proves that these labors were undertaken for the most part in the local household, since women were not wont to seek employment too often outside the house" (195).

12. The stereotype of the female-as-consumer in reconstructions of this period of Jewish history is in contrast with the stereotype of the working wife and mother that is common in accounts of post-medieval Jewish history. See the following sources for descriptions of women at work. Merchants: tBaba Kamma 11.7, mKetubot 9.4, mTohorot 7.9; textile sales: mBaba Kamma 10.9; bread sales: mHallah 2.7; selling calves: mBaba Kamma 10.9; selling clothing: mKilayim 9.5; selling olives (in a husband's shop): tBaba Qamma 10.9; bread production: mOhalot 5.4; baking assistants: tHallah 2.8; grinding at millstone:

tNiddah 4.9; spinning yarn: mNegaim 2.4, tKelim Baba Batra 6.1, 4.8, mSotah 6.1, mKetubot 7.6, tKetubot 7.6, and see R. Raabe, ed., *Petrus der Iberer,* (Leipzig, 1895), 28–29, in which the impoverished Melania is said to have spun wool for sale in Jerusalem. On egg-hatching, see tBaba Metzia 4.24–25 (I thank Judith Hauptman for this last reference). Linen production: mNegaim 2.4, tNegaim1.8, tTohorot 4.11; glassmaking: private conversation with Marianne Stern, Toledo Museum of Art, who has found evidence for female glassmakers in Roman Palestine and elsewhere. Wet nursing: mAvodah Zarah 2.1, tKetubot 5.5; midwifery: mAvodah Zarah 2.1, mShabbat 18.3, mRosh Hashana 2.5; textile laundering: mMoed Qatan 3.2; teaching: mQiddushin 4.13; hairdressing: mKelim 4.12; innkeeping: mYebamot 16.7, mDemai 3.5; funeral undertaking and the preparation of corpses for burial: mShabbat 23.5. Also, ritual wailing: mKetubot 4.4, mKelim 15.6; managing the affairs of a husband's estate: mShebuot 7.8; and charity distribution: mTohorot 7.9.

13. Although rabbis imagine that women will grind using a hand grinder, thus making a distinction between tools used by women and men; see mKetubot 5.5.

14. Clement of Alexandria *Paedagogus* 2.11–12.

15. For a critical reading of the tension of particularity and universalism for Jews see Daniel Boyarin, *A Radical Jew: Paul and the Politics of Identity.* On some of the ramifications of the Hellenic/Hebraic split, note Vassilis Lambropoulos, *The Rise of Eurocentrism:* "The exhaustion of Hebraism and Hellenism may finally allow Jews and Greeks to live and create like every other people, without the self-enslaving and -extermination advantages accorded to their ideal types by Protestantism" (331).

For examples of how the Hellenic/Hebraic distinction has worked vis-à-vis discussions by Jews of Jewish women, note Theodore Friedman, "The Shifting Role of Women," and Judith Romney Wegner, "Philo's Portrayal of Women: Hebraic or Hellenic?"

16. Thus, constructions of gender and sexuality are another way to think about how Jewish elites fashioned themselves as variously and simultaneously similar to and different from the culture of Rome they might have known. I return to this point in later chapters, through discussions of rabbinic arguments for female domesticity. Furthermore, I stress Rome, and not Christianity, as the dominant culture, because I concur that the tendency to compare Jews and Christians comes more from modern fetishes (of ecumenicism, of self-differentiation, and so on). At least during the second and early third century, the period in which early Rabbinic Judaism is emerging, Christianity is not yet a dominant religion. Its major texts have not yet been canonized, and Christians themselves seem to be more oppressed as religious minorities than Jews, although this situation would change in the fourth century.

17. Suetonius *De Grammaticus et Rhetoribus* 23.

18. Martial 12.59.6.

19. CIL 6:11602. Tr. Natalie Kampen, *Image and Status,* 122–123. Kampen argues convincingly that this inscription does not record a female worker's occupation but record a compliment given to a wife or woman.

20. In the original, *domum servavit, lanam fecit* (CIL 1.(2).1211). Marcel Durry, ed., *Eloge funèbre d'une matrone romaine.* Translation from Sarah

Pomeroy, *Goddesses, Whores, Wives, and Slaves,* 199. Kampen, *Image and Status,* dates this inscription to the first century B.C.E..

21. See Erik Wistrand, *The So-called Laudatio Turiae.* Earlier scholarship identified the husband as the Roman consul of 18 B.C.E., G. Lucretius Vespillo, and his wife, Turia, but more recent scholarship has questioned the identification.

22. Suetonius *De Vita Caesarium, Divus Augustus* 2.64.

23. Terence *Andria* 74–79.

24. Livy *History (Ad Urbe Condita)* 1.57.

25. See Stephanie Jed, *Chaste Thinking: The Rape of Lucretia and the Birth of Humanism,* and Sandra Joshel, "The Body Female and the Body Politic: Livy's Lucretia and Verginia," in Amy Richlin, ed., *Pornography and Representation in Greece and Rome,* 112–130, who stresses the role that Lucretia's raped and dead body played in inspiring male military action and the building of the Empire.

26. Ovid *Fasti* 2.720–783; Dionysius of Halicarnassus *Antiquitates Romanae* 4.64–67. Accounts of Lucretia vary; the rape and her spinning occur in some but not all versions, and not necessarily together. I am interested in the proliferation of tales, of course, as evidence of a repeated telling and liveliness to the story that transcends its appearance in any one written text.

27. d'Ambra and others note that Domitian's concern with urban renewal was partnered with an urgent sense of cultural renewal; see Eve d'Ambra, *Private Lives, Imperial Virtues,* 5. Cultural renewal was built on Domitian's understanding of Augustan visions of piety, morality, and behavior fitting the collected memory of Rome's past.

28. On Pallas and Arachne: Ovid *Metamorphoses* VI.53–68. The coins that depict Rome as a woman provide other examples of a particular construction of the female body that stands for Rome. For an artistic depiction of Arachne on an Antioch mosaic pavement, see Doro Levi, *Antioch Mosaic Pavements,* II: pls. 27, 28 (from the House of Dionysus and Ariadne).

If with regard to elite women the trope of spinning and weaving suggested uncertainty, then regarding freed woman, poor women, and slaves it signified the ease with which women could betray social expectations of their sexuality.

29. In my translation, I differ from the reading by P. Kyle McCarter in his Anchor Bible commentary, *II Samuel.* McCarter translates the phrase *maḥaziq ba-pelek* as "clings to a crutch." McCarter opts for the Phoenician "crutch," *plkm,* but his choice ignores the feminizing effect of the curse, which he seems to understand since his notes refer to the effeminacy of its Ugaritic (*plk*) and Akkadian (*pilakku*) meanings, and its appearance in Proverbs 31.19 to signify the distaff or spindle that a woman uses to spin.

The curse of feminization conveyed by using the spindle was not limited to Israelite culture. See the Hittite prayer to Ishtar of Nineveh: "Take from (their) men masculinity, prowess, robust health, swords (?), battle-axes, bows, arrows and dagger(s)! And bring them to Hatti! Place in their hands the spindle and mirror of a woman! Dress them as women!" And note a loyalty oath for Hittite soldiers that placed a soldier near a distaff, mirror, and set of women's clothing and pronounced these words: "Are not these (you see here) the fine garments of a woman? We leave them (here) for (the ceremony of taking) the oath. Therefore, whoever breaks these oaths and plots evil against the kind, queen and princes, let these oaths change him from a man into a woman! Let them change his troops into women, let them dress in the fashion of women and put on their heads the *kureššar* headdress! Let them [who break the oath] break the bows, arrows, (and) weapons of their hands, and let them put in their hands distaff and mirror." Translations from Harry Hoffner, Jr. "Symbols for Masculinity and Femininity: Their Use in Ancient Near Eastern Sympathetic Magic Rituals."

30. This passage is not the only place where rabbinic writing engages these questions. In subjecting it to extended analysis, I do not mean to imply that this is "the" rabbinic position. As I read it, early rabbinic writing does not have the kind of philosophical coherence that some other scholars see, nor does it need to display this cultural standard and practice. The discussion in m/tQiddushin is one early rabbinic response to the predicament of gender, which is, paradoxically, a predicament that rabbis themselves have constructed. That is to say that not only the resolutions but the predicaments are less than inevitable.

31. yQiddushin 1.7.2, a comment on 2 Samuel 3.29.

32. ySotah 3.19a, bSotah 20a and bYoma 60b. This pattern of assigning women to weaving and spinning, and placing this in opposition to men's learning and wisdom, is a wider pattern. See the tale of Hipparchia in Diogenes Laertius *Lives of Eminent Philosophers* in which the philosopher responds to challenges by the atheist Theodorus—"Is this she who quit woof and warp and comb and loom?"—with the words "It is I, Theodorus—but do you suppose that I have been ill advised about myself, if instead of wasting further time upon the loom I spent it in education?" See also M. E. Waithe, ed., *History of Women Philosphers,* vol. 1, *Ancient Women Philosophers.*

33. Even women who study are never represented inside the bet-midrash.

THREE: WEAVERS AT THEIR LOOMS

1. Sulpicia *Elegies* 3.16 in Tibullus, *Elegies* 3.16. Composed in the first century C.E., Sulpicia's elegies are the only example of Latin poetry written by a woman; see C. U. Merriam, "Some Notes on the Sulpicia Elegies" and H. M. Currie, "The Poems of Sulpicia," 1751–1764.

2. Tobit 2.11–12, dated to the late third and early second centuries B.C.E. See minor variations in Robert Hanhart, *Tobit,* 76.

3. Artemidorus Daldianus *Oneirokritika* 3.36.

4. Pliny *Naturalis Historia* 8.194; Plutarch "Quaestiones Romanae," 31; Varro, *De Lingua Latina* 5.61. See Susan Treggiari, *Roman Marriage,* 166–168.

5. Apuleius *Metamorphoses* 9.5–7. Although Apuleius himself was from the province of Africa, the novel is set in Macedonia and in Achaea, and is built around a preexisting Greek narrative (see H. J. Mason, "Fabula Graecanica"). On the trope of the woman for whom even spinning does not ensure chastity, note examples from chapter 2 (Terence, "Lady of Andros," and Suetonius *De Vita Caesarium*). In "Andros" an honest woman made a meager living as a wool worker. Yet, even the association with wool cannot keep her sexually pure, and she becomes a prostitute (74–79).

Lower-class women are portrayed as more sexually transgressive than upper-class women, but the insecurity regarding upper-class women provides a continuum for the pattern, as opposed to a separate class-based iconography. Note a similar twist in Propertius: "I sat up over my loom, trying to stave off sleep / then tired of that and played the lyre a little" (1.3.35–44); as Elaine Fantham et al. note in *Women in the Classical World:* "But the loom, symbol of the honest wife, and the lyre, symbol of the entertainer, are as incongruous a combination as Propertius' protestations of loyalty and his bouts of wild infidelity" (285–287).

6. Pliny *Naturalis Historia* 19.16–18. In general, Pliny is concerned with asserting differences between women and men. Pliny's text offers an example of writing that is meant to be read in similar ways to the Mishnah, not theatrically or in a linear fashion, but "in specialized segments or homogenous stretches and consulted episodically and punctually." See Gian Biagio Conte, *Genres and Readers,* 69, and Andrew Wallace-Hadrill, "Pliny the Elder and Man's Unnatural History."

7. In the words of Virginia Woolf, "Let us not take it for granted that life exists more fully in what is commonly thought big than in what is commonly thought small," from "Modern Fiction" in *Collected Essays,* 2: 107.

8. The Hierocles text was preserved in the fourth-century Stobaeus; see Otto Hense and Curt Wachsmuth, eds., *Ioannis Stobaei,* vol. 3. Also, Eusebius, *De Vita Constantini* ii.34, in which wool work is demeaning for men.

9. Diocletian *Price Edict* 26. The document expresses the values of its own time, but based on comparison with anecdotal accounts from the earlier centuries, the distinction between wool and linen seems apt. See Siegfried Lauffer, ed. *Diokletians Preisedikt;* English translation in Tenney Frank, *Economic Survey of Ancient Rome,* vol. 5. On the distinction see also R. Pfister, *Textiles de Palmyre.*

10. In biblical culture, *shaatnez,* the distinction between flax and wool and the usual prohibition on mixing them, is articulated in Deuteronomy 22.11. Thus a categorical and binary distinction is made, one that can be easily mapped with gender and other differences. Note the remark from Pirke de Rabbi Eliezer that Cain brought an offering of flax seeds, and Abel brought an offering of wool. Biblical writings do not seem to make gender an explicit part of this difference. However, in the second century, flax production was developed in Palestine. By the third and fourth centuries it became a well-known export industry. The equation of women and wool happens during this rise in the profitability of flax. As discussed in chapter 4, mKetubot 5.5 cites "wool work" as the matronly task par excellence; tKetubot 5.4 glosses this with an admonition from Rabbi Yehudah that the husband cannot force his wife to spin flax, since flax lacerates the mouth and makes the lips stiffen. The reference points to the practice in which a spinner pulls the combed fibers through the mouth onto the spindle in order to moisten and keep the fibers together as they are spun into thread. For examples, see the description of the Muses spinning in Catullus *Poems* 64.303–322, and the Orvieto vase figured in Charles Daremberg and Edmond Saglio, *Dictionnaire des Antiquites Grecques et Romaines,* 1426, fig. 3382. I am not arguing that the distinction that men worked in flax and women in wool is absolute; in any case, tTohorot 4.11 considers a case of a menstruating woman who spins flax.

In these texts rabbinic desires to protect and ornament the female body collide with the desire to make the female body work. Women's work is not supposed to disfigure her, even to the point of making her lips coarse. In this instance, set amid the rise in the flax industry, the discourse that desires women to be ornamental and beautiful is directly engaged in removing women from competition with men for viable and lucrative economic participation, and in placing her at home. Taking this discourse in another direction, note also the shared resonance in both Roman and Jewish culture of wool with thrift and simplicity: Suetonius's portrait of Augustus wearing homespun wool; and ySanhedrin 2.8, 20c, where Judah ha-Nasi wears a linen garment to meet Rabbi Yoḥanan and is told that it was more proper for a patriarch to wear clothes made of wool. Wearing wool—the less expensive and luxurious material—demonstrates humility and eschews the extravagance associated with linen, as articulated by Clement (*Paedagogus* 2.20), who admonishes Egyptian women for their extravagance in wearing linen garments from the "land of the Hebrews."

11. See Miriam Peskowitz, "Family/ies in Antiquity." For comparable arguments regarding Roman Egypt, see Keith Bradley, *Discovering the Roman Family,* and for an argument specific to textile trades in Egypt see Ewa Wipszycka, *L'industrie textile dans l'Egypte romaine.*

12. When thinking from within the pervasive logic of advanced capitalism in Europe and the United States, it might seem possible to argue that these divisions were in place because they were efficient modes of production. Yet, as argued by several scholars of Roman economy, the motivation of economic efficiency did not have the same function in Rome as it sometimes does in twentieth-century economics. Furthermore, as feminist historians of labor such as Alice Kessler-Harris and Ava Baron have shown, gender divisions of labor have rarely enabled efficient productivity, and more often than not have hindered it. Writing about nineteenth-century America, in *A Woman's Wage,* Kessler-Harris argues that "to put it another way, the economic inefficiency that frequently defined the sexual division of labor was sustained only by the ideological conviction (and it was no less than ideological) that the separate spheres were naturally ordained" (62).

Arguments are still proffered that spinning and weaving are essentially female, and that they are logically assigned to women because women engage in child raising and must do tasks that are both easily interrupted and allow women to stay close to home. These derive from problematic anthropology and suspect assumptions about work and subjectivity. On initial formulations, see Judith Brown, "A Note on the Division of Labor by Sex." Unfortunately these essentialized notions have received renewed popularity—as feminist positions—in E. J. W. Barber's *Women's Work: The First 2000 Years.*

13. Readers interested in more details should consult Peskowitz, "The Work of Her Hands," chap. 4. With particular reference to talmudic sources, see Samuel Krauss, *Talmudische Archäologie;* and Abraham Samuel Hirschberg (Herszberg), *Hayye ha-Tarbut be-Yisrael bi Tekufat ha-Mishna ve-ha-Talmud.* These texts contain a wealth of useful as well as incorrect detail; hence I cite them sparingly. Their use of evidence is mixed with the very positivist and gender-stereotypical assumptions I have set out to critique.

These studies form a separate scholarly tradition from studies of ancient technology, weaving, and looms in Greece, Rome, and the rest of Europe. See Hugo Blümner, *Technologie und Terminologie der Gewerbe und Künste bei Griechen und Römern;* R. J. Forbes, *Studies in Ancient Technology,* vol. 4, with a forthcoming revision by J. P. Wild; Marta Hoffmann, *The Warp-Weighted Loom;* Wild, *Textile Production in the Northern Roman Provinces* and idem, "The Roman Horizontal Loom"; Lillian Wilson, *The Clothing of the Ancient Romans;* Wipzsycka, *L'industrie textile dans l'Egypte romaine;* Grace M. Crowfoot, "Of the Warp-Weighted Loom" and idem, "The Vertical Loom in Palestine and Syria"; Henry L. Roth, *Ancient Egyptian and Greek Looms;* R. Patterson, "Spinning" in C. Singer et al., eds., *A History of Technology,* vol. 1. More recently, see E. J. W. Barber, *Prehistoric Textiles,* 79–125, and D. L. Carroll, *Looms and Textiles of the Copts.*

14. Sources: Seneca *Ad Lucilium, Epistulae Morales* 90.20 refers to the two-beam loom by quoting Ovid's account of Pallas and Arachne (*Metamorphoses* 6:53–68) during which the weavers stretch the warp so that the web was bound between two beams. On Pollux, see *Onomasticon* 8.36. By the early fourth century, Servius *Ad Aeneid* 7.14 would remember that "once upon a time" weavers would stand and weave upward. Also worthy of mention is Festus *Pauli Exc* 286–289 (dated to the late second century C.E.), who recalled that the warp-weighted loom was then being used to weave garments for special occasions. A bride's tunic or yellow veil might be woven on an archaic loom, as would the *tunica recta* for boys reaching adulthood. The textual problems and transmission of Festus's writings are legion, however, since the work was redacted/edited by Paulus Diaconus in the eighth century.

Sources for the first-century date for the technological shift include the following: Corinth excavations show a decline of loom weights at this time; see G. R. Davidson, *Corinth,* 147. A tombstone from Burgos (Lara de Los Infantes), Spain, depicts a warp weighted loom. The stone is dated to the second or first century B.C.E., and thus is not of much help in securing a latest date; see C. A. Giner, *Tejido y cestería en la península ibérica,* 93, 105, pl. 7. Excavations at Hellenistic and Roman Tarsus, in Asia Minor, showed a decline in the quantity of loom weights after the Hellenistic-Roman stratum; see Hetty Goldman, ed., *Excavations at Gözlü Kule, Tarsus,* vol. 1/2: 394, n. 6. At Herculaneum, Italy, the excavation of rows of clay loom weights at several houses indicate that warp-weighted looms had been set up in courtyards. This attests to the use of this technology in the years up to 79 C.E.; see Amedeo Maiuri, *Ercolano: I Nuovi Scavi,* 430.

In artistic depictions, the two-beam loom appears beginning in the late first century. Note the depiction of a two-beam loom on the frieze of the Forum of Nerva in Rome, dated to 96–98 C.E.; see Peter Heinrich von Blanckenhagen, *Flavische Architektur,* 118–127, esp. 124, taf. 40–42. Depictions become more common in the third century. These include: a wall painting in the Hypogeum of the Aurelii, Rome, dated 220 C.E. (see Nikolaus Himmelmann, *Das Hypogaum der Aurelier am Viale Manzoni,* and the reproduction in Wild, *Textile Manufacture,* pl. XIb, and Wilson, *Clothing,* 22, pl. 10, fig. 2); the tombstone of Severa Seleuciana, dated 279 C.E. (pictured in Goffredo Bendinelli, "An Underground Tomb"); and an illuminated manuscript of Virgil (*Aeneid,* 7.5–10) that depicts Kirke at her loom, dated to 400 C.E. (Codex Vaticanus MSS 3225, picture 39; in Wild, *Textile Manufacture*, fig. 60). Note the historical anomaly of illustrating Circe with a two-beam instead of a warp-weighted loom.

Rabbinic evidence for Palestine: for the two-beam loom: mNegaim 11.9 and mKelim 21.1, which describe the lower and upper beams (*kôbed hataḥětôn/kôbed hāʿelyôn*. On the absence of terminology for loom weights: Krauss, *Talmudische Archäologie*, 150–151, incorrectly translates the Hebrew word *makbēš* as *Gewichten* (weight); Marcus Jastrow, *A Dictionary*, 781, is more correct in translating *makbēš* as a "clothes press" or "fuller's press," or more generally as a mechanism which requires that screws be tightened and loosened, as fits the contexts of mKelim 20.5 and mShabbat 20.5.

15. In "Of the Warp-weighted Loom" Grace Crowfoot guesses this is the reason for its large-scale extinction, despite the fact that other "primitive" technologies survived. She writes, "[W]e can imagine how gratefully Greek and Roman women would welcome a more restful position; one that would not call forth that often heard complaint, 'I've been on my feet from morning till night' " (47).

16. I thank Toni Weaver at the Textile Museum, Washington, D.C., for demonstrating and explaining this to me.

17. This note is for readers interested in the genealogy of micro-"truths." Grace Crowfoot dated the appearance and popularity of the two-beam loom in Palestine as early as the second century B.C.E. This has been repeated by scholars who have uncritically cited Crowfoot's work. Crowfoot's early date was based on the mishnaic reference I cite below. Crowfoot relied on the early dating of the Mishnah by Gustaf Dalman, *Arbeit und Sitte in Palästina*, 5:63. Dalman himself relied on Danby's dating of parts of the Mishnah to the second century B.C.E.; see Herbert Danby, *The Mishnah*, ix. The incorrect dating of the shift from the warp-weighted loom was based on an obsolete view of the Mishnah's own antiquity.

18. mNegaim 2.4: "How [does one perform] the inspection for leprosy? The man is inspected as he hoes or as he harvests olives. The woman [is inspected] as she kneads [dough for bread, cakes] or as she nurses her child, as she weaves at the 'loom' (*běʿômdîn*), for [the inspection] of the right armpit. Rabbi Yehudah says, also, as she spins flax (*ṭôweh běpištān*), [for the inspection] of the left [arm, hand or armpit]."

The passage is based on the purity considerations of Leviticus 13.47–59, 14.34–57 and Exodus 4.6. (N.B. Leviticus 13.47–59 and the question of leprosy in wool or linen, or in warp or woof thread.) On what "leprosy" may have been, see Julius Preuss, *Biblical and Talmudic Medicine*, and Mirko Grmek, *Greek Diseases in the Ancient Greek World*, 152–176. The Tosefta's gloss works differently. tNegaim 1.8 repeats and highlights only the last two poses for women, those of weaving and spinning. This further limits the imagination of women's work to these tasks, as it describes the leprosy exam through more clearly feminized tasks, using this legal passage to construct a narrower notion of a female subject. But the Tosefta takes the weaving pose, which is unattributed in the Mishnah, and attributes it to Rabbi Meir. It then invokes the explicit approval of Rabbi Judah ha-Nasi for this procedure. The passage in question is as follows: "One who weaves at the ʿômdîn, [this position allows inspection] for [signs in] the armpit, [these are] the words of Rabbi Meir. Rabbi Yehudah says, one who spins flax, [this position allows inspection] for [signs in] the left [arm]. The two positions for the inspection are approved by Rabbi." A slightly later text, Sifra Leviticus, Parshat Negaim, Pereq 4 (on Leviticus 13.12) repeats mNegaim 2.4, but without additional comment.

19. On women harvesting olives, see mYebamot 15.2 and tEduyot 1.12. On men weaving: mEduyot 1.3., tEduyot 1.3, tQiddushin 5.14, and below, mZabim 3.2. On men baking bread, and the market production of bread: mKelim 15.2, 15.3; mBaba Batra 2.3; tAvodah Zarah 7.2, and in particular, mErubim 7.11, in which a woman gives an amount of money to a baker to bake loaves for her; also, mHallah 1.7, 2.7, 3.1–3.3. Bread was also produced at homes: see bBaba Metzia 2.2, 2.3; mBetsah 5.4 in which a woman borrows water and salt for her dough; and mPesah 3.4, which describes women kneading dough together. For another alternative, note the production of bread by slaves and servants in mBetsah 2.6, set in Rabban Gamliel's household. Given the ideological import of bread making as a female and domestic task (mShabbat 23.1), and hallah as a mitzvah directed particularly to women, these references should be approached as a complexly layered continuum of realia and metaphor. Against the gendering of olive and grape production as masculine and bread production as feminine (as in mShabbat 23.1), note the way mTaharot 9.3 places vats of olives in the process of softening inside the household, and on its roofs, part of the space rabbis also filled with women.

On wet nursing (*nutrix*): Although later rabbis will argue that it is a wife's duty to her husband to breast-feed their children, wet nurses were allowed in the case of twins. But rabbinic direction is in some ways beside the point; wet nursing was common throughout the Roman empire. See Keith Bradley, "Wet-Nursing at Rome: A Study in Social Relations," 201–229 and "Sexual Regulations in Wet-Nursing Contracts from Roman Egypt," 321–325; Suzanne Dixon, *The Roman Mother*. See Soranus of Ephesus (98–117 C.E.), who suggests that in breast-feeding, the best person, of the appropriate age and properly nourished, and not necessarily the mother, should feed the child: "the mother will fare better with a view to her recovery and further childbearing, if she is relieved of having her breasts distended, as well" (trans. Owsei Temkin et al., *Soranus' Gynecology*, Baltimore: Johns Hopkins University Press, 1956), 90.

20. Tractate Zabim treats the problems of ritual impurity and transmission of impurity incurred by genital discharges. The terms *zāb* (masc.) and *zābâ* (fem.) designate that a man or woman who experiences three drips of a genital discharge, other than menstrual blood, on one day or on consecutive days, will be in a state of ritual impurity. When the discharges cease, the person observes seven dripless days, washes the garments, and immerses in the *miqveh*. On the eighth day, the person brings two pigeons (or two turtledoves) to the Temple (a cultural memory by the second century); one is a sin-offering, the other a burnt-offering. The chapters preceding mZabim 3.2 classify the various situations and combinations of discharges, discuss the variable kinds of susceptivity to this form of ritual impurity, and address the primary and secondary channels of transmission. For example, a man with a discharge (such as from gonorrhea) sat on a linen bed-covering. Then he stood and walked out into the courtyard. Later, a child entered the room and, unknowingly, lay down on the bed. The impurity is transmitted to the child, in secondary fashion, because the child

touched a cloth made impure by the man. The general principle is that the impurity is transmitted not just through touch, but through the exchange of pressure and energy.

21. For the philological argument see Peskowitz, "The Work of Her Hands," 187–191. The translation of ʿômdîn as "upright loom" in Jastrow, *Dictionary,* 1052 is too vague, as both looms were nominally vertical, and because the definition does not attend to the specific technological differences of the warp-weighted and two-beam looms. The entry for this word should be amended, with ramifications for its translation as "upright loom" in Danube, *Mishnah;* Phillip Blackman, *Mishnayot;* and Jacob Neusner, *The Mishnah. A New Translation.* A second rendering of the term as "vertical loom" appears in Neusner, *A History of the Mishnaic Law of Purities,* 6:46, but even this translation does not encapsulate the technological description that is a necessary part of understanding the passages in which this word appears. On *yôšbîn* as a self-supported loom with its own base, see two occurrences, in mKelim 2.2 and mKelim 10.1. Both describe a vessel that rests on its own base and does not lean on something else for support. Hanoch Albeck, *Shishah Sidrei Mishnah,* 6:444–445, is more correct in explicating the difference between the words as "whether they weave on a loom which stands before them, or whether they weave at a loom which sits upon the ground (my translation)," but still remains ambiguously vague and lacks the technological referent.

22. In *The Warp-Weighted Loom* Marta Hoffman describes her observations of warp-weighted weaving in modern Scandinavia. She notes the practice of two or more weavers working together on the warp-weighted loom in order to manipulate the heddle back and forth (thus creating the shed and countershed) and controlling the weighted warp threads.

23. Hellenistic I and II and Roman I weights may be found most visibly among the remains of Tel Anafa, Beth-Shean, Tel Mikal (Persian-Hellenistic), Bet-Yerah, Ashdod, Arad, and Gamla. An example of a set of twenty Roman I loom weights comes from Samaria-Sebaste; see John W. Crowfoot et al., *Samaria-Sebaste,* vol. 3, *The Objects from Samaria,* 399, fig. 92a.

24. I thank Orit Shamir for sharing her insights into these materials. See the preliminary report by Yigael Yadin, *The Finds from the Bar Kokhba Period in the Cave of Letters.* Building XI (Roman I) contained charred loom weights. Locus 1108 contained loom weights found below the remains of a burnt loom. Additional loom weights were excavated but remain unpublished in the recent final reports from this site.

25. Yadin, *Finds from the Bar Kokhba Period in the Cave of Letters,* 130. The excavator designated Hall C as the site of what he called a "household textile industry."

26. Listed variously as *mishkolot, mishkol nol, mishkolot nol,* or *mishkol arigah.* See also Orit Shamir, "Nol ha-Mishkolot," 32–34.

27. My point throughout is that the performative context of the Mishnah and Tosefta is the third century and later. I am less interested in the purity of the "original" contexts of "early" passages transmitted in "later" texts than in the cultural work accomplished when these texts are repeated for centuries. Some might argue that it is possible that fragments from these texts come from earlier decades; that is, some of the passages in question could have been origi-

nally compiled or imagined at a time when both looms were in use. This would place mNegaim 2.4 and mZabim 3.2 into the mid-second century or earlier. However, even the best arguments for seeing and unraveling layers in the Mishnah rely on notions about the development of legal logic. The various arguments for locating layers claim certain configurations of what constitutes critical method for studying rabbinic texts. Even within these, the argument has not been made that within allegedly early passages, the details of realia are also unchanged. Even within their "internal" chronology, these passages are "late": when tNegaim 1.8 comments upon the positions women should use for the purity exam, Rabbi Yehudah ha-Nasi's approval is cited. tNegaim 1.8 repeats only the last two positions, and ascribes them to Rabbi Meir (mid-second century); see note 18 above. One could argue that the attribution to Meir places the reference into a time frame closer to the actual use of the warp-weighted loom. However, the Tosefta repeats the two positions, and cites the approval of Rabbi. It effectively recasts Meir into a new literary and historical context. Regarding the third passage, tKelim Baba Batra 1.2 comments on and adds to the early mishnaic description of the two-beam loom. The Tosefta's comment is even further from the date of the warp-weighted loom's usage than mNegaim 2.4 and tNegaim 1.8.

28. Herodotus *History* 2.35.

29. In *The Mirror of Herodotus* François Hartog uses this passage to demonstrate Herodotus's pattern of translating differences through inversion, "whereby otherness is transcribed as anti-sameness," and comments upon how the formula is an easy and familiar one for "travelers' tales and utopias . . . since it constructs an otherness that is transparent for the listener or reader; it is no longer a matter of *a* and *b*, simply of *a* and the converse of *a*" (212–217).

30. Rashi on bShabbat 105a.

31. Theophylactus *Ad Johan*, XIX, 23.

FOUR: DOMESTICITY

1. The woman is referred to as ʾēšet ḥayil, commonly translated into English as "good wife," "worthy wife," or "woman of valor." The Hebrew root ḥyl has additional meanings related to battles and warriors, such as "strong," "firm," and "mighty." Against the tendency to "feminize" according to stereotypes of what femininity is and should be, the Septuagint's translation of Hebrew to Greek is instructive: *gynaikas andreias*, "a masculine, manly woman."

2. Various dates have been proposed for Targum Proverbs: Kaminka proposes the third century B.C.E.; in his introduction to *The Targum of Proverbs*, John Healey argues for the second century C.E. at the earliest. I will not overinterpret the lack of elaboration on chapter 31; in general it contains little of the expansion of biblical text that makes the Targum so interesting as still another textual voice within Judaism of the Roman and Byzantine periods.

3. Much of the extensive scholarship on Proverbs 31.10–31 is concerned with its female personifications and with the female figure of wisdom. See for example, Claudia Camp, *Wisdom and the Feminine in the Book of Proverbs;* Bernhard Lang, *Wisdom and the Book of Proverbs;* and Thomas McCreesh, "Wisdom as Wife: Proverbs 31:10–31."

4. Or, if she were unmarried and a minor in her father's house, to her father (see discussion in chapter 5). In more complicated cases, her labors were owned by her sons (if she were a widow with children), or by her brother-in-law (if she were a childless widow).

5. As such, I am extending Wegner's argument (in *Chattel or Person?*) that to ascertain a woman's status according to mishnaic law, it is necessary to find the man (husband, father, etc.) who has legal control of a woman's sexuality. Wegner argues for quite a strong connection between gender, legal status, and the control of sexuality. This insight and its ramifications have been extremely helpful and necessary for my own work. I am arguing throughout that early rabbinic Judaism constructs gender as a wider variety of bodily disciplines. In contrast to the tendency to focus only on sexuality, I am arguing for the ways in which gender is constituted through masculinist control and ownership of the female laboring body, and for how control of the laboring body is imbricated with the sexed/biological body.

6. On the innovations regarding the husband's control of old property, see chapter 1.

7. It has become popular to define mKetubot 5.5 as a household code, in part since doing so places it among other Roman-period household codes and allows analysis. See Colossians 3.18–4.1; 1 Peter; Pseudo-Phocylides *Maxims* 175–227; Philo *Apologia for the Jews,* 7.3; Josephus *Against Apion* 2.189–209; Philo *Decalogue* 165–167; Plutarch *Mulierum virtutes;* Iamblichus *Life of Pythagoras* 54–57; Plutarch *Advice to Bride and Groom,* 138b–146a; Callicratidas *On the Happiness of Households,* 105.20–22, and of course, the ever-repeated guide to household management, Aristotle *Politics* 1. 1253b 1–14. In particular, mKetubot 5.5 had close parallels in Hierocles *Oikonomikos,* a second-century C.E. Stoic tractate. In the *Oikonomikos,* the wife's domestic tasks are outlined as spinning wool, making bread, and cooking, followed by a general statement that her work includes everything of a domestic nature; see the edition of Hense and Wachsmuth 3:679–701.

On Roman-period household codes, see David Balch, "Household Codes" and *Let Wives Be Submissive: The Domestic Code in 1 Peter;* Kathleen O'Brien Wicker, "First Century Marriage Ethics"; and Dieter Luehrmann, "Neutestamentliche Haustafeln und Antike Okonomie." Balch in particular has argued that household codes were used by minority groups in the Roman Empire to display their respectability according to what they perceived as Roman and elite standards; as such, they are an apologetic response to real or perceived critique.

8. Tosefta Ketubot 5.4 begins its comment on this passage by noting that the Mishnah had classified seven labors but did not assign the rest; tKetubot 5.4 concludes its list of labors by noting how the ethos of a place matters. Where wives do not usually do certain kinds of labors, her husband must not force her to do so. Thus, the details of domesticity will vary according to a woman's economic status and according to the cultural customs of the place where she and her husband reside.

9. However, unlike other constructions of this metaphor, mKetubot 5.5 does not seem to attach any ambivalence to it. For the rabbis, the metaphor works. See the discussion of ambivalence in chapter 2 and below.

10. Variations on this idea of protection appear both in the Mishnah and in

scholarly accounts of the Mishnah. In the latter, arguments about protecting women appear as "normal" explanations, such that often the ancient rabbinic discourse is not recognized as distinctive at all. An illustration of this comes from Ze'ev Falk, *Introduction to Jewish Law of the Second Commonwealth*, 292: "the following rule [mKetubot 5.5] defined the duties of a wife and prevented exaggerated demands on the part of the husband." In its depiction of the uncontrollable man and the vulnerable woman, such a scenario constructs (for them and for us) women as in need of protection by "good" men (in this case, the rabbis), who will protect Jewish women from other "bad" men (including their husbands). It simultaneously forges a distinction between rabbis and other Jewish men, so that the former are morally heroic and the latter are in need of control.

11. The passage, which remands a wife's new property to her husband, continues on into a discussion of who owns the compensation for more overt violences to her body. The first position is that compensation for indignities to her, and damages for injury to her body, belong to the woman (mKetubot 6.1 end). The dissenting position argues that these payments should be split in differing proportions between the woman and her husband, or alternately, that her portion of the damages must be used to purchase land, of which the husband will enjoy the usufruct.

12. A corollary passage, mKetubot 9.4, provides a policing mechanism whereby the husband can put his wife under oath to insure that she accurately reports her earnings to him; also mShebuot 7.8. Regarding the status of finds (*mĕṣîʾāh*), see mBaba Metzia 1.3–1.4, 2.1–2.2, mGittin 5.8, and mMakorot 2.8–2.10. The examples used to discuss finds are mundane objects that are either found by chance or collected and gathered. For all objects, the early rabbinic process is to attempt to locate the owner before taking possession. The male head of household owns things found by his wife, by his minor sons and daughters, and by male and female non-Jewish slaves. Finds by adult sons and daughters, male and female Jewish slaves, and a divorced wife awaiting her marriage settlement belong to the finders. There is no scriptural authority for his control over the finds of the other family members; on slaves and servants, see Leviticus 25.39–43 (on "Hebrew" slaves) and Leviticus 25.44–46 (on "Canaanite" slaves).

13. Once again, the notion is long-standing and widespread, especially in texts which understand domesticity and women's education to be opposites: Musonius *That Women Too Should Study Philosophy;* Diogenes Laertius on Hipparchia in his *Lives of Eminent Philosophers;* Plutarch's fulminations when Fulvia leaves the loom; and as well, in his *Orations,* Libanius's positive assessment of women who leave the loom to help the community.

14. Her needs: *ṣārkāh*. See the expansion of the list of third-party or guardian support in tKetubot 5.8–9. The list of materials ends with reference to the daughter of Naqdimon ben Gurion, a childless widow who, while awaiting a levirate marriage to her brother-in-law, contests the amount of her maintenance. The text considers the maintenance award more than sufficient (noting it in the exaggerated terms of five hundred dinarii per day for spices alone, but see parallel texts), and the tale ends with her downfall into poverty, in which she must pick barley pieces from waste. The discussion about maintaining wives and

other dependent women concludes with a sense of rabbinic mistrust of these women and cautions about the possibility of female greed.

15. On the upright looms in use, warp thread hangs vertically. Warp thread is thicker and heavier than woof thread, which is woven in and out, horizontally. The passage explains the relation between the two forms of spun wool as a 1:2 ratio, in which five *selaim* of vertical warp will equal (in weight? in time spent in production?) ten *selaim* of horizontal woof.

16. This section links a wife's paid and unpaid labor, and also associates these with elements of control in another way. Textually, her labors are the beginning and end points of a discussion that ranges through the overlapping issues of work, sex, and gender. The discussion of household labors (mKetubot 5.5) is connected to the principle of the work of her hands (6.1) through a series of discussions. The literary pathway from household labors to the control of a wife's new property takes a reader through vignettes of laboring wives; to leisurely wives with sexual temptations; to the possibility that a husband might use a vow to restrict his sexual intercourse with his wife (5.6); to the rebellious wife (*môredet*) who loses money from her ketubbah (and any forthcoming inheritance) for each week of her rebellion (5.7); and to lists of maintenance (*mezônôt*), food, provisions, clothing, and support that a husband must provide for his wife (5.8–5.9). The path moves from the household labors (5.5) to sexual intercourse to domestic control of the unruly wife to the husband's material protection of her, and finally, in mKetubot 6.1, to the principle that all her profits, products, and wages belong to him. The interconnection of all these things is a reminder that rabbinic writing carefully crafted these layers of marriage.

17. A philological note: The terminology used by Proverbs 31 for female labor is related to that used in early rabbinic texts, but the lack of actual overlap is significant. In Proverbs 31.31, references to female work use these phrases: *maʿăśêhā* (her work) and *pĕrî yādêhā* (the fruits of her hands). The phrase common in rabbinic writing—*maʿaśēh yādê*—is absent from Proverbs. A version of the phrase does appear in Isaiah 45.11, where it refers to male labor. In the Mishnah/Tosefta the same phrase is used specifically to refer to female labor.

The much later Midrash Mishle (Midrash on Proverbs) (ninth and tenth centuries) clarifies one change in how rabbis read this part of Proverbs. The worthy wife of Proverbs 31.10 is read both as an actual woman (as the second interpretation of the phrase, a tale of Rabbi Meir's wife, makes clear) and at the same time (in the first interpretation) the worthy wife is allegorized into Torah. Then, reading Proverbs 31.30 ("It is for her fear of the Lord that a woman is to be praised"), the midrash substitutes Moses for the terms "her" and "a woman." To the question "Why are the prophets compared to women?" comes the answer: "Just as such a woman is not embarrassed to demand the needs of her household from her husband, so were the prophets not shy about demanding Israel's needs from God." This analogy makes the position of husbands parallel to the position of God. Significantly, in this reading of Proverbs the husband is the gateway between a wife and the marketplace/economy. In contrast to the biblical text, in which the women's access to the market was not mediated by her husband, this later rabbinic ethos makes clear that the husband controls the material and fiscal resources of the household. Thus, the much-commented-upon representation in Proverbs of a wife's independence and economic agency is here transformed into a relation that demands her to be dependent upon her husband and asserts his control over her. See S. Buber, *Midrasch Mischle;* Burton Visotzky, "Midrasch Mishle" and *The Midrash on Proverbs.*

18. See the discussion of 2 Samuel 3.29 in chapter 2.

19. Livy *History (Ad Urbe Condita)* 1.57; Columella *De Re Rustica* 12, preface; II Baruch 10.19; Jerome *Instructions for Rearing a Virgin Christian Daughter* 107.

20. North of Palestine, in Palmyra, funerary portraits of women placed spindles and distaffs in their hands. These monuments and portraits have not been fully gathered and studied, but see Robert Ousterhout and Ann Terry, "Souvenir of a World in Transition: A Late Roman Grave Stele from Phrygia." A collection of Palmyrene funerature displayed in the new wing of the Istanbul Archaeological Museum contains some important examples. See also the third-century grave relief from Palmyra at the Nelson Gallery–Atkins Museum in Kansas City, Missouri.

21. Petronius *Satyricon* 132.2; Apuleius *Metamorphoses* 9.5; Pausanius *Descriptio Graeciae* 7.21.14, on female cloth workers at Patrae, Egypt; *Petrus der Iberer* 28–29. Also, Susan Treggiari, "Lower-class Women in the Roman Economy."

22. On the Fates spinning, see Catullus *Epithalamium of Peleus and Thetis* 64.303–382 and Plato *Republic* 616 c,d. On Minerva as *lanifica* see Ovid *Metamorphoses* 6; on the story of the Virgin Mary picked to weave the Temple curtains, Proto-Evangelium Jacobi 10.1.

23. See Susan Treggiari, "Family Life among the Staff of the Volusii," and J. P. Wild, "The Gynaceum at Venta and Its Context." See Theodosian Code 10.20.3; Petronius 132; Tibullus 4.10.3; and Lactantius *De Mortibus Persecutorum* 21.4 on Christian women who were captured and sent to work in the gynaceum.

FIVE: CONTESTATIONS

1. Judith Romney Wegner, *Chattel or Person?* 75.

2. bKetubot 47b.

3. It strikes me that analyses such as these show the extent to which commentators on Jewish traditions have a long history of sacrificing asking hard questions about women's lives in favor of supporting a benign notion of rabbinic law.

4. bKetubot 58b. Because I am focusing on earlier developments, I will not offer extensive discussion of these Babylonian passages, which postdate the Mishnah by several centuries, nor do I wish to enter into theoretical discussions of dating layers of Talmud, nor do I accept arguments that a baraita (such as bKetubot 47b) dates to the early rabbinic period. A brief survey of these talmudic texts shows that the argument continues over these economic relations of marriage. Here, the primary question is their origin (either in scripture or as rabbinic innovation). Here the two passages diverge again, with bKetubot 58b–59a finding a rabbinic origin, and bKetubot 47b–48a exegeting the duty of maintenance from Exodus 21.20. In finding the supposed origins of laws, and

in assessing the relations of different laws to each other, bKetubot 58b posits that the husband's duty to maintain his wife is the primary obligation, and in return for this, he receives her earnings. Furthermore, the wife can waive her right to the husband's support, and in return, keep her earnings (although the husband still has the right to her finds, to the profits from her old property, and to her household labors). Because the husband is obligated to maintain the wife, he cannot renounce the arrangement; this renunciation only comes from her (although there is some disagreement on this point, namely that he can initiate the renunciation contractually). Some scholars are currently arguing that this mechanism wherein the wife can renounce the arrangement and keep her earnings is liberatory. My response is that even if a wife renounces support, in societies which devalue women's labor and in which women are limited to certain kinds of labors, most women are not able to find the kinds of economic advantage they receive through their husbands. See also bKetubot 66a and bGittin 11b–12b.

5. Boaz Cohen, *Jewish and Roman Law* 1:273. The pattern is widespread. See Louis Epstein, The *Jewish Marriage Contract*, 154, in which the wife gives her finds to her husband because "peace in the family required such a concession to the husband." Invoking notions of marital distrust, the treacherous wife, and the need to discipline wives, he continues: "without this grant to the husband the wife would have every chance to steal from him and protect her booty by the claim that she found it." Again, modern scholars have, unfortunately and sometimes despite their best intentions, been complicit with the worst misogyny of the ancients; note that Cohen writes elsewhere that "the husband shares his wife's earnings in return for fulfilling the Biblical obligation that compels him to support his wife, in order to lighten, so to speak, the burdens of matrimony" (*Jewish and Roman Law* 1:218). On this inversion (in which the husband—not the wife, and not even the two of them—bears marriage's burdens) and on the notion of marriage as burden, note the similarity with the Roman jurist Ulpian. See below, the discussion of mKetubot 4.6 and 13.1.

6. As Amy Richlin argues in "Zeus and Metis: Foucault, Feminism, Classics," analyses of power that do not consider gender to be central will never "get to" gender. See also her introduction to the 1992 revised edition of *The Garden of Priapus: Sexuality and Aggression in Roman Humor.*

7. The Tosefta uses *parnasah* instead of the Mishnah's *mezônôt*.

8. Unlike the similar legislation for wives, the halakah for daughters is eventually assigned a biblical prooftext, Exodus 21.7, in which a father sells his daughter to be a maidservant. In this proof, daughters are compared to maidservants whose labor is explicitly owned. The analogy is brought that if a father can sell a daughter, then just as he can sell a maidservant and owns her labor, the father owns the daughter's labors. On vows, see Numbers 30.6. On the exchange of women from father to husband, or husband to father, note Deuteronomy 24.2: "And she leaves his house, and she becomes another man's wife." As other passages clarify, this applies to daughters who are minors, not those who have reached adulthood (at age 12½). As Wegner makes clear, the daughter who becomes an adult and remains unmarried is emancipated from the father.

9. See also tKetubot 4.1–2.

10. A wife's obligation to nurse young children and to take care of the house is directed to her husband, not to the children. On filial service, see tQiddushin 1.11. The lack of a father's legal obligation to support his children is fairly straightforward in the Mishnah but was seen as problematic for other rabbinic interpretation, beginning with the Tosefta. In tTemurot 1.13, a father might give to his children a "treasure" so that they might support themselves; bKetubot 49a–50a argues that support of one's children is a valued act of charity. See Israel Lebendinger's classic "The Minor in Jewish Law." In modern scholarship, note the tendency to elevate the father's moral sense of obligation to children as an innate characteristic, a tendency that derives from a certain apology from what to many of us seems like a curious shortcoming. For example, Ze'ev Falk, in *Introduction to Jewish Law of the Second Commonwealth:* "No duty is mentioned, but only the religious precept of charity, since in most cases the father's compassion for his children is a sufficient motive for him to care for their needs of his own volition" (325). Here, compassion is seen as an essential part of being a Jewish father, a characteristic that predates law and society. In contrast, the critical issue is how early rabbinic law constructed a notion and practice of fatherhood that would leave the father largely free of legal responsibilities to maintain his children but see fit to legislate other family members' responsibilities to the father.

On sons, note that early rabbinic law accorded sons greater economic privileges than sons in a comparable period of Roman law. This could suggest a rabbinic desire to constitute the Jewish man with advantageous economic potential (although the Roman institution of *peculium* would make it difficult to assess how the two systems would have compared in practice). It is significant that as a minority law in the Roman Empire, early rabbinic law gave its sons more economic privilege vis-à-vis its daughters, and vis-à-vis the sons of Roman law.

11. mBaba Batra 8.1–3; see Numbers 27.8. The sons take precedence over the daughters. If the father had sons who are deceased at the time of the father's death, the sons' children take precedence over the daughters. If there are no sons and no descendants of sons, the daughters inherit.

12. The sons' right to inheritance is biblical, and daughters' maintenance (after the father's death) is narrated by the Mishnah (mKetubot 4.11) as enjoined by the Court; it can also be contracted.

13. See sources in Keith Bradley, "Child Labor in the Roman World," in his *Discovering the Roman Family,* 103–124.

14. See David Daube, "Texts and Interpretation in Roman and Jewish Law"; Bernard Jackson, "Legalism and Spirituality"; Daniel Boyarin, *Intertextuality and the Reading of the Midrash;* and the writing of Jacob Neusner.

15. This strategy of inversion is found also in a short judgment attributed to the second-century Roman jurist Ulpian (floruit 193–211), who ruled that the profits on a married woman's dowry belonged to her husband. "Equity demands that the profits on a dowry shall belong to the husband. Since he bears the burdens of marriage it is only fair that he receives the profits" (Digest 23.3.7; see Mommsen et al., *The Digest of Justinian,* 670). Ulpian's reasoning resorts to a concept of fairness and equity: a man bears the burdens of a marriage, therefore he should receive the profits. At first glance this formulation

seems rational, equitable, and commonsensical. It starts to seem less fair and rational when placed into a context. Absent from Ulpian's reasoning is a cognizance of burdens borne by the wife and restrictions placed upon her in Roman society; Ulpian's ruling seems not to consider that marriage might be a burden for the wife. Considering Ulpian and the early rabbis together, it becomes necessary to remember the second century as a period in which relatively more systematic law codes were being developed. The *Institutes of Gaius* date to this period, as does the Mishnah. If Ulpian and the world of Roman lawyers at first seem remote from the rabbis in Palestine, note the presence of Roman law and its advocates in the Eastern provinces, as well as Ulpian's personal links with nearby Tyre, where his father was a citizen (see Tony Honoré, *Ulpian*) and note Richard Hanson's numismatic arguments for the connections between Tyre and Galilee. These similarities between the narratives of gender in Roman and early rabbinic law should be interpreted in light of other arguments for and apparent instances of rabbinic knowledge of, and similarities to, Roman law. See Saul Lieberman, "Roman Legal Institutions in Early Rabbinics and in the Acta Martyrum" and *Hellenism in Jewish Palestine,* 6 ff.; Boaz Cohen, *Jewish and Roman Law;* Bernard Jackson, "On the Problem of Roman Influence on the Halakhah and Normative Self-Definition in Judaism."

16. Naphtali Lewis and Jonas Greenfield, eds., *The Documents from the Bar Kokhba Period from the Cave of Letters,* 76–82; the text under consideration is PY 18. See also Lewis et al., "Papyrus Yadin 18."

17. Lewis and Greenfield, *Documents from the Bar Kokhba Period,* 37: PY 37.

18. Lewis and Greenfield, *Documents from the Bar Kokhba Period,* 80–81, and A. Yardeni, "The Aramaic and Hebrew Documents in Cursive Script from Wadi Murabba'at and Nahal Hever and Related Material."

19. An additional complexity is that the document is not per se a "Jewish" marriage document. However, Judah (the bride's father) used a ketubbahfor his own marriage, and this suggests an element of consciousness in his agreement to a non-Jewish document for his daughter's marriage.

20. Raphael Taubenschlag, *The Law of Greco-Roman Egypt in the Light of the Papyri,* 142.

21. Ranon Katzoff, "Legal Analysis," in Lewis et al., "Papyrus Yadin 18"; A. Wasserstein, "A Marriage Contract from the Province of Arabia Nova"; and Katzoff, "Papyrus Yadin 18 Again: A Rejoinder."

22. Nahal Hever 10. The maintenance arrangement is not found in biblical sources, despite the attempt by rabbinic exegetes to locate it in Exodus 21.10. For references, see Epstein, *Jewish Marriage Contract,* 149 n. 27.

23. Katzoff, "Papyrus Yadin 18 Again," 175.

24. I also find troubling the invocation of "an economic standard" of Greek legal custom. This rests on the assumption that Greek difference would have been easily distinctive. But in Roman Palestine and Roman Arabia, the term "Greek" would include a range of ethnic peoples, customs, and ideas about these peoples. It is not reasonable to assume that all "Greeks" would have had a higher standard of living than all "Jews." It cannot be shown that the economic living standards of Roman Palestine and Roman Arabia varied exclusively by ethnicity.

25. In mKetubot 12.1–2 a woman can contract with her husband (either through the ketubbah or through a document written later) that the husband will provide maintenance of the daughter for a specified amount of time. Maintenance of sons is not mentioned in the Mishnah, but in tKetubot 13.1 this kind of written contract includes both sons and daughters. See also tKetubot 10.2, in which the father cannot force the children to work in exchange for their maintenance.

26. *hā-ʾāb ʾênô ḥayāb.* See also tKetubot 4.17. The debate over the maintenance of daughters continues in the Talmud (see bKetubot 49a), where the consensus will be similar to the Tosefta's ruling, using a minor (daughter) to major (son) argument. Also, see Saul Lieberman, *Tosefta Ki-Fshutah* 6:245. The basis for the discussion in tKetubot 4.8 is a legal story about nonrabbinic Jewish life and its practices. This is clarified in the next passage, tKetubot 4.9, which adduces a proof wherein Hillel bases a ruling on a written marriage document; tKetubot 4.8 argues for the father's obligation to support daughters and sons, and bases this (commandment for sons and obligation for daughters) on what it posits as the authority of Jews' practices. The term *ḥôbāh* recalls the obligatory sacrifices presented at the Temple.

SIX: GOSSIP

1. mSotah 6.1: "Whoever had voiced suspicions concerning his wife [with regard to her extramarital sexual actions], and she continued [her actions] secretly: even if he heard [about her secretive sexual actions] from a flying bird, he may divorce her and [if he does, he] must give [her] the ketubbah, [this is the] opinion of Rabbi Eliezer. Rabbi Joshua says [he may divorce her, and if he does, he must give her the ketubbah] when the [women] spinners (*môzĕrôt*) argue and repeat [tales] about her by the moonlight."

I use the phrase "gossip" as an English translation of "argue and repeat tales." This phrase should not be confused with the expression *lāšôn hārā,* or more colloquially, *lashon hara,* "evil or slanderous speech," as in ARN A.19. Also, the term *môzĕrôt* (see ySotah 6.20d) differs from the more usual terms for spinning built on the roots *ṭwh* and *šzr* (as in mKelim 9.6, mShabbat 7.2, tKelim Baba Batra 1.6, tNegaim 1.8 and elsewhere).

2. Lee Levine, *The Rabbinic Class of Roman Palestine in Late Antiquity,* 67 and 134. But see Martin Goodman, *State and Society in Roman Galilee* and Bernard Jackson, "On the Problem of Roman Influence in the Halakhah and Normative Self-Definition in Judaism," 159–172. On the general lack of policing see Fergus Millar, "The World of the Golden Ass."

3. In many traditions, gossip is feminized and devalued as the talk of women. Note the Oxford English Dictionary definition of a *gossip* as "a person, mostly a woman, of light and trifling character, esp., one who delights in idle talk, a newsmonger, a tattler," with the additional meaning: "applied to a woman's female friends invited to be present at a birth." Note the Christian meaning, now archaic: "One who has contracted spiritual affinity by acting as a sponsor at a baptism." The association holds in the currently constructed culture of Judaism as well, as this rabbinic commentator notes: "Women are inclined to gossip, elaborating and exaggerating the most ordinary occurrences.

This gossiping trait in some women is a classic theme in many cultures, particularly in the Orient. In the words of Ben Sirah: 'a silent woman is a gift from the Lord'" (Menachem M. Brayer, *The Jewish Woman in Rabbinic Literature* 1:232). The citations offered are Sirach 23.5, Deuteronomy Rabbah 6, and bNedarim 21b. Readers will note the unsubtle combination of both an unreflective essentialized masculinism with an unreflective orientalism.

Whereas the primary way that I invoke gossip in this chapter is as a mode of social control, it is also the case that for people in subordinate positions, gossip can be a form of resistance, a necessary way to circulate information. As Patricia Meyer Spacks argues in *Gossip:* "Fostering re-descriptions of reality, it allows fiction-makers to utilize its often subversive activities."

4. Based on Numbers 5.11–31. In *The Law of Jealousy,* Adriana Destro argues that this level of detail has to do with the significance of the topic for rabbinic writers, who kept elaborating and reflecting upon a rite that was practically difficult but symbolically necessary. In her words, "a married woman who fails to demonstrate solidarity with her husband highlights elements of crisis within the entire religious and social system" (ix). To consider sotah in context of other disciplines of adultery, see Peter Garnsey, "Adultery Trials and the Survival of the *Quaestiones* in the Severan Age" and Tikva Frymer-Kensky, "The Strange Case of the Suspected Sotah."

5. Although see mSotah 3.4; the rabbis are concerned that despite the accused woman's guilt, her merits might prevent the waters from working.

6. Historically archaic because of the destruction of the Temple. See mSotah 9.9 where the cause of cessation is not the (external) Roman-imposed destruction but an (internal) decision by Yoḥanan ben Zakkai to stop the rite. In this narration, rabbis wrest control of many things—including control over their uncontrolled women—away from the ramifications of Roman conquest. Note that Sotah is arguably a composite text, but in light of the tenuous truth claims of text criticism of Mishnah, I will locate it for the purposes of this argument in the general period of the second and third century in which other mishnaic tractates are usually located. Little of the argument I develop rests on absolute (and impossible) accuracy and exact dating of this text.

7. Josephus *Antiquities* 20.17–96. See Josephus *Wars* 5.55, 5.119, 5.147, 5.253, and 6.355 for references to Helene's contributions to the architecture of Jerusalem through building a palace and monuments. For other ancient sources on Helene, see the commentary in Menahem Stern, *Greek and Latin Authors on Jews and Judaism,* 2:197, on Pausanias's *Descriptio Graeciae.*

8. mYoma 3.10. The text of the plaque is unknown. The talmudic discussion (bYoma 37b–38a) wonders whether the entire set of verses were used, or just their abbreviation; presumably the text in question is Numbers 5.19–22, the oath for the rite of bitter waters. See also tYoma/Kippurim 2.3, tSukkah 1.1, mNazir 3.6, and tPeah 4.18.

9. Yoma/Kippurim 2.3

10. The time of sunrise is linked with the time for reciting Shema each morning; see mBerahot 1.

11. Susan Grossman, "Women and the Jerusalem Temple," in Grossman and Haut, eds., *Daughters of the King: Women and the Synagogue,* 15–49.

12. For recent arguments dating the ketubbah to the late first century, see

Michael Satlow, "Reconsidering the Rabbinic *Ketubah* Payment," in Shaye J. D. Cohen, ed., *The Jewish Family in Antiquity.*

13. See also tKetubot 12.3.

14. For an alternate analysis, see Judith Romney Wegner, *Chattel or Person?* 84.

15. For another passage in which women are divorced without *ketubbah,* see tKetubot 7.4.

On tithing and the separation of *terumot* and *maᶜaserot,* Numbers 18.21; *niddah* (conditions of menstrual impurity), Leviticus 18.19; on the separation of *ḥallah,* Numbers 15.20; on vows, Numbers 30.3.

16. On *dat yĕhûdît* and its transformation in tKetubot 7.6 and elsewhere as *dat yisraᵓel,* see M. T. Friedman, *Jewish Marriage in Palestine,* 162–167. The most common translation of *dat yĕhûdît* is "Jewish custom" (see Louis Epstein's "breaches of accepted Jewish custom" in *Jewish Marriage Contract*). Whereas in the development of rabbinic law, custom (*minhag*) will at times have the force of law, to most English-speaking readers, custom and law mean very different things, and rely on different authorities. The word *dat* has a range of meanings, including "law," "custom," and "judgment." It is authorized, but not in the same way as mitzvot or halakah (although note that in its rabbinic invocation it effectively becomes halakah). In mKetubot 7.6, the parallel equivalency with *dat moseh* suggests a greater force than the usual English "custom." For this reason, and in order to remind us that early rabbinic law was not the only "law" that circulated for Jews in the Roman period, I translate the term *dat* as "law." See also Tobit 7.13 (*kata ton nomon Moiseos*), yYebamot 15.3.14d and yKetubot 4.8.28d.

17. See Saul Lieberman, *Tosefta Ki-Fshutah* 6.291. The proscription against female spinning in the marketplace takes on new meanings in light of my arguments about the cultural and economic decommodification of female labor. In this passage, a married woman and her productive labor (denoted in the metaphor of spinning) is banned from the marketplace, one of the necessary places of economic participation.

18. There is much unresolved debate over whether, where, how, and when Jewish women covered their hair or heads. In *Her Share of the Blessings,* Ross Kraemer suggests that "respectable" women, no matter what their communal loyalties, covered their heads or hair in some way. See Cynthia Thompson, "Portraits from Roman Corinth: Hairstyles, Headcoverings, and St. Paul" and Jerome Neyrey, "Body Language in 1 Corinthians." Selected sources: mShabbat 6.1; 1 Corinthians 11; Tertullian *The Veiling of Virgins;* Plutarch *Quaestiones Romanae* 267a; and Dio Chrysostomus 33d Discourse. See also Ramsay MacMullen, "Women in Public in the Roman Empire" and Howard Eilberg-Schwartz and Wendy Doniger, eds., *Off With Her Head!*

19. bKetubot 72b will understand this as a prohibition based on physical movements: to spin, she lifts her arm and thus shows some skin. This explanation has been remarkably intransigent and continues to appear. The emphasis on the physical sexuality of the woman's body (and the unspoken assumption of a male gaze and male desire for her) effaces the simultaneous rabbinic concern to constrict her economic and laboring body. The prohibition of spinning in the marketplace constrains her "women's work" to the home, where she is in

the domain of the husband, and where he mediates between the wife's labors
and its economic rewards (for him). Restricting her "spinning"—the metonym
for women's labors—from the marketplace effectively contains her sphere of
economic activity. For references to sources, I thank Eliyana Adler and Deborah
Budner, for showing me their unpublished paper "Take Back the Shuk! Approaches to Images and Realities of Jewish Women in the Ancient Marketplace." See also bGittin 4a, ySotah 5.7, Testament of Job 25.2.

Furthermore, tSotah 5.9 is a gloss on mSotah 6.1 (above) that uses some of
the language from mKetubot 7.6. The point made at the end of tSotah 5.9 elides
the tenor of the phrase "a husband may divorce" his wife into the more force-
ful, "a husband must divorce." For reference, tSotah 5.9:

Rabbi Meir said: As there are diverse tastes in regard to food, so there are
diverse tastes regarding women.
You can find a man around whose cup a fly flits by, and he will put [the cup]
aside and won't even taste what is in that cup. This one is a bad lot for women,
for he is always contemplating divorcing his wife.
You can find a man in whose cup a fly takes up residence. So he tosses [the fly]
out and does not drink what is in [the cup]. Such a one is like Pappos ben Judah,
who used to lock his door to keep his wife inside when he went out.
And you can find a man into whose cup a fly falls, and he tosses [the fly] away,
and drinks what is in the cup. This is the trait of the ordinary man, who sees
his wife talking with her neighbors or with her relatives, and leaves her be.
And you have a man into whose meal a fly falls, and he picks it up and sucks
[the fly], and tosses it away, and then eats what is on his plate. This is the trait
of a bad man, who sees his wife going around with her hair unkempt, with
her shoulders uncovered, having no shame before her male servants, having no
shames before her female servants, going out and doing her spinning in the
marketplace, bathing, [and] talking with anybody at all.
It is a commandment to divorce such a wife. As it is said: *When a man takes a
wife and marries her, if then she finds no favor in his eyes because he has found
indecency in her, and he writes her a bill of divorce and puts it in her hand and
sends her out of his house, and she departs from his house* (Deuteronomy 24.1).

20. See mKetubot 1.8, which questions the virginity of an unmarried
woman found in the marketplace talking to a man. On the marketplace as the
opposite of the secluded and chaste home, and ramifications for women who
flaunt these domains, note the pattern that appears in Philo *Special Laws*
3.169–177, itself a gloss on Deuteronomy 25.11. A wife "whose hands were
trained to spin and weave, not to inflict pain" ventures into the market. Her
husband has been insulted. As she rushes to defend him, her hands touch a
man's penis, a transgression for which her hand will be amputated.

21. For example, see Shaye J. D. Cohen, "Epigraphical Rabbis," 1–17.

22. Citations from Michel de Certeau, "The Scriptural Economy," in his
The Practice of Everyday Life, 141.

23. Michel Foucault, "The Eye of Power," 155.

24. For theoretical explication see Judith Butler, *Gender Trouble;* Jacques
Derrida, *Devant la Loi;* and Vicki Schultz, "Women 'Before' the Law."

25. Avot de Rabbi Natan (hereafter ARN), B.21, end. The figure of workers wearing signs of their trades is found also in mShabbat 1.3, tShabbat 1.8, 1.9. The comparable section of ARN A contains a much shorter analysis of the questions of labor. See Solomon Schechter, *Aboth de-Rabbi Nathan;* Louis Finklestein, *Mavo le-Massekhtot Avot ve-Avot de Rabbi Natan;* Judah Goldin, "The Two Versions of Abot de Rabbi Natan"; Anthony Saldarini, *Scholastic Rabbinism* and *The Fathers According to Rabbi Nathan (Abot de Rabbi Nathan) Version B.* Although ARN B had been dated to the seventh to ninth centuries, recent and persuasive arguments have redated it to the third century, a position that is broadly consensual: see Saldarini, *Fathers,* 10–14; H. L. Strack and G. Stemberger, *Introduction to the Talmud and Midrash,* 245–247; and M. B. Lerner, "The External Tractates," 367–403. Notes Saldarini, "These arguments only pertain to ARN as probably existing with approximately the same structure as it has now. It may have been in a much earlier and less extensive form. The argument does not automatically allow us to prove that any individual passage of ARN is from the Tannaitic period" (*Fathers,* 14). Lerner argues differently: "the final redaction of Avot de-R. Natan, version B took place in the Land of Israel in Amoraic times, probably towards the end of the third century. However, the bulk of the material is of decidedly earlier vintage" ("External Tractates," 377). Readers unfamiliar with these texts should be aware of the differences between ARN A and ARN B: ARN A relies on the mishnaic tractate Pirke Avot while ARN B relies upon a different version of that tractate, one regarded as earlier than the version incorporated in the Mishnah.

26. ARN B.21, beginning; commenting on Pirke Avot 1.10. On the fiction of "oral law" see the recent arguments by Martin Jaffee, "How Much 'Orality' in Oral Torah?"

27. On the popularity of the image that Adam ha-Rishon (the first man) worked to produce all his needs (in contrast to the putative laziness of "modern" men, who have all conveniences brought to them) see tBerahot 7.5 and parallels: "How long did the first man labor until he could don one simple garment? Until he sheared and cleaned and combed and dyed and spun and wove and sewed. Only after all this could he wear [the garment]. And I arise each morning and I find that all this [work has been done] for me."

28. *běnê 'ādām.* Saldarini translates the phrase as the gender-inclusive "human beings." I retain the masculine gendering of the phrase because it seems to represent more accurately the fact that gender and its distinctions were important to rabbis and should not be effaced through our practices of translation. On similar texts about women talking, see tKetubot 7.4, where the wife's reputation among the neighboring women is at issue.

29. The association of an idle man with hunger was widespread and long-standing. Proverbs 28.19: "One who cultivates the land has plenty to eat; idle pursuits lead to poverty"; 2 Thessalonians 3.10: "The man who will not work will not eat"; Pseudo-Phocylides 153–158: "Work hard so that you can live from your own means; for every idle man lives from what his hands can steal; [a craft maintains a man, but an idle man is oppressed by hunger]. Eat not the leavings of another man's meal, but eat without shame what you have earned yourself."

On the trope of the laboring male and the woman under surveillance see

tQiddushin 1.11: "And whoever does not have a trade—to what is he compared? To a woman who has a husband. Whether she ornaments herself or nor,
people don't stare at her. And if she doesn't ornament herself, [the husband]
curses her. And whoever does not have a trade—to what is he compared? To a
woman who has no husband. Whether she ornaments herself or not, everybody
stares at her. And if she doesn't ornament herself, he doesn't curse her."

30. tKetubot 4.9, mKetubot 7.6. See also Philo *Special Laws (Spec Leg)*
3.169–177, in which men belong in the marketplaces, council chambers, courts,
and open air gatherings, and women belong in the interior rooms of homes.
Women (*i.e.*, respectable women) should frequent the marketplace only when
absolutely necessary (on the way to or from a temple) and should choose times
when the marketplace is least crowded.

31. mBaba Kamma 8.6; ARN B.9 and 42; mKetubot 7.6.

32. The parallels drawn between male labor and female modesty have further ramifications for the interarticulation of work, sexuality, and gender (as
discussed in chapter 2). The formula that compares female modesty with male
labor also posits modesty—desisting from sexual promiscuity—as an aspect of
female labor. Thus, for women, modesty and sexual virtue comprise the surplus
value of their labor. In this formula, the category of worker is masculinized.
One result: a human is either a (male) worker or a woman. Productive or service
labor—that which helps a human attain food and drink—becomes different
from, but the equivalent to, female labors of modesty.

The widespread categorization of worker as male will present problems for
ARN A.11, as the text wends its way through elaborations of men and work,
and then afterward asks: What are the examples for women? As it is said, "Let
neither man nor woman make any more work for the offering of the Sanctuary"
(Exodus 36.3). And as to the children: "And the people were restrained from
bringing" (Exodus 36.6). The rabbinic text was aware that its operating definition of worker was "male worker." Both passages emerge from a similar discourse in which the equation of worker and man was invisible (i.e,, not articulated) yet operative nonetheless. Women and children are the additions, that
which is not automatically part of the definition.

33. The methodological implications are important. Law has been privileged as the mode for reconstructing and writing the history of Jewish religious
culture. Law has been used both to describe the details of lives lived or to document Jewish lives as a composite. The historical preferences of elite and educated rabbinic Jewish men, of course, should not continue to prescribe the values and presuppositions of those who write about rabbis.

34. de Certeau, "Scriptural Economy," 143.

35. R. E. Tringham, "Households with Faces: The Challenge of Gender in
Prehistoric Architectural Remains," in *Engendering Archaeology*, ed. Joan Gero
and Margaret Conkey, 93–94.

36. For information on the state of the Parthenon's reconstruction I thank
Jean O'Barr. See also Fitzgerald, "The Cult and Culture of Classical Sites: The
Parthenon Fiasco."

37. I wrote part of this chapter while living in Cedar Key, Florida, a very
small fishing village on the Gulf of Mexico. My daily walks through town,
punctuated with chats with neighbors, made clear the variety, amount, and

tenor of events and issues that never made it into the typeset pages of the local paper, *The Beacon*.

38. The seclusion of women was more likely a useful literary trope than a common practice, although I wish not to make too large a distinction between these two things, and of course the differences of economic access, architectural traditions, and class status would have much to do with the possibility of enacting the seclusion of women. On the physical enforcement of ideas about gendered space and the "protection" of women's sexuality, see Pseudo-Phocylides 215–216: "Guard a virgin in firmly locked rooms, and do not let her be seen before the house until her wedding day" or 2 Maccabees 3.19: "In the distressed city, women in sackcloth, their breasts bare, filled the streets; unmarried girls who were kept in seclusion ran to the gates or wall of their houses." See also Philo *In Flaccum* 89; 3 Maccabees 1.18–19; and 4 Maccabees 18.7.

EPILOGUE: BURYING SPINDLES WITH THE DEAD

1. On "home," see Laura Levitt, *Jews and Feminism: The Ambivalent Search for Home*.

2. In writing this epilogue I am indebted to ongoing and spirited conversations with my friends Rob Baird, Nadia Abu El-Haj, and Laura Levitt, and to discussions about women and antiquity with Rebecca McKee. Several books and articles have been indispensable to my process of framing this chapter, although they do not appear as specific citations: Amitav Ghosh, *In an Antique Land*; Michel-Rolph Trouillot, *Silencing the Past: Power and the Production of History*; Patricia Williams, *The Alchemy of Race and Rights*; and Amy Richlin's many writings.

3. The distinction between looking with and looking at comes from Caroline Walker Bynum, "Women's Stories, Women's Symbols": "What I am suggesting is exactly that Turner looks *at* women; he stands with the dominant group (males) and sees women (both as symbol and fact) as liminal to men. In this he is quite correct of course, and the insight is a powerful one. But it is not the whole story. The historian or anthropologist needs to stand *with* women as well" (33).

4. I cannot in a short paragraph do justice to this argument, which reaches to the key category constructions of Jewish Studies, and of history, religion, and the humanities more generally. See Howard Eilberg-Schwartz, *The Savage in Judaism*; Maurice Olender, *The Languages of Paradise: Race, Religion, and Philology in the Nineteenth Century*; Léon Poliakov, *The Aryan Myth: A History of Racist and Nationalist Ideas in Europe*; and Vassilis Lambropoulos, *The Rise of Eurocentrism: Anatomy of Interpretation*.

5. Nadia Abu El-Haj, *Excavating the Land, Creating the Homeland: Archaeology, the State, and the Making of History in Modern Jewish Nationalism*, and Albert Glock, "Archaeology as Cultural Survival: The Future of the Palestinian Past."

6. See Laurence Silberstein, "Toward a Postzionist Discourse," in Peskowitz and Levitt, *Judaism Since Gender*; Jonathan Boyarin, *Storm from Paradise: The Politics of Jewish Memory*; and David Myers, *Re-inventing the Jewish Past: European Jewish Intellectuals and the Zionist Return to History*.

7. Here and at every stage of this book, my everlasting gratitude goes to Laura Levitt and our ongoing conversations. For this argument I am particularly indebted to her essay "(The Problem With) Embraces." There she articulates what it might mean to engage Jewish Studies as a feminist practice. My thoughts have emerged from the discussions that preceded, accompanied, and resulted from her writing of that piece.

8. Pierre Bogaert, *Apocalypse de Baruch,* 1:222–241. In "2 (Syriac Apocalypse of) Baruch," 615–652, A. F. J. Klijn argues for its close links to rabbinic literature, based on the theological and metaphoric parallels discussed by Louis Ginzberg in "Baruch, Apocalypse of (Syriac)," 2.551–556.

9. On virgins spinning in the Temple, see also Protoevangelium of James, in W. Schneemelcher, ed., *New Testament Apocrypha,* 1:370–388, in which as a young girl, Mary, mother of Jesus, is chosen for this Temple service. On gold from Ophir, see I Kings 9.28, 10.11, 22.48; I Chronicles 29.4; II Chronicles 8.18; Job 22.24, Psalms 45.9, and Isaiah 13.12 ("I will make men more scarce than fine gold, more rare than gold of Ophir").

10. For references, see Miriam Peskowitz, "The Work of Her Hands," 252–257. On Iron age burials, see Elizabeth Bloch-Smith, *Judahite Burial Practices and Beliefs about the Dead,* 93.

11. Jerusalem: E. L. Sukenik, "Kever Yehudi Zafonit-Maarvit Le-yerushalayim," 122–124. Amman: G. L. Harding, "A Roman Family Tomb in Jebel Joph, Amman," 81–94. Meiron: Eric M. Meyers, James F. Strange, and Carol L. Meyers, *Excavations at Ancient Meiron,* 111 and 119 (Locus TI.5.3). Identification numbers for the whorls are IAA/Romema 80–429 and IAA/Romema 80–428 (viewed by permission of excavator). Silet edh-Dahr, near Nablus: O. R. Seller and D. C. Baramki, *A Roman-Byzantine Burial Cave in Northern Palestine,* 21–25; the contents described are from tomb 10, dated fifth to sixth centuries C.E. Naf: Varda Sussman, "A Tomb at Naḥf," 31–32; dated second to fourth centuries C.E.

The preceding examples comprise only a fraction of excavated grave goods from this region. For additional data, see unpublished author's notes, based on archival research at the Israel Antiquities Authority, Jerusalem. I thank Ruth Peled, Joe Zias, Maarva Baluka, and Orit Shamir of the IAA for their help. For additional technical details, I refer readers to Peskowitz, "The Work of Her Hands" (chap. 6) and a forthcoming technical article on spindle whorls. For comparison to these Palestinian grave goods, M. Capitanio, "La necropoli romana di Portorecanati," 142 ff., offers a grave-by-grave catalogue from a site in central Italy, dated first to second centuries C.E.

In general, grave goods have not been well studied. For Palestine see the following, on the practice of placing keys in graves, Shmuel Yeivin, "The Origin of an Ancient Jewish Burial Custom" and G. Alon, "Burial Customs in Early Israel." More recently, see Rachel Hachlili's reports on the Jericho excavations, and Rachel Hachlili and Ann Killebrew, "Was the Coin-on-Eye Custom a Jewish Burial Practice in the Second Temple Period?" and responses. On the broader context of funerary rites, see Eric M. Meyers, *Jewish Ossuaries;* the research of Amos Kloner; and the brief synthetic article by Ze'ev Weiss, "Social Aspects of Burial in Beth She'arim: Archaeological Finds and Talmudic Sources," in Lee

Levine, ed., *The Galilee in Late Antiquity,* 357–371. More comparatively, see Walter Burkert, *Greek Religion,* 192.

12. Contra Rachel Hachlili. Grave goods have been feminized through modern discourse. See my argument in "The Burial of Gender and the Gendering of Burial" (forthcoming).

13. On minor objects, see the critique of M. J. Chavane, *Salamine de Chypre,* 6:1–2.

14. The rods were often made of perishable wood and in most burial contexts only the whorls survive, since they were made of more durable materials. The whorls measure roughly 25 centimeters in diameter, are 1 to 2 centimeters high, and weigh usually between 11 and 22 grams.

15. See Siegfried Lauffer, ed. *Diokletian's Preisedikt.* English translation in E. R. Graser, ed., "The Edict of Diocletian on Maximum Prices," in Tenney Frank, *Economic Survey of Ancient Rome,* vol. 5. On spindles and whorls, see 13.5–6; needles, 16.9, wine, 2.2; eggs, 6.43; pomegranates, 6.71; stone mason, 7.2; weaver, 21.1–6.

16. Digest 11.7.14.5.

17. Europe: J. P. Wild, *Textile Manufacture in the Northern Roman Provinces.* Amman: Harding, "A Roman Tomb in Amman," 30–32; 2 steatite whorls, one from loculus C18, one from tomb floor J46. Pella: R. H. Smith, *Pella of the Decapolis,* 1:187; 2 whorls, dated second to fourth centuries C.E. Whorl 78:316 was the only remnant of grave goods found in grave 3. Whorl 78:318 was found in grave 1, with a lamp. Cyprus: J. du Plat Taylor, "Roman Tombs at 'Kambi,' Vasa." Glass spindle whorls were excavated amid large quantities of grave goods, dated third to fourth centuries C.E. Meroe: John Garstang, *Meroe: The City of the Ethiopians,* 47; the dating of the tombs includes a large span of centuries. See John W. Crowfoot, "Christian Nubia," 150; black-clay whorls were found, both baked and unbaked. The whorls are decorated, but the excavator does not describe the decorations.

18. See Sandra Joshel, *Work, Identity, and Legal Status at Rome.*

19. Rome, dated to the Flavian period. Translated by Richard Lattimore in his *Themes in Greek and Latin Epigraphs,* 298. The epitaph is replete with difficult readings, but the sections significant to my argument are relatively secure.

20. CIL 1.2.1211.

21. CIL 6.11602, translated by Natalie Kampen in her *Image and Status,* 122–123.

22. F. Noack, "Dorylaion. II. Grabreliefs," 315–334, esp. 322–323 and figs. 4–5. See Michael Rostovtzeff, *Social and Economic History of the Roman Empire,* pl. 46.2. In *Hellenica* 10:249, L. Roberts lists similar decoration found on steles in the eastern parts of Lydia, in Phrygia, and in Bithynie, as also reported by Paul Trebilco, *Jewish Communities in Asia Minor,* 61. See A. Joubin, "Stèles funéraires de Phrygie."

23. Roberts, *Hellenica* 10:249, pl. 33. Also, W. H. Buckler and W. M. Calder, eds., *Monumenta Asiae Minoris Antiqua,* 6:116, no. 335a, and Trebilco, *Jewish Communities,* 61, n.14.

24. Buckler and Calder, *Monumenta Asiae Minoris Antiqua,* 6:113–114, no. 325. The inscription is identified as "Jewish" through language that seems

biblically influenced, but the stone does not contain conventionally "Christian" designations; this identification could be easily challenged. See *Bulletin de Correspondence Hellenique* 17 (1893): 273, no. 63 and W. M. Ramsay, *Cities and Bishoprics of Phrygia* (Oxford: Clarendon Press, 1895–1897), 615, no. 526.

25. Hava Weissler reminds me that not all attempts to "find women" and to salvage ancient images assume that women share an essential identity.

26. A burial from sixth-century Beth Shean may provide evidence of spindles being buried with men. However, the conditions of excavation and reporting render it difficult to interpret. One spindle whorl was found in a tomb along with other grave goods. The tomb is enclosed by edifice K. On the outside of the south wall of edifice K is an inscription that contains a prayer for the exprefect John, who, according to the tomb's excavator, "may be supposed to have built the monument as a burial-place for himself." If this is the grave of John, then we are presented with an example of a whorl being buried with a male skeleton. However, the grave contained bones and two skulls, one set above the other. The excavator posits the second burial (denoted by the second skull) to have been placed in the tomb at a much later date than the seventh-century burial of John (if John were indeed buried in this tomb). The report does not detail the precise burial with which the various grave goods were associated. Nor have the bones been analyzed to determine the biological sex of the skeletons in question. These ambiguities make the evidence of Beth Shean such that one can neither challenge nor confirm the association of whorls exclusively with the burial of women and girls. On Beth Shean see G. M. Fitzgerald, *A Sixth-Century Monastery at Beth-Shan (Scythopolis)*, 4, 11, 14. Because of the patterns and politics of excavation, there are, in fact, no examples of single burials that include both spindles/spindle whorls and skeletal bones positively identified as female.

27. Meyers et al., *Excavations at Ancient Meiron*.

28. Or as Ross Kraemer aptly puts it in *Her Share of the Blessings,* religious women in antiquity were stuck "between a rock and a hard place."

29. Moshe Malka, responsa of 7 Shvat 5733 to Azriel Licht. I thank Susan Shapiro for bringing this responsa to my attention.

References and Select Bibliography

Aberbach, Moshe. *Labor, Crafts and Commerce in Ancient Israel.* Jerusalem: Magnes Press, 1994.

Abu El-Haj, Nadia. "Excavating the Land, Creating the Homeland: Archaeology, the State, and the Making of History in Modern Jewish Nationalism." Ph.D. diss., Duke University, 1995.

Adan-Bayewitz, David. "The Itinerant Peddler in Roman Palestine." In *Jews in Economic Life: Collected Essays in Memory of Arkadias Kahan (1920–1982),* ed. Nachum Gross. Jerusalem: Zalman Shazar Center for the Furtherance of the Study of Jewish History, 1985.

———. *Common Pottery in Roman Galilee: A Study of Local Trade.* Ramat-Gan, Israel: Bar-Ilan University Press, 1993.

Adler, Eliyana, and Deborah Budner. "Take Back the Shuk! Approaches to Images and Realities of Jewish Women in the Ancient Market-place." Unpublished paper, Brandeis University, 1994.

Agrell, Goran. *Work, Toil, and Sustenance: An Examination of the View of Work in the New Testament, Taking into Consideration Views Found in Old Testament, Intertestamental, and Early Rabbinic Writings.* Stockholm: Verbum, 1976.

Aharoni, Yohanan. "The Caves of Nahal Hever." ʿAtiqot, English ser., 3 (1961): 148–75.

Albeck, Hanoch. *Shisheh Sidre Mishnah.* Jerusalem: Mosad Bialik, 1958.

Alcalay, Ammiel. *After Jews and Arabs: Remaking Levantine Culture.* Minneapolis: University of Minnesota Press, 1993.

Alon, Gedalia. "Burial Customs in Early Israel" (in Hebrew). *Bulletin of the Jewish Palestine Exploration Society* 9 (1941): 107–12.

———. *Toldot ha-Yehudim be-Erets-Yisrael bi-tekufat ha-Mishnah veha-Talmud* (translated as *The Jews in Their Land in the Talmudic Age*). Jerusalem: Magnes Press, 1989.

Andersen, F. G. *Shiloh. The Danish Excavations at Tall Sailun, Palestine in 1926, 1929, 1932 and 1963.* Vol. 2, *The Remains from the Hellenistic to the Mamluk Periods.* Copenhagen: The National Museum of Denmark, 1985.

Applebaum, Shimon. "Economic Life in Palestine." In *The Jewish People in the First Century,* vol. 2, ed. Shmuel Safrai and Menahem Stern. Philadelphia: Fortress Press, 1976.

———. "Judaea as a Roman Province: The Countryside as a Political and Economic Factor." In *Aufsteig und Neidergang der Römischen Welt* 2.8. Berlin: de Gruyter, 1977.

———. "Syria-Palaestina as a Province of the Severan Empire." In *Judaea in Hellenistic and Roman Times: Historical and Archaeological Essays.* Leiden: Brill, 1989.

Apuleius. *Metamorphoses.* 2 vols. Cambridge, Mass.: Harvard University Press, 1989.

Archer, Léonie. "The Role of Jewish Women in the Religion, Ritual and Cult of Graeco-Roman Palestine." In *Images of Women in Antiquity,* ed. A. Cameron and A. Kuhrt. Detroit: Wayne State University Press, 1983.

———. "The Virgin and the Harlot in the Writings of Formative Judaism." *History Workshop* 24 (1987): 1–16.

———. *Her Price Is Beyond Rubies: The Jewish Woman in Graeco-Roman Palestine.* Sheffield: Sheffield Academic Press, 1990.

Archer, Léonie, Susan Fischler, and Maria Wyke, eds. *Women in Ancient Societies: "An Illusion of the Night."* New York: Routledge, 1994.

Arendt, Hannah. *The Human Condition: A Study of the Central Dilemmas Facing Modern Man.* New York: Doubleday, 1959.

———. "Thinking and Moral Consideration." *Social Research* 38 (1971).

Artemidorus Daldianus. *Oneirokritika (The Interpretation of Dreams).* Trans. Robert White, *The Interpretation of Dreams, by Artemidorus. Translation and Commentary.* Torrance, Calif.: Original Books, 1990 [1975].

Asad, Talal. *Genealogies of Religion: Discipline and Reasons of Power in Christianity and Islam.* Baltimore, Md.: Johns Hopkins University Press, 1993.

Avi-Yonah, Michael. "Trade, Industry and Crafts in Palestine." *Antiquity Library of Palestinology* 9–10 (1937): 94–98.

———. *The Holy Land from the Persian to the Arab Conquests (536 B.C. to A.D. 640): A Historical Geography.* Grand Rapids, Mich.: Baker Book House, 1966.

———. *The Jews of Palestine: A Political History from the Bar Kokhba War to the Arab Conquest.* New York: Schocken, 1976.

Ayali, Meir. *Otsar kinuye ovdim be-sifrut ha-Talmud veha-Midrash (A Nomenclature of Workers and Artisans in the Talmudic and Midrashic Literature).* Tel Aviv: ha-Kibuts ha-Meuhad, 1984.

Babbitt, F. C. *Plutarch's Moralia.* Vol. 4. Cambridge, Mass.: Harvard University Press, 1972.

Bagatti, Bellarmino. *Excavations in Nazareth.* Jerusalem: Franciscan Press, 1969.

Bagatti, Bellarmino, and J. T. Milik. *Gli Scavi del "Dominus Flevit."* Jerusalem: Studium Biblicum Franciscanum, 1958.

Baird, Robert J. *Inventing Religion in the Western Imaginary.* Princeton: Princeton University Press, forthcoming.

Balch, David. *Let Wives Be Submissive: The Domestic Code in 1 Peter.* Atlanta, Ga.: Scholars Press, 1981.

———. "Household Codes." In *Greco-Roman Literature and the New Testament,* ed. David Aune. Atlanta, Ga.: Scholars Press, 1988.

Balsdon, J. P. V. D. *Roman Women: Their History and Habits.* New York: Barnes & Noble Books, 1983 [1962].

Bamberger, B. "Qetanah, Na'arah, Bogereth." *Hebrew Union College Annual* 32 (1961): 281–94.

Baramki, Dimitri. "Note on a Cemetery at Karm al-Shaikh, Jerusalem." *Quarterly of the Department of Antiquities of Palestine* 1 (1932): 3–10.

Baras, Zvi, et al. *Eretz Israel from the Destruction of the Second Temple to the Muslim Conquest* (in Hebrew). Jerusalem: Yad Izhak ben Zvi, 1982.

Barber, E. J. W. *Prehistoric Textiles: The Development of Cloth in the Neolithic and Bronze Ages with Special Reference to the Aegean.* Princeton: Princeton University Press, 1991.

———. *Women's Work, The First 20,000 Years: Women, Cloth and Society in Early Times.* New York: W. W. Norton, 1994.

Baron, Ava, ed. *Work Engendered: Toward a New History of American Labor.* Ithaca: Cornell University Press, 1991.

Barrett, Michèle. "Ideology and the Cultural Production of Gender." In *Feminist Criticism and Social Change. Sex, Class and Race in Literature and Culture,* ed. Judith Newton and Deborah Rosenfelt. New York: Methuen, 1985.

———. *Women's Oppression Today: The Marxist/Feminist Encounter.* London: Verso, 1988 [1980].

Baskin, Judith. "The Separation of Women in Rabbinic Judaism." In *Women, Religion, and Social Change,* ed. Yvonne Yazbeck Haddad and Ellison Banks Findly. Albany: State University of New York Press, 1985.

———. "Silent Voices: Women as Wives in Rabbinic Literature." In *Active Voices: Women in Jewish Culture,* ed. Maurie Sacks. Urbana: University of Illinois Press, 1995.

Baskin, Judith., ed. *Jewish Women in Historical Perspective.* Detroit: Wayne State University Press, 1991.

Ben-David, Arye. *Talmudische Okonomie. Die Wirtschaft des Judischen Palastina zur Zeit der Mischna und des Talmud.* Hildesheim: Georg Olms, 1974.

Bendinelli, Goffredo. "An Underground Tomb with Important Fresco Decoration Recently Discovered in Rome," *Art and Archaeology* 11 (1921): 169–72.

Benjamin, Walter. *Illuminations: Essays and Reflections.* Ed. Hannah Arendt. New York: Schocken, 1968.

Bennett, Judith. "'History That Stands Still': Women's Work in the European Past." *Feminist Studies* 14 (1988): 269–83.

———. "Feminism and History." *Gender and History* 1 (1989): 251–72.

Benoit, Pierre, J. T. Milik, and Roland de Vaux. *Discoveries in the Judaean Desert.* Vol. 2, *Les Grottes de Murabbaat. Planches.* Oxford: Clarendon Press, 1961.

Berger, Adolf. *Encyclopedic Dictionary of Roman Law.* Philadelphia: American Philosophical Society, 1980 [1952].

Berman, Saul. "The Status of Women in Halakhic Judaism." *Tradition* 14 (1973): 5–28.

Bernstein, Michael André. *Foregone Conclusions: Against Apocalyptic History.* Berkeley and Los Angeles: University of California Press, 1994.

Biale, Rachel. *Women and Jewish Law: An Exploration of Women's Issues in Halakhic Sources.* New York: Schocken, 1984.

Birks, Peter, and Grant McLeod. *Justinian's Institutes.* Ithaca: Cornell University Press, 1987.

Blackman, Phillip. *Mishnayot.* London: Judaica Press, 1990 [1963].

Blanckenhagen, Peter Heinrich von. *Flavische Architektur und ihre Dekoration Untersucht am Nervaforum.* Berlin: Mann, 1940.

Bland, Kalman. "Medievals Are Not Us." *Shofar* 14 (1995): 35–44.

Bloch-Smith, Elizabeth. *Judahite Burial Practices and Beliefs about the Dead.* Sheffield: Sheffield Academic Press, 1992.

Blok, Josine and Peter Mason. *Sexual Asymmetry: Studies in Ancient Society.* Amsterdam: Glieben, 1987.

Blümner, Hugo. *Technologie und Terminologie in der Gewerbe und Künste bei Griechen und Römern.* 4 vols. New York: Arno Press, 1979 [Leipzig: B. G. Teubner, 1875–1887].

Boardman, John, and Donna Kurtz. *Greek Burial Customs.* London: Thames and Hudson, 1971.

Boatwright, M. T. "The Imperial Women of the Early Second Century A.D." *American Journal of Philology* 112 (1991): 513–40.

Bogaert, Pierre. *Apocalypse de Baruch, introduction, traduction du Syriaque et commentaire.* 2 vols. Paris: Cerf, 1969.

Bokser, Baruch. "Rabbinic Responses to Catastrophe: From Continuity to Discontinuity." *Proceedings of the American Academy for Jewish Research* 50 (1983): 37–61.

Bottini, A., and E. Greco. "Tomba a camera dal territorio pestano: alcune considerazioni sulla posizioni della donna." *Dialoghi di Archeologia* 8 (1974–75): 231–74.

Bowersock, Glen. *Hellenism in Late Antiquity.* Ann Arbor: University of Michigan Press, 1990.

Boyarin, Daniel. *Intertextuality and the Reading of the Midrash.* Bloomington: Indiana University Press, 1990.

———. *Carnal Israel: Reading Sex in Talmudic Culture.* Berkeley and Los Angeles: University of California Press, 1993.

———. *A Radical Jew: Paul and the Politics of Identity.* Berkeley and Los Angeles: University of California Press, 1994.

Boyarin, Jonathan. *Storm from Paradise: The Politics of Jewish Memory.* Minneapolis: University of Minnesota Press, 1992.

Bradley, Keith. "Sexual Regulations in Wet-Nursing Contracts from Roman Egypt," *Klio* 62 (1980): 321–5.

———. "Wet-Nursing at Rome: A Study in Social Relations." In *The Family in Ancient Rome,* ed. Beryl Rawson. London: Croom Helm, 1986.

——. *Discovering the Roman Family: Studies in Roman Social History.* New York: Oxford University Press, 1991.

Brayer, Menachem. *The Jewish Woman in Rabbinic Literature: A Psychosocial Perspective.* 2 vols. Hoboken, N.J.: Ktav, 1986.

Brommer, Frank. *Vasenlisten zur griechischen Heldensage.* Marburg: N. G. Elwert, 1973.

Brooten, Bernadette. *Women Leaders in the Ancient Synagogue: Inscriptional Evidence and Background Issues.* Atlanta, Ga.: Scholars Press, 1982.

——. "Early Christian Women and Their Historical Contexts. Issues of Method in Historical Reconstruction." In *Feminist Perspectives on Biblical Scholarship,* ed. A. Y. Collins. Atlanta, Ga.: Scholars Press, 1985.

——. "Jewish Women's History in the Roman Period: A Task for Roman Theology." *Harvard Theological Review* 79 (1986): 22–30.

Brown, Cheryl Anne. *No Longer Be Silent: First Century Jewish Portraits of Biblical Women.* Louisville, Ky.: Westminster/John Knox Press, 1992.

Brown, Judith. "A Note on the Division of Labor by Sex." *American Anthropologist* 72 (1970): 1073–78.

Brown, Peter. *The World of Late Antiquity,* A.D. *150–170.* London: Harcourt Brace Jovanovich, 1971.

Buber, S. *Midrasch Mischle.* Warsaw, 1893.

Büchler, Adolf. *The Political and the Social Leaders of the Jewish Community in Sepphoris in the Second and Third Centuries.* Oxford: Hart at the University Press, 1909.

——. *The Economic Conditions of Judaea after the Destruction of the Second Temple.* London: Jews College Publications, 1912.

Buckler, W. H., and W. M. Calder, eds. *Monumenta Asiae Minoris Antiqua.* Vol. 6, *Monuments and Documents from Phrygia and Caria.* Manchester: Manchester University Press, 1939.

Bulz, E. "The Earnings of Women According to Jewish Rabbinical Jurisdiction." *Proceedings of the Fifth World Congress of Jewish Studies.* Jerusalem: World Congress of Jewish Studies, 1972.

Burford, Alison. *Craftsmen in Greek and Roman Society.* Ithaca: Cornell University Press, 1972.

Burkert, Walter. *Greek Religion.* Cambridge, Mass.: Harvard University Press, 1985.

Burnley, James. *The History of Wool and Wool-Combing.* New York: A. M. Kelly, 1969 [1889].

Butler, Judith. *Gender Trouble: Feminism and the Subversion of Identity.* New York: Routledge, 1990.

——. "Against Proper Objects." *Differences* 6.2–3 (1994): 1–26.

Butler, Judith, and Joan W. Scott, eds. *Feminists Theorize the Political.* New York: Routledge, 1992.

Bynum, Caroline Walker. "Introduction: The Complexity of Symbols." In *Gender and Religion: On the Complexity of Symbols,* ed. Caroline Walker Bynum, Stevan Harrell, and Paula Richman. Boston: Beacon Press, 1986.

——. "Women's Stories, Women's Symbols: A Critique of Victor Turner's Theory of Liminality." In *Fragmentation and Redemption: Essays on Gen-*

der and the Human Body in Medieval Religion. New York: Zone Books, 1992.

———. "Why All the Fuss about the Body: A Medievalist's Perspective." *Critical Inquiry* 22 (1995): 1–33.

Camp, Claudia. *Wisdom and the Feminine in the Book of Proverbs.* Decatur, Ga.: Almond Press, 1985.

Cantarella, Eve. *Pandora's Daughters: The Role and Status of Women in Greek and Roman Antiquity.* Baltimore, Md.: Johns Hopkins University Press, 1987.

Capitanio, M. "La necropoli romana di Portorecanati," *Notizie degli Scavi* 28 (1974): 142 ff.

Carroll, D. L. "Dating the Foot-Powered Loom: The Coptic Evidence." *American Journal of Archaeology* 89 (1985): 168–73.

———. *Looms and Textiles of the Copts.* San Francisco: California Academy of Sciences, 1988.

Casson, Lionel. *Travel in the Ancient World.* Baltimore, Md.: Johns Hopkins University Press, 1994 [1974].

Castelli, Elizabeth. "Virginity and Its Meaning for Women's Sexuality in Early Christianity." *Journal of Feminist Studies in Religion* 2 (1986): 61–88.

———. *Imitating Paul: A Discourse of Power.* Louisville, Ky.: Westminster/John Knox Press, 1991.

Chakrabarty, Dipesh. "Postcoloniality and the Artifice of History: Who Speaks for "Indian" Pasts?" *Representations* 37 (1992): 1–26.

Chapkis, Wendy, and Cynthia Enloe. *Of Common Cloth: Women in the Global Textile Industry.* Amsterdam and Washington, D.C.: Transnational Institute, 1983.

Chavane, M.-J. *Salamine de Chypre.* Vol. 6, *Les Petits Objets.* Paris: Diffusion de Boccard, 1975.

Clark, Gillian. *Women in Antiquity: Pagan and Christian Life-Styles.* New York: Oxford University Press, 1993.

Clarke, E. G. *Targum Pseudo-Jonathan of the Pentateuch: Text and Concordance.* Hoboken, N.J.: Ktav, 1984.

Cohen, Beth, ed. *The Distaff Side: Representing the Female in Homer's Odyssey.* New York: Oxford University Press, 1995.

Cohen, Boaz. *Mishnah and Tosefta: A Comparative Study. Part I: Shabbat.* New York: Jewish Theological Seminary of America, 1935.

———. "Usufruct in Jewish and Roman Law." *Revue Internationale des Droits de l'Antiquite* 1 (1954): 173–93.

———. *Jewish and Roman Law: A Comparative Study.* 2 vols. New York: Jewish Theological Seminary of America, 1966.

Cohen, Shaye J. D. "Epigraphical Rabbis." *Jewish Quarterly Review* 72 (1981): 1–17.

———. "The Destruction: From Scripture to Midrash." *Prooftexts* 2 (1982): 18–39.

———. "The Origins of the Matrilineal Principle in Rabbinic Law." *Association for Jewish Studies Review* 10 (1985): 19–53.

———. *From the Maccabees to the Mishnah.* Louisville, Ky.: Westminster/John Knox Press, 1987.

——. "'Those Who Say They Are Jews and Are Not': How Do You Know a Jew in Antiquity When You See One?" In *Diasporas in Antiquity*, ed. Shaye J. D. Cohen and Ernest Frerichs. Atlanta, Ga.: Scholars Press, 1993.

Cohen, Shaye J. D, ed. *The Jewish Family in Antiquity*. Atlanta, Ga.: Scholars Press, 1993.

Colt, H. D. *Excavations at Nessana (Auja Hafir, Palestine) 1936-1937*. London: British School of Archaeology in Jerusalem, 1962.

Conder, Claude Reignier, and Horatio Herbert Kitchener. *The Survey of Western Palestine: Memoirs of the Topography, Orthography, Hydrography and Archaeology*. 7 vols. London: Committee of the Palestine Exploration Fund, 1881-1883.

Conkey, Margaret W., and Spector, Joan D. "Archaeology and the Study of Gender." *Advances in Archaeological Method and Theory* 7 (1984): 1-38.

Conte, Gian Biagio. *Genres and Readers: Lucretius' Love Elegy and Pliny's Encyclopedia*. Trans. Glenn W. Most. Baltimore, Md.: Johns Hopkins University Press, 1994.

Corpus Inscriptionum Latinarum (abbreviated as CIL). Berlin: Berolini, apud Reimerum, 1862.

Corte, Matteo della. *Case ed abitanti di Pompei*. Rome, 1954 [Valle de Pompei: Sicignano, 1927].

Courtney, Edward. *A Commentary on the Satires of Juvenal*. London: Athlone Press, 1980.

Crowfoot, Elizabeth. "Textiles." In *Discoveries in the Wadi ed-Daliyeh*, ed. Paul W. Lapp and Nancy Lapp. Cambridge, Mass.: American Schools of Oriental Research, 1974.

Crowfoot, Grace M. *Methods of Hand-Spinning in Egypt and the Sudan*. Halifax: Bankfield Museum Notes, 1931.

——. "Of the Warp-Weighted Loom." *Annual of the British School at Athens* 37 (1936): 36-47.

——. "The Vertical Loom in Palestine and Syria." *Palestine Exploration Quarterly* (1945): 141-51.

——. "Linen Textiles from the Cave of Ain Feshka in the Jordan Valley." *Palestine Exploration Quarterly* (1951): 5-31.

Crowfoot, John W. "Christian Nubia." *Journal of Egyptian Archaeology* 13 (1927): 141-50.

Crowfoot, John W., Grace M. Crowfoot, and Kathleen Kenyon. *Samaria-Sebaste*. Vol. 3, *The Objects from Samaria*. London: Palestine Exploration Fund, 1957.

Crowfoot, John W., and Gerald Milnes Fitzgerald. *Excavations in the Tyropoeon Valley, Jerusalem, 1927*. London: Palestine Exploration Fund, 1929.

Curchin, Leonard. "Men of the Cloth: Reflexions on the Roman Linen Trade, Based on a New Document from Bordeaux." *Liverpool Classical Monthly* 10 (1985): 34-35.

Currie, H. M. "The Poems of Sulpicia." In *Aufsteig und Neidergang der Römischen Welt* 2.30.3. Berlin: de Gruyter, 1983.

Dalman, Gustaf. *Arbeit und Sitte in Palästina*. Gutersloh: Bertelsmann, 1937.

d'Ambra, Eve. *Private Lives, Imperial Virtues: The Frieze of the Forum Transitorium in Rome.* Princeton: Princeton University Press, 1993.

Danby, Herbert. *The Mishnah.* London: Oxford University Press, 1933.

Dar, Shimon. "Horvat Sumaqa—Settlement from the Roman and Byzantine Periods in the Carmel." *Bulletin of the Anglo-Israel Archaeological Society* 8 (1988): 34–48.

Daremberg, Charles, and Edmond Saglio. *Dictionnaire des Antiquites Grecques et Romaines.* Paris: Hachette, 1877–1919.

Daube, David. *Collaboration with Tyranny in Rabbinic Law.* London: Oxford University Press, 1965.

———. "Texts and Interpretation in Roman and Jewish Law." In *Essays in Greco-Roman and Related Talmudic Literature,* ed. H. Fischel. Hoboken, N.J.: Ktav, 1977.

———. "Johanan ben Beroqa and Women's Rights." In *Zeitschrift der Savignystiftung fur Rechtsgeschichte,* ed. Th. Mayer-Maly et al. Vienna: Hermann Bohlaus, 1982.

Dauphin, Claude, and J. Schonfield. "Settlements of the Roman and Byzantine Periods on the Golan Heights: Preliminary Report on Three Seasons of Survey (1979–1981)." *Israel Exploration Journal* 33 (1983): 189–206.

Davidman, Lynn, and Shelly Tenenbaum, eds. *Feminist Perspectives on Jewish Studies.* New Haven: Yale University Press, 1994.

Davidson, G. R. *Corinth.* Vol. 12, *The Minor Objects.* Princeton: American Schools of Classical Studies at Athens, 1952.

Davis, Dona. "When Men Become 'Women': Gender Antagonism and the Changing Sexual Geography of Work in Newfoundland." *Sex Roles* 29 (1993): 457–76.

Davis, Joseph. "Literary Studies of Aggadic Narrative: A Bibliography." In *New Perspectives in Ancient Judaism,* vol.3, ed. Jacob Neusner. Lanham, Md.: University Press of America, 1987.

de Certeau, Michel. *The Practice of Everyday Life.* Berkeley and Los Angeles: University of California Press, 1984.

de Lauretis, Teresa. *Technologies of Gender.* Bloomington: Indiana University Press, 1987.

Derrida, Jacques. "Devant la Loi." Trans. Avital Ronell. In *Kafka and the Contemporary Critical Performance: Centenary Readings,* ed. Alan Udoff. Bloomington: Indiana University Press, 1987.

Destro, Adriana. *The Law of Jealousy: The Anthropology of Sotah.* Atlanta, Ga.: Scholars Press, 1989.

Diogenes Laertius. *Lives of Eminent Philosophers.* 2 vols. London: William Heinemann, 1925.

Dionysus of Halicarnassus. *Roman Antiquities (Antiquitates Romanae).* 7 vols. Cambridge, Mass.: Harvard University Press, 1937.

Dixon, Suzanne. "Polybius on Roman Women and Property." *American Journal of Philology* 106 (1985): 147–70.

———. *The Roman Mother.* Norman: University of Oklahoma Press, 1988.

———. *The Roman Family.* Baltimore, Md.: Johns Hopkins University Press, 1992.

Dominguez, Virginia. "Invoking Culture: The Messy Side of 'Cultural Politics.'" In *Eloquent Obsessions: Writing Cultural Criticism,* ed. Marianna Torgovnick. Durham, N.C.: Duke University Press, 1994.

Dothan, Moshe. *Hammath Tiberias: Early Synagogues and the Hellenistic and Roman Remains.* Jerusalem: Israel Exploration Society, University of Haifa, and the Israel Department of Antiquities and Museums, 1983.

Douzinas, Costas, and Ronnie Warrington with Shaun McVeigh. *Postmodern Jurisprudence: The Law of Text in the Texts of Law.* New York: Routledge, 1991.

Downey, G. "Libanius' Oration in Praise of Antioch (Oration XI)." *Proceedings of the American Philosophical Society* 103 (1959): 652–86.

Dupont, Florence. *Daily Life in Ancient Rome (La vie quotidienne du citoyen romain sous la République).* Oxford: Basil Blackwell, 1992 [1989].

Durry, Marcel, ed. *Eloge funèbre d'une matrone romaine.* Paris: Budé, 1950.

Ebert, Teresa L. "Ludic Feminism, the Body, Performance, and Labor: Bringing Materialism Back into Feminist Cultural Studies." *Cultural Critique* 23 (1992–1993): 5–50.

———. *Ludic Feminism and After: Postmodernism, Desire and Labor in Late Capitalism.* Ann Arbor: University of Michigan Press, 1996.

Eichenauer, Monika. *Untersuchungen zur Arbeitswelt der Frau in der Romsichen Antike.* Frankfurt am Main: P. Lang, 1988.

Eilberg-Schwartz, Howard. *The Savage in Judaism: An Anthropology of Israelite Religion and Ancient Judaism.* Bloomington: Indiana University Press, 1990.

———. "People of the Body: The Problem of the Body for the People of the Book." *Journal of the History of Sexuality* 2 (1991): 1–25.

Eilberg-Schwartz, Howard, and Wendy Doniger, eds. *Off with Her Head! The Denial of Women's Identity in Myth, Religion, and Culture.* Berkeley and Los Angeles: University of California Press, 1995.

Eitan, Avraham. "Excavations at the Foot of Tel Rosh Ha'ayin." *ʿAtiqot,* Hebrew ser., 5 (1969): 49–68.

Elman, Yaacov. *Authority and Tradition: Toseftan Baraitot in Talmudic Babylonia.* New York: Yeshiva University Press, 1994.

Epstein, Louis. *The Jewish Marriage Contract: A Study in the Status of the Woman in Jewish Law.* New York: Jewish Theological Seminary of America, 1927.

———. *Marriage Laws in the Bible and Talmud.* Cambridge, Mass.: Harvard University Press, 1942.

———. *Sex Laws and Customs in Judaism.* New York: Bloch Publishing, 1948.

Falk, Ze'ev. "Mutual Obligation in the Ketubah." *Journal of Jewish Studies* 7 (1957): 215–17.

———. *Introduction to Jewish Law of the Second Commonwealth.* Leiden: Brill, 1978.

Fantham, Elaine, Helene Peet Foley, Natalie Boymel Kampen, Sarah Pomeroy, and H. A. Shapiro. *Women in the Classical World: Image and Text.* New York: Oxford University Press, 1994.

Felson-Rubin, Nancy. "Behind the Poet's Back: Characters Who Spin." In *Tex-*

tual Fidelity and Textual Disregard, ed. Bernard Dauenhauer. New York: Peter Lang, 1990.

———. *Regarding Penelope: From Character to Poetics.* Princeton: Princeton University Press, 1994.

Ferguson, Kathy. *The Man Question: Visions of Subjectivity in Feminist Theory.* Berkeley and Los Angeles: University of California Press, 1993.

Fiensy, David. *The Social History of Palestine in the Herodian Period: The Land Is Mine.* Lewiston, N.Y.: Edwin Mellen Press, 1991.

Fildes, Valerie. *Wet-nursing: A History from Antiquity to the Present.* Oxford and New York: Basil Blackwell, 1988.

Finkelstein, Louis. *Mabo le-Massekhtot Abot we-Abot de Rabbi Natan.* New York: Jewish Theological Seminary of America, 1950.

Fitzgerald, G. M. *A Sixth-Century Monastery at Beth-Shan (Scythopolis).* Philadelphia: University of Pennsylvania Press, 1939.

Fitzgerald, Gerald. "The Cult and Culture of Classical Sites: The Parthenon Fiasco." *Public Culture* 8 (1995): 177–85.

Flesher, Paul V. M. "Are Women Property in the System of the Mishnah?" In *From Ancient Israel to Modern Judaism,* vol. 1, ed. Jacob Neusner, Ernest Freirichs, and Nahum Sarna. Atlanta, Ga.: Scholars Press, 1988.

Forbes, R. J. *Studies in Ancient Technology.* Vol. 4. Leiden: Brill, 1964.

Foucault, Michel. *The History of Sexuality,* vols. 1, 3. New York: Vintage Books, 1980.

———. "The Eye of Power." In *Power/Knowledge: Selected Interviews and Other Writings (1972–1977).* New York: Pantheon Books, 1980.

Fraade, Steven. *From Tradition to Commentary: Torah and Its Interpretation in the Midrash Sifre to Deuteronomy.* Albany: State University of New York Press, 1991.

Frank, Tenney. *Economic Survey of Ancient Rome.* 6 vols. Baltimore, Md.: Johns Hopkins University Press, 1940.

Frazer, J. G. *Pausanias's Description of Greece.* 2 vols. New York: Biblio and Tannen, 1965.

Frey, Jean-Baptiste, ed. *Corpus Inscriptionum Iudaicarum.* Rome: Institute of Christian Archaeology, 1952 [1936].

Friedman, Mordechai A. *Jewish Marriage in Palestine: A Cairo Geniza Study.* Tel Aviv and New York: Jewish Theological Seminary of America, 1980.

Friedman, Theodore. "The Shifting Role of Women: From the Bible to Talmud." *Judaism* 36 (1987): 479–87.

———. "Babatha's Ketubba: Some Preliminary Observations." *Israel Exploration Journal* 46 (1996): 55–77.

Frymer-Kensky, Tikva. "The Strange Case of the Suspected Sotah (Numbers 5.11–31)." *Vetus Testamentum* 34 (1984): 11–26.

Furtwängler, Adolf. *Griechische Vasenmalerai.* Munich: Bruckmann, 1932.

Gafni, Isaiah. "The Institution of Marriage in Rabbinic Times." In *The Jewish Family: Metaphor and Memory,* ed. David Kraemer. New York: Oxford University Press, 1989.

Gal, Zvi. "Loom Weights or Jar Stoppers?" *Israel Exploration Journal* 39 (1989): 281–83.

Gardner, Jane, and Thomas Wiedemann. *The Roman Household: A Sourcebook.* New York: Routledge, 1991.

Garnsey, Peter. "Adultery Trials and the Survival of the *Quaestiones* in the Severan Age." *Journal of Roman Studies* 57 (1967): 56–60.

———. "Where did Italian Peasants Live?" *Proceedings of the Cambridge Philological Society* 29 (1979): 1–25.

———. *The Roman Empire: Economy, Society, and Culture.* Berkeley and Los Angeles: University of California Press, 1987.

Garnsey, Peter, ed. *Non-Slave Labour in the Greco-Roman World.* Cambridge: Cambridge Philological Society, 1980.

Garnsey, Peter, Keith Hopkins, and C. R. Whittaker. *Trade in the Ancient Economy.* Berkeley and Los Angeles: University of California Press, 1983.

Garnsey, Peter, and C. R. Whittaker, ed. *Imperialism in the Ancient World.* New York: Cambridge University Press, 1978.

Garstang, John. *Meroe: The City of the Ethiopians.* Oxford: Clarendon Press, 1911.

Geller, Markham. "New Sources for the Origins of the Rabbinic Ketubah." *Hebrew Union College Annual* 49 (1978): 227–45.

Gero, Joan, and Margaret Conkey, eds. *Engendering Archaeology.* Oxford: Basil Blackwell, 1991.

Ghosh, Amitav. *In an Antique Land.* New York: Knopf, 1993.

Gibbs, L. "Identifying Gender Representation in the Archaeological Record: A Contextual Study." In *The Archaeology of Contextual Meanings,* ed. Ian Hodder. New York: Cambridge University Press, 1986.

Giner, C. A. *Tejido y cestería en la península ibérica: Historia de su tecnica e industrias desde la prehistoria hasta la romanizacion.* Madrid: Bibliotheca Praehistorica Hispana, 1984.

Ginzberg, Louis. "Baruch, Apocalypse of (Syriac)." *Jewish Encyclopedia,* 2: 551–56. New York and London: Funk & Wagnalls, 1902.

Glock, Albert. "Archaeology as Cultural Survival: The Future of the Palestinian Past." *Journal of Palestine Studies* 23 (1994): 70–84.

Goldenberg, Robert. "Early Rabbinic Explanations of the Destruction of Jerusalem." *Journal of Jewish Studies* 33 (1982): 518–25.

Goldin, Judah. "The Two Versions of Abot de Rabbi Natan." *Hebrew Union College Annual* 19 (1945–1946): 97–120.

———. "Of Change and Adaptation in Judaism." *History of Religions* 4 (1965): 269–294.

Goldman, Hetty, ed. *Excavations at Gözlü Kule, Tarsus.* Vols. 1, 2, *The Hellenistic and Roman Periods, Texts and Plates.* Princeton: Princeton University Press, 1950.

Goodblatt, David. "The Beruriah Traditions." *Journal of Jewish Studies* 26 (1975): 68–85.

Goodman, L. "The Biblical Laws of Diet and Sex." *Jewish Law Association Studies* 2 (1986): 17–57.

Goodman, Martin. "Review of *Jews of Palestine,* by M. Avi-Yonah." *Journal of Jewish Studies* 28 (1977): 85–88.

———. *State and Society in Roman Galilee, A.D. 132–212.* Totowa, N.J.: Rowman & Allanheld, 1983.

Gophna, Ram, and Varda Sussman. "A Jewish Burial Cave of the Roman Period at the Foot of Tel Halif." ʿAtiqot, Hebrew ser., 7 (1984): 69–76.

Gordon, Leonard D. "Towards a Gender-Inclusive Account of Halakhah." In Gender and Judaism: The Transformation of Tradition, ed. T. M. Rudavsky. New York: New York University Press, 1995.

Gordon, W. M., and O. F. Robinson. The Institutes of Gaius. Ithaca: Cornell University Press, 1988.

s.v. "gossip." Oxford English Dictionary. 2d ed. Oxford: Clarendon Press, 1989.

Grafton, Anthony. New Worlds, Ancient Texts: The Power of Tradition and the Shock of Discovery. Cambridge, Mass.: Belknap Press of Harvard University Press, 1992.

Grant, Michael. The Antonines: The Roman Empire in Transition. New York: Routledge, 1994.

Gratwick, A. S. "Free or Not So Free? Wives and Daughters in the Late Roman Republic." In Marriage and Property, ed. E. M. Craik. Aberdeen: Aberdeen University Press, 1984.

Green, William Scott. "Storytelling and Holy Men." In Take Judaism for Example, ed. Jacob Neusner. Atlanta, Ga.: Scholars Press, 1992.

Green, William Scott, ed. Law as Literature. Semeia 27. Atlanta, Ga.: Scholars Press, 1983.

Greene, Kevin. The Archaeology of the Roman Economy. Berkeley and Los Angeles: University of California Press, 1986.

Grmek, Mrko. Greek Diseases in the Ancient Greek World (Les Maladies: à l'aube de la civilisation occidentale). Trans. Mireille Muellner and Leonard Muellner. Baltimore, Md.: Johns Hopkins University Press, 1989.

Groh, Dennis. "Galilee and the Eastern Roman Empire in Late Antiquity." Explor 3 (1977): 78–92.

———. "Jews and Christians in Late Roman Palestine—Towards a New Chronology." Biblical Archaeologist 51 (1988): 86–91.

Gross, Nachum, ed. Economic History of the Jews. New York: Schocken, 1975.

Grossman, Susan, and Rivka Haut, eds. Daughters of the King: Women and the Synagogue. Philadelphia: Jewish Publication Society, 1992.

Gunther, Rosmarie. Frauenarbeit, frauenbindung: Untersuchungen zu unfreien und freigelassenen Frauen in der Stadtromischen Inschriften. Munchen: W. Fink, 1987.

Guttmann, Alexander. "Participation of the Common People in Pharisaic and Rabbinic Legislative Process." Jewish Law Association Studies 1 (1985): 41–51.

Haas, Peter. "Women in Judaism: Reexamining an Historical Paradigm." Shofar 10 (1992): 35–52.

Habicht, Christian. Pausanias' Guide to Ancient Greece. Berkeley and Los Angeles: University of California Press, 1985.

Hachlili, Rachel. "A Jerusalem Family in Jericho." Bulletin of the American Schools of Oriental Research 230 (1978): 45–56.

———. "The Goliath Family in Jericho: Funerary Inscriptions from a First-Century Monumental Tomb." Bulletin of the American Schools of Oriental Research 235 (1979): 31–66.

———. "A Second Temple Period Necropolis in Jericho." *Biblical Archaeologist* 43 (1980): 235–40.

———. *Ancient Jewish Art and Archaeology in the Land of Israel.* Leiden: Brill, 1988.

Hachlili, Rachel, and Ann Killebrew. "Was the Coin-on-Eye Custom a Jewish Burial Practice in the Second Temple Period?" *Biblical Archaeologist* 46 (1983): 147–83.

Halivni, David Weiss. "The Reception Accorded to Rabbi Judah's Mishnah." In *Jewish and Christian Self-Definition.* Vol. 2, *Aspects of Judaism in the Graeco-Roman Period,* ed. E. P. Sanders. Philadelphia: Fortress, 1981.

Hallett, Judith. *Fathers and Daughters in Roman Society: Women and the Elite Family.* Princeton: Princeton University Press, 1984.

Halliday, W. R. *The Greek Questions of Plutarch with a New Translation and Commentary.* New York: Arno Press, 1975.

Hamel, Gildas. *Poverty and Charity in Roman Palestine, First Three Centuries, C.E.* Berkeley and Los Angeles: University of California Press, 1990.

Hamer, Mary. *Signs of Cleopatra: History, Politics, Representation.* London: Routledge, 1993.

Hammon, N. G. L., and H. H. Scullard, eds. *The Oxford Classical Dictionary.* 2d ed. Oxford: Clarendon Press, 1970.

Hammond, P. C. "Three Workshops at Petra (Jordan)." *Palestine Exploration Quarterly* 1986/87: 130–38.

Hanhart, Robert, ed. *Tobit.* Gottingen: Vanderhoeck & Ruprecht, 1983.

Hanson, Richard. *Tyrian Influence in the Upper Galilee.* Cambridge, Mass.: American Schools of Oriental Research, 1980.

Harding, G. Lankester. "A Roman Family Tomb in Jebel Joph, Amman." *Quarterly of the Department of Antiquities in Palestine* 14 (1950): 81–94.

———. "A Roman Tomb in Amman." *Annual of the Department of Antiquities of Jordan* 1 (1951): 30–33.

Hartog, François. *The Mirror of Herodotus: The Representation of the Other in the Writing of History.* Berkeley and Los Angeles: University of California Press, 1988.

Hauptman, Judith. "Women's Liberation in the Talmudic Period: An Assessment." *Conservative Judaism* 26 (1972): 22–28.

———. "Maternal Dissent: Women and Procreation in the Mishna." *Tikkun* 6 (1991): 81–82, 94–95.

———. "Feminist Perspectives on Rabbinic Texts." In *Feminist Perspectives on Jewish Studies,* ed. Lynn Davidman and Shelly Tenenbaum. New Haven: Yale University Press, 1994.

Healey, John. *The Targum of Proverbs.* Collegeville, Minn.: The Liturgical Press, 1991.

Heinemann, J. H. "The Status of the Labourer in Jewish Law and Society in the Tannaitic Period." *Hebrew Union College Annual* 25 (1954): 263–325.

Helly, Dorothy, and Susan Reverby, eds. *Gendered Domains: Rethinking Public and Private in Women's History.* Ithaca: Cornell University Press, 1992.

Hengel, Martin. *Judaism and Hellenism.* Philadelphia: Fortress Press, 1974.

———. *The Hellenization of Judaea in the First Century after Christ.* London and Philadelphia: SCM Press and Trinity Press International, 1989.

Hense, Otto, and Curt Wachsmuth, eds. *Ioannis Stobaei. Anthologium.* 5 vols. Berlin: Weidmannsche Verlagsbuchhandlung, 1958 [Berolini and Weidman, 1884–1912].

Herbert, Sharon. "Tel Anafa 1978: Preliminary Report." *Bulletin of the American Schools of Oriental Research* 234 (1979): 67–83.

Herlihy, David. *Opera Muliebra: Women and Work in Medieval Europe.* Philadelphia: Temple University Press, 1990.

Herodotus. *Herodotus.* 4 vols. Cambridge, Mass.: Harvard University Press, 1920.

Herzog, Isaac. *The Main Institutions of Jewish Law.* London: Soncino Press, 1965 [1936].

Heschel, Susannah. "Women's Studies." *Modern Judaism* 10 (1990): 243–58.

Himmelmann, Nikolaus. *Das Hypogaum der Aurelier am Viale Manzoni: Ikonographische Beobachtungen.* Wiesbaden: Akademie der Wissenschaften und der Literatur, 1975.

Hirschberg (Herszberg), Abraham Samuel. *Hayye ha-Tarbut be-Yisrael bi Tekufat ha-Mishna ve-ha-Talmud.* Warsaw, 1924.

Hirschfeld, Yizhar. *Dwelling Houses in Roman and Byzantine Palestine* (in Hebrew). Jerusalem: Yad Ishak Ben Zwi, 1987.

Hobson, D. "Women and Property Owners in Roman Egypt." *Transactions of the American Philological Association* 113 (1983): 311–21.

Hoffmann, Marta. *The Warp-Weighted Loom: Studies on the History and Technology of an Ancient Implement.* Oslo, Norway: Robin and Russ Handweavers, 1974.

Hoffner, Harry, Jr. "Symbols for Masculinity and Femininity: Their Use in Ancient Near Eastern Sympathetic Magical Rituals." *Journal of Biblical Literature* 85 (1966): 326–34.

Holum, Kenneth et al. *King Herod's Dream: Caesarea by the Sea.* New York: W. W. Norton, 1988.

Honig, B. "Toward an Agonistic Feminism: Hannah Arendt and the Politics of Identity." In *Feminists Theorize the Political,* ed. Judith Butler and Joan W. Scott. New York: Routledge, 1992.

Honoré, Tony. *Ulpian.* New York: Oxford University Press, 1982.

Hopkins, Keith. "Rules of Evidence." *Journal of Roman Studies* 68 (1978): 178–86.

———. "Taxes and Trade in the Roman Empire (200 B.C.—A.D. 400)." *Journal of Roman Studies* 70 (1980): 101–25.

———. *Death and Renewal.* New York: Cambridge University Press, 1983.

Humphreys, Sarah C. *The Family, Women, and Death: Comparative Studies.* New York: Routledge, 1983.

Hyman, Paula. "Gender and Jewish History." *Tikkun* 3 (1988): 35–38.

Ilan, Tal. "The Social Status of Women in Jewish Palestine in the Hellenistic-Roman Period (330 B.C.E.—200 C.E.)." Ph.D. diss., Hebrew University, 1990.

———. *Jewish Women in Greco-Roman Palestine: An Inquiry into Image and Status.* Tübingen: J. C. B. Mohr, 1995.

Irigaray, Luce. "Equal to Who?" *Differences* 1 (1989): 59–75.

Irvin, Dorothy. "The Ministry of Women in the Early Church: The Archaeological Evidence." *Duke Divinity School Review* 45 (1980): 76–86.

Isaac, Benjamin. "Judaea after A.D. 70." *Journal of Jewish Studies* 35 (1984): 44–50.

———. *The Limits of Empire: The Roman Army in the East.* Oxford: Clarendon Press, 1990.

Isaac, Benjamin, and Isaac Roll. "Judaea in the Early Years of Hadrian's Reign." *Latomus* 38 (1979): 54–66.

Jackson, Bernard. "On the Problem of Roman Influence on the Halakhah and Normative Self-Definition in Judaism." In *Jewish and Christian Self-Definition.* Vol. 2, *Aspects of Judaism in the Graeco-Roman Period,* ed. E. P. Sanders. Philadelphia: Fortress Press, 1981.

———. "Legalism and Spirituality: Historical, Philosophical, and Semiotic Notes on Legislators, Adjudicators, and Subjects." In *Religion and Law: Biblical-Judaic and Islamic Perspectives,* ed. E. Firmage et al. Winona Lake, Ind.: Eisenbrauns, 1990.

Jaffee, Martin. "How Much 'Orality' in Oral Torah? New Perspectives on the Composition and Transmission of Early Rabbinic Tradition." *Shofar* 10 (992): 53–72.

Jastrow, Marcus. *A Dictionary of the Targumim, the Talmud Babli and Yerushalmi, and the Midrashic Literature.* New York: Judaica Press, 1985 [1903].

Jed, Stephanie. *Chaste Thinking: The Rape of Lucretia and the Birth of Humanism.* Bloomington: Indiana University Press, 1989.

Jolowicz, Herbert F. *Historical Introduction to the Study of Roman Law.* New York: Cambridge University Press, 1967.

Jones, A. H. M. "The Cloth Industry Under the Roman Empire." *The Economic History Review,* 2d ser., 13.2 (1960): 183–92.

———. *Cities of the Eastern Roman Provinces.* 2d ed. Oxford: Clarendon Press, 1971.

Jongman, Willem. *The Economy and Society of Pompeii.* Amsterdam: Gieben, 1988.

Josephus. *The Jewish War.* 8 vols. Cambridge, Mass.: Harvard University Press, 1989 [1927].

———. *Jewish Antiquities.* 8 vols. Cambridge, Mass.: Harvard University Press, 1991 [1930].

Joshel, Sandra. *Work, Identity, and Legal Status at Rome: A Study of the Occupational Inscriptions.* Norman: University of Oklahoma Press, 1992.

Joubin, A. "Stèles funéraires de Phrygie." *Revue archéologique,* 3d ser., 24 (1894): 181–83.

Juvenal. *Juvenal and Perseus.* Cambridge, Mass.: Harvard University Press, 1918.

Kaminka, A. "Septuaginta und Targum zu Proverbia." *Hebrew Union College Annual* 8 (1931): 169–91.

Kampen, Natalie. *Image and Status: Roman Working Women in Ostia.* Berlin: Mann, 1981.

Kasovsky, Ch. *Thesaurus Mishnae.* 4 vols., rev. ed. Tel Aviv: Masadah, 1957–1961.

Katz, Marylin. *Penelope's Renown: Meaning and Indeterminacy in the Odyssey.* Princeton: Princeton University Press, 1991.

Katzoff, Ranon. "Papyrus Yadin 18 Again: A Rejoinder." *Jewish Quarterly Review* 82 (1991): 171–76.

Kelly, Joan. *Women, History, and Theory.* Chicago: University of Chicago Press, 1984.

Kenyon, Kathleen. *Excavations at Jericho.* Vol. 2, *The Tombs Excavated in 1955–58.* London: British School of Archaeology in Jerusalem, 1965.

Kessler-Harris, Alice. *Women Have Always Worked: A Historical Overview.* Old Westbury, N.Y.: The Feminist Press, 1981.

———. *A Woman's Wage: Historical Meanings and Social Consequences.* Lexington: University Press of Kentucky, 1990.

Kirschner, Robert. "Apocalyptic and Rabbinic Responses to the Destruction of 70." *Harvard Theological Review* 78 (1985): 27–46.

Kleiman, E. "Markets and Fairs in the Land of Israel in the Period of the Mishnah and the Talmud." *Zion* 51 (1986): 471–86.

Kleiner, D. E. E. "Women and Family Life on Roman Imperial Funerary Altars." *Latomus* 46 (1987): 545–54.

Klijn, A. F. J. "2 (Syriac Apocalypse of) Baruch: A New Translation and Introduction." In *The Old Testament Pseudepigrapha,* ed. James Charlesworth. New York: Doubleday, 1983.

Kofsky, A. S. "A Comparative Analysis of Women's Property Rights in Jewish Law and Anglo-American Law." *Journal of Law and Religion* 6 (1988): 317–53.

Konstans, David, and Martha Nussbaum. "Preface to 'Sexuality in Greek and Roman Society.'" *Differences* 2 (1990): iii.

Koortbojian, Michael. *Myth, Meaning and Memory on Roman Sarcophagi.* Berkeley and Los Angeles: University of California Press, 1995.

Kosovsky, Binyamin. *Otsar leshon ha-Tanaim.* 4 vols. Jerusalem: Bet hamidrash le-rabanim ba-Amerikah, 1965–1974.

Kraemer, Ross. "Women in the Religions of the Greco-Roman World." *Religious Studies Review* 9 (1983): 127–39.

———. *Her Share of the Blessings: Women's Religions Among Pagans, Jews, and Christians in the Greco-Roman World.* New York: Oxford University Press, 1992.

Krauss, Samuel. *Talmudische Archäologie.* 2 vols. Leipzig: Buchhandlung Gustav Fock, 1910.

Labovitz, Gail. "Arguing for Women in Talmud." *Shofar* 14 (1995): 72–79.

Lamberton, Robert, and John Keaney, eds. *Homer's Ancient Readers: The Hermeneutics of Greek Epic's Earliest Exegetes.* Princeton: Princeton University Press, 1992.

Lambropoulos, Vassilis. *The Rise of Eurocentrism: Anatomy of Interpretation.* Princeton: Princeton University Press, 1993.

Lang, Bernhard. *Wisdom and the Book of Proverbs: A Hebrew Goddess Redefined.* New York: Pilgrim, 1986.

Lapp, Nancy, ed. *The Third Campaign at Tell el-Ful: The Excavations of 1964.* Cambridge, Mass.: American Schools of Oriental Research, 1981.

Lapp, Paul W., and Nancy Lapp. *Discoveries in the Wadi Ed-Daliyeh.* Cambridge, Mass.: American Schools of Oriental Research, 1974.

Laqueur, Thomas. *Making Sex: Body and Gender from the Greeks to Freud.* Cambridge, Mass.: Harvard University Press, 1990.

Lattimore, Richard. *Themes in Greek and Latin Epigraphs.* Urbana: University of Illinois Press, 1962.

Lauffer, Siegfried, ed. *Diokletians Preisedikt.* Berlin: de Gruyter, 1971.

Lauterbach, J. Z. *Mekhilta de-Rabbi Ishmael.* 3 vols. Philadelphia: Jewish Publication Society, 1933-1935.

Lebendiger, I. "The Minor in Jewish Law, I–III." *Jewish Quarterly Review* 6 (1915): 459-93.

———. "The Minor in Jewish Law, IV-VI." *Jewish Quarterly Review* 7 (1916): 89-111, 145-74.

Lefebvre, Henri. "The Everyday and Everydayness." *Yale French Studies* 73 (1987): 7-11.

Lerner, M. B. "The External Tractates." In *The Literature of the Sages. First Part: Oral Tora, Halakha, Mishna, Tosefta, Talmud, External Tractates,* ed. Shmuel Safrai. Compendia Rerum Iudaicarum as Novum Testamentum. Philadelphia: Fortress Press, 1987.

Levi, Doro. *Antioch Mosaic Pavements.* Princeton: Princeton University Press, 1967.

Levine, Amy-Jill. "Second Temple Judaism, Jesus, and Women: Yeast of Eden." *Biblical Interpretation* 2.1 (1994): 8-33.

Levine, Amy-Jill, ed. *"Women Like This": New Perspectives on Jewish Women in the Greco-Roman World.* Atlanta, Ga.: Scholars Press, 1991.

Levine, Baruch. "Mulugu/Melug: The Origins of a Talmudic Legal Institution." *Journal of the American Oriental Society* 88 (1968): 271-84.

Levine, Lee. *The Rabbinic Class of Roman Palestine in Late Antiquity.* New York: Jewish Theological Seminary of America, 1989 [Jerusalem: Yad Izhak ben-Zvi, 1985].

Levine, Lee, ed. *The Galilee in Late Antiquity.* New York: Jewish Theological Seminary of America, 1992.

Levine, Lee, and Ehud Netzer. *Excavations at Caesarea Maritima. 1975, 1976, 1979—A Final Report.* Jerusalem: Hebrew University, 1986.

Levitt, Laura. "(The Problem With) Embraces." In *Judaism Since Gender,* ed. Miriam Peskowitz and Laura Levitt. New York: Routledge, 1997.

———. *Jews and Feminism: The Ambivalent Search for Home.* New York: Routledge, 1997.

Levitt, Laura, and Miriam Peskowitz, eds. "Engendering Jewish Knowledges." *Shofar* 14 (1995).

Levy, Edmond, ed. *La Femme dans les Societes Antiques.* Strasbourg: Institut d'Histoire Romaine, 1983.

Lewis, Naphtali. *Life in Egypt Under Roman Rule.* Oxford: Clarendon Press, 1983.

Lewis, Naphtali, and Jonas Greenfield, ed. *The Documents from the Bar Kokh-*

ba Period from the Cave of Letters. The Greek Documents. Jerusalem: Israel Exploration Society, 1989.

Lewis, Naphtali, Ranon Katzoff, and Jonas Greenfield. "Papyrus Yadin 18." *Israel Exploration Journal* 37 (1987): 229–50.

Lewis, T. N. "Women Under Rabbinic Judaism." Ph.D. diss. Hebrew Union College–Jewish Institute of Religion, 1949.

Lieberman, Saul. *Greek in Jewish Palestine: Studies in the Life and Manners of Jewish Palestine in the II–IV Centuries C.E.* New York: Jewish Theological Seminary of America, 1942.

———. "Roman Legal Institutions in Early Rabbinics and in the Acta Martyrum." *Jewish Quarterly Review* 35 (1944–1945): 1–57.

———. "Palestine in the Third and Fourth Centuries." *Jewish Quarterly Review* 36 (1945–1946): 329–79.

———. "Palestine in the Third and Fourth Centuries." *Jewish Quarterly Review* 37 (1946–1947): 31–54.

———. *Hellenism in Jewish Palestine: Studies in the Literary Transmission, Beliefs and Manners of Palestine in the I Century B.C.E.–IV Century C.E.* New York: Jewish Theological Seminary of America, 1950.

———. *Tosefta Ki-Fshutah.* New York: Jewish Theological Seminary of America, 1955–1982.

Lightstone, Jack. "The Dead in Late Antique Judaism: Homologies of Society, Cult, and Cosmos." In *Survivre . . . La Religion et la Mort,* ed. Raymond Lemieux and Réginald Richard. Montreal: Bellarmin, 1955.

Linder, Amnon. *The Jews in Roman Imperial Legislation.* Detroit: Wayne State University Press, 1987 [Jerusalem: The Israel Academy of Sciences and Humanities, 1983].

Lissarrague, François. "Figures of Women." In *A History of Women in the West.* Vol. 1, *From Goddesses to Christian Saints,* ed. Pauline Schmitt Pantel. Cambridge, Mass.: Harvard University Press, 1992.

Liu, Raymond. "Spindle Whorls: Pt. 1. Some Comments and Speculations." *Bead Journal* 3 (1978): 87–103.

Livy. *Livy in fourteen volumes.* Cambridge, Mass.: Harvard University Press, 1976.

Loewe, Raphael. *The Position of Women in Judaism.* London: SPCK, 1966.

Lowy, S. "The Extent of Jewish Polygamy in Talmudic Times." *Journal of Jewish Studies* 9 (1958): 115–38.

Luehrmann, Dieter. "Neutestamentliche Haustafeln und Antike Okonomie." *New Testament Studies* 27 (1980): 83–97.

Lyapustin, B. S. "Women in the Textile Industry: Production and Morality." *Journal of Ancient History* (Moscow) 174 (1985): 36–44 (English Abstract 45–46).

MacMullen, Ramsay. "Rural Romanization." *Phoenix* 22 (1968): 337–41.

———. "Market-Days in the Roman Empire." *Phoenix* 24 (1970): 333–41.

———. *Roman Social Relations.* New Haven: Yale University Press, 1974.

———. "Women in Public in the Roman Empire." *Historia* 29 (1980): 208–18.

———. *Changes in the Roman Empire: Essays in the Ordinary.* Princeton: Princeton University Press, 1990.

Mactoux, Marie-Madeleine. *Penelope: Légende et Mythe*. Paris: Centre de Re-
cherches d'Histoire Ancienne, 1975.

Magnus, Shulamit. "'Out of the Ghetto': Integrating the Study of Jewish
Women into the Study of 'The Jews.'" *Judaism* 39 (1990): 28–36.

Maiuri, Amedeo. *Ercolano: I Nuovi Scavi (1927–1958)*. Rome: Istituto poli-
grafico dello Stato, Libreria della Stato, 1958.

Malherbe, Abraham J. *The Cynic Epistles*. Atlanta, Ga.: Scholars Press, 1977.

Mason, H. J. "Fabula Graecanica: Apuleius and His Greek Sources." In *Aspects
of Apuleius' Golden Ass: A Collection of Original Papers*, ed. B. L. Hijmans
and R. Th. van der Paardt. Groningen: Bouma's Boekhuis, 1978.

Mayer, Gunter. *Die Judische Frau in der Hellenistich-Romischen Antike*.
Stuttgart: Kohlhammer, 1987.

Mazar, Amihai. "Tombs of the Roman Period at Caesarea." ʿ*Atiqot*, Hebrew
ser., 21 (1992): 105–8.

Mazar, B. *Beth Shearim*. Vol. 1, *Catacombs 1–4*. Jerusalem and New Brunswick:
Israel Exploration Society, 1973.

McCarter, P. Kyle. *II Samuel: A New Translation with Introduction, Notes and
Commentary*. New York: Doubleday, 1984.

McCreesh, Thomas. "Wisdom as Wife: Proverbs 31: 10–31." *Revue Biblique*
92 (1985): 25–46.

Merino, Luis Diez. *Targum de Proverbios. Edicion Principe del Ms. Villa-Amil
no. 5 de Alfonso de Zamora*. Madrid: Instituto "Francisco Suarez," 1984.

Merriam, C. U. "Some Notes on the Sulpicia Elegies." *Latomus* 44 (1990): 95–
98.

Metcalf, Peter, and Richard Huntington. *Celebrations of Death: The Anthropology of Mortuary Ritual*, 2d ed. New York: Cambridge University Press,
1991.

Meyer, Gunter. *Die Jüdische Frau in der Hellenistich-Romischen Antike*.
Stuttgart: Kohlhammer, 1987.

Meyer, Seligmann. *Arbeit und Handwerk im Talmud*. Berlin: Julius Benzian,
1878.

Meyers, Carol. *Discovering Eve: Ancient Israelite Women in Context*. New
York: Oxford University Press, 1988.

Meyers, Eric M. *Jewish Ossuaries: Reburial and Rebirth*. Rome: Biblical Institute Press, 1971.

———. "The Use of Archaeology in Understanding Rabbinic Materials." In
Texts and Responses, ed. Michael Fishbane and Paul Flohr. Leiden: Brill,
1975.

———. "Galilean Regionalism as a Factor in Historical Reconstruction." *Bulletin of the American Schools of Oriental Research* 221 (1976): 93–101.

———. "The Cultural Setting of Galilee: The Case of Regionalism and Early
Judaism." *Aufsteig und Neidergang der Römischen Welt* 2.19.1. Berlin: de
Gruyter, 1979.

———. "Galilean Regionalism: A Reappraisal." In *Approaches to Ancient Judaism*, vol. 5, ed. William Scott Green. Atlanta, Ga.: Scholars Press, 1985.

Meyers, Eric M., Arthur T. Kraabel, and James F. Strange. *Ancient Synagogue
Excavations at Khirbet Shemaʿ: Upper Galilee, Israel 1970–1972*. Durham,

N.C.: American Schools of Oriental Research and Duke University Press, 1976.

Meyers, Eric M., and Carol Meyers, with James F. Strange. *Excavations at the Ancient Synagogue of Gush Halav.* Winona Lake, Ind.: Eisenbrauns and American Schools of Oriental Research, 1990.

Meyers, Eric M., and James F. Strange. *Archaeology, the Rabbis and Early Christianity: The Social and Historical Setting of Palestinian Judaism and Christianity.* Nashville: Abingdon, 1981.

Meyers, Eric M., James F. Strange, and Carol L. Meyers. "Preliminary Report on the 1980 Excavations at en-Nabratein." *Bulletin of the American Schools of Oriental Research* 244 (1980): 1–25.

———. *Excavations at Ancient Meiron, Upper Galilee, Israel, 1971–72, 1974–75, 1977.* Cambridge, Mass.: American Schools of Oriental Research, 1981.

———. "Second Preliminary Report on the 1981 Excavations at en-Nabratein, Israel." *Bulletin of the American Schools of Oriental Research* 246 (1982): 35–54.

Millar, Fergus. "The World of the Golden Ass." *Journal of Roman Studies* 71 (1981): 63–75.

———. *The Roman Near East 31 B.C.—A.D. 337.* Cambridge, Mass.: Harvard University Press, 1993.

Millar, Fergus, and Erich Segal, eds. *Caesar Augustus: Seven Aspects.* Oxford: Clarendon Press, 1984.

Minnen, Peter van. "Urban Craftsmen in Roman Egypt." *Munsterische Beitrage zur Antiken Handelsgeschichte* 6 (1987): 31–88.

Moeller, Walter O. "The Male Weavers at Pompeii." *Technology and Culture* 10 (1969): 561–6.

———. *The Wool Trade of Ancient Pompeii.* Leiden: Brill, 1976.

Mommsen, Theodor, Paul Kreuger, and Alan Watson. *The Digest of Justinian.* Philadelphia: University of Pennsylvania Press, 1985.

Morris, Ian. *Death Ritual and Social Structure in Classical Antiquity.* New York: Cambridge University Press, 1992.

Myers, David. *Re-inventing the Jewish Past: European Jewish Intellectuals and the Zionist Return to History.* New York: Oxford University Press, 1995.

Nemoy, Leon. "A Modern Egyptian-Karaite Digest of the Duties and Rights of Husband and Wife." In *Occident and Orient: A Tribute to the Memory of Alexander Scheiber,* ed. Robert Dan. Leiden: Akadémiai Kiadó and Brill, 1988.

Neusner, Jacob. *A History of the Mishnaic Law of Purities.* Vol. 6. Leiden: Brill, 1977.

———. "Women in the System of the Mishnah." *Conservative Judaism* 33 (1980): 3–13.

———. "Mishnah on Women: Thematic or Systematic Description?" *Marxist Perspectives* 3 (1980): 78–99.

———. *Judaism: The Evidence of the Mishnah.* Chicago: University of Chicago Press, 1981.

———. "What Is at Stake in the Debate on Whether to Represent Judaism as a Religion of Pots and Pans or as a Religion of Sanctification and Salvation?"

and "The Debate on Pots and Pans." In *A Religion of Pots and Pans? Modes of Philosophical and Theological Discourse in Ancient Judaism,* ed. Jacob Neusner. Atlanta, Ga.: Scholars Press, 1988.

———. *The Mishnah. A New Translation.* New Haven: Yale University Press, 1988.

———. *The Economics of the Mishnah.* Chicago: University of Chicago Press, 1990.

———. *Judaism and Story: The Evidence of the Fathers According to Rabbi Nathan.* Chicago: University of Chicago Press, 1992.

———. "The Feminization of Judaism: Systematic Reversals and Their Meaning in the Formation of the Rabbinic System." In *Formative Judaism,* 7th ser. Atlanta, Ga.: Scholars Press, 1993.

Neyrey, Jerome. "Body Language in 1 Corinthians." *Semeia* 35 (1986): 129–70.

Noack, F. "Dorylaion. II. Grabreliefs." *Mittheilungen des Kaiserlich Deutschen Archaeologischen Instituts* 19 (1894): 315–34.

Oakman, Douglas. *Jesus and the Economic Questions of His Day.* Lewiston, N.Y.: Edwin Mellen Press, 1986.

Ohrenstein, Roman, and Barry Gordon. *Economic Analysis in Talmudic Literature: Rabbinic Thought in the Light Modern Economics.* Leiden: Brill, 1992.

Olender, Maurice. *The Languages of Paradise: Race, Religion and Philology in the Nineteenth Century.* Cambridge, Mass.: Harvard University Press, 1992.

Ophir, Adi. "From Pharaoh to Saddam Hussein: The Reproduction of the Other in the Passover Haggadah," in *The 'Other' in Jewish History and Thought,* ed. Laurence Silberstein and Robert Cohn. New York: New York University Press, 1994.

Oppenheim, A. C. "A Note on *son barzel.*" *Israel Exploration Journal* 5 (1955): 89–92.

Oren, Eliezer, and Uriel Rappaport. "The Necropolis of Maresha-Beth Guvrin." *Israel Exploration Journal* 34 (1984): 114–153.

Ousterhout, Robert, and Ann Terry. "Souvenir of a World in Transition: A Late Roman Grave Stele from Phyrgia." *Krannert Art Museum Bulletin* (1979).

Overman, J. Andrew. "Recent Advances in the Archaeology of the Galilee in the Roman Period." *Current Research in Biblical Studies* 1 (1993): 35–57.

Ovid. *Ovid in six volumes.* Cambridge, Mass.: Harvard University Press, 1986–88.

Pantel, Pauline Schmitt, ed. *A History of Women in the West.* Vol. 1, *From Ancient Goddesses to Christian Saints.* Cambridge, Mass.: Harvard University Press, 1992.

Patterson, R. "Spinning and Weaving." In *A History of Technology.* Vol. 1, *From Early Times to the Fall of Ancient Empires,* ed. Charles Singer et al. Oxford: Clarendon Press, 1954.

Pauly, August Friedrich von, Georg Wissowa, and W. Kroll. *Real-Encyclopedia der classischen Alterthumswissenschaft.* 1970.

Pausanias. *Description of Greece (Descriptio Graeciae).* 2 vols. Cambridge, Mass.: Harvard University Press, 1961.

s.v. "Penelope." Robert E. Bell. *Women of Classical Mythology: A Biographical Dictionary.* New York: Oxford University Press, 1993 [1991].

Peskowitz, Miriam. "'The Work of Her Hands': Gendering the Everyday in Roman Palestine (70–250 C.E.), Using Textile Production as a Case Study." Ph.D. diss., Duke University, 1993.

———. "'Family/ies' in Antiquity: Evidence from Tannaitic Literature and Roman Galilean Architecture." In *The Jewish Family in Antiquity*, ed. S. J. D. Cohen. Providence, R.I., and Atlanta, Ga.: Brown Judaic Studies and Scholars Press, 1993.

———. "Spinning Tales and Crafting Identities: Gender, Otherness, and the Interpretation of Tannaitic Texts from Roman-period Judaism." In *The 'Other' in Jewish Thought and History*, ed. Laurence Silberstein and Robert Cohn. New York: New York University Press, 1994.

———. "Engendering Jewish Religious History." *Shofar* 14 (1995): 8–34.

———. "Imagining the Rabbis." *Religious Studies Review* 21 (1995): 285–90.

Peskowitz, Miriam, and Laura Levitt, eds. *Judaism Since Gender.* New York: Routledge, 1997.

Petrie, W. M. Flinders. *Tools and Weapons.* London: British School of Archaeology in Egypt, 1912.

———. *Objects of Daily Use.* London: British School of Archaeology in Egypt, 1927.

Pfister, R. *Textiles de Palmyre.* Paris: Les Editions d'art et d'histoire, 1934.

———. *Textiles de Halabiyeh (Zenobia). Decouverts par le Service des Antiquities de la Syrie dans la necropole de Halabiyeh sur l'Euphrate.* Paris: Geuthner, 1951.

Pfister, R., and Louisa Bellinger. "The Textiles." *The Excavations at Dura Europos. Final Report 4, Part 2.* New Haven: Yale University Press, 1945.

Philo. *Philo.* Vol. 7, *Special Laws.* Cambridge, Mass.: Harvard University Press, 1984.

Pliny. *Natural History (Naturalis Historia).* Cambridge, Mass.: Harvard University Press, 1961.

Plutarch. *The Greek Questions of Plutarch.* Oxford: Clarendon Press, 1928.

———. "Quaestiones Romanae." In F. C. Babbitt, *Plutarch's Moralia.* Vol. 4. Cambridge, Mass.: Harvard University Press, 1972.

———. *Advice to Bride and Groom. Moralia.* Vol. 2. Cambridge, Mass.: Harvard University Press, 1976.

Poliakov, Léon. *The Aryan Myth: A History of Racist and Nationalist Ideas in Europe.* Edinburgh: Sussex University Press, 1971.

Pomeroy, Sarah. *Goddesses, Whores, Wives and Slaves: Women in Classical Antiquity.* New York: Schocken, 1975.

Pomeroy, Sarah, ed. *Women's History and Ancient History.* Chapel Hill: University of North Carolina Press, 1991.

Porath, Yosef, and Yossi Levy. "Mughar el-Sharaf: A Cemetery of the Roman and Byzantine Periods in the Sharon." ʿAtiqot, Hebrew ser., 22 (1993): 29–42.

Prager, Susan Westerberg. "Shifting Perspectives on Marital Property Law." In *Rethinking the Family: Some Feminist Questions,* ed. Barrie Thorne with Marilyn Talon. New York: Longman, 1982.

Preuss, Julius. *Biblical and Talmudic Medicine.* New York: Sanhedrin Press, 1978, and Northvale, N.J.: Jason Aronson, 1993.

Pritchard, James B. *The Excavation at Herodian Jericho, 1951.* New Haven, Conn.: American Schools of Oriental Research, 1958.

Propertius. *Elegies.* Cambridge, Mass.: Harvard University Press, 1952.

Proto-Evangelium Jacobi. "Proto-evangelium of James." In *New Testament Apocrypha,* ed. W. Schneemelcher. Louisville, Ky.: Westminster/John Knox Press, 1963–66.

Pseudo-Phocylides. In *Old Testament Pseudepigrapha,* Vol. 2, ed. James Charlesworth. New York: Doubleday.

Rabbinovicz, Raphael Nathan. *Dikdukei sofrim/Variae lectiones.* 16 vols. Munich-Przemysi, 1867–1897.

Rabinowitz, Nancy Sorkin, and Amy Richlin, eds. *Feminist Theory and the Classics.* New York: Routledge, 1993.

Rahmani, L. Y. "Jewish Rock Cut Tombs in Jerusalem." ʿAtiqot, English ser., 3 (1961): 93–120.

Rappaport, Uriel. "How Anti-Roman was the Galilee?" In *The Galilee in Late Antiquity,* ed. Lee Levine, 1992.

Raymond, Louis. *Spindle Whorls in Archaeology.* Greeley, Colo.: University of Northern Colorado, Museum of Anthropology, 1984.

Rhode, Deborah. "Feminist Critical Theories." *Stanford Law Review* 42 (1988): 617–38.

Rich, John W., and Andrew Wallace-Hadrill, eds. *City and Country in the Ancient World.* New York: Routledge, 1991.

Richlin, Amy "Zeus and Metis: Foucault, Feminism, Classics." *Helios* 18 (1991): 160–80.

———. *The Garden of Priapus: Sexuality and Aggression in Roman Humor.* 2d ed. rev. New York: Oxford University Press, 1992 [1983].

———. "Hijacking the Palladium: Feminists in Classics." *Gender and History* 4 (1992): 70–83.

Richlin, Amy, ed. *Pornography and Representation in Greece and Rome.* New York: Oxford University Press, 1992.

Rieger, Paul. *Versuch einer Technologie und Terminologie der Handwerke in der Mishnah.* Breslau: Gross, Barth & Comp, 1894.

Roberts, C. "Die Fusswaschung des Odysseus auf zwei Reliefs des fünften Jahrhunderts." *Athensiche Mitteilungen* 25 (1900): 325–38.

Roberts, L. *Hellenica. Recueil d'epigraphie de numismatique et d'antiquités grecques.* Vol. 10. Paris: Librairie d'Amérique et d'orient, 1955.

Robinson, David M. *Excavations at Olynthus.* Part 10. Baltimore, Md.: Johns Hopkins University Press, 1941.

Roebuck, Carl. *The Muses at Work: Arts, Crafts, and Professions in Ancient Greece and Rome.* Cambridge: M.I.T. Press, 1969.

Roscher, Wilhelm Heinrich. *Ausfurliches Lexikon der griechischen und romischen Mythologie.* 6 vols. Leipzig: B. G. Teubner, 1884–1937.

Rose, H. J. *The Roman Questions of Plutarch.* New York: Biblio & Tannen, 1974.

Rostovtzeff, Michael. *The Social and Economic History of the Roman Empire.* 2d ed. Oxford: Clarendon Press, 1957 [1937].

Roth, Henry Ling. *Studies in Primitive Looms.* Halifax: Bankfield Museum Notes, 1918.

Roth, Martha Tobi. *Babylonian Marriage Agreements. Seventh to Third Centuries B.C.* Neukirchen-Vluyn: Neukirchener, 1989.

Safrai, Shmuel. "Was There a Women's Gallery in the Synagogue in Antiquity?" *Tarbiz* 32 (1963): 329–38.

——. "The Small Village in Eretz Israel During the Period of the Mishnah and Talmud." *Proceedings of the Eighth World Congress of Jewish Studies.* Jerusalem: Magnes Press, 1982.

Safrai, Ze'ev. *The Economy of Roman Palestine.* London: Routledge, 1994.

Safrai, Ze'ev, and M. Linn. "The Economic Basis of Geva." In *Geva,* ed. Benjamin Mazar. Ramat Gan: ha-Kibuts ha-Meuhad, 1988.

Saldarini, Anthony. *The Fathers According to Rabbi Nathan (Abot de Rabbi Nathan) Version B. A Translation and Commentary.* Leiden: Brill, 1975.

——. *Scholastic Rabbinism: A Literary Study of the Fathers According to Rabbi Nathan.* Atlanta, Ga.: Scholars Press, 1982.

Saller, Richard. "Patria Potestas and the Stereotype of the Roman Family." *Continuity and Change* 1 (1986): 21–34.

——. "Men's Age at Marriage and Its Consequences in the Roman Family." *Classical Philology* 82 (1987): 21–34.

Saller, Sylvester. *Excavations at Bethany (1949–1953).* Jerusalem: Franciscan Press, 1957.

Sanders, E. P. *Judaism: Practice and Belief 63 BCE to 66 CE.* London and Philadelphia: SCM Press and Trinity Press International, 1992.

Sanders, E. P., ed., with A. I. Baumgarten and Alan Mendelson. *Jewish and Christian Self-Definition.* Vol. 2, *Aspects of Judaism in the Graeco-roman Period.* Philadelphia: Fortress Press, 1981.

Schäfer, Peter. "Hadrian's Policy in Judaea and the Bar Kokhba Revolt: A Reassessment." In *A Tribute to Geza Vermes: Essays on Jewish and Christian Literature and History,* ed. Philip Davies and Richard White. Sheffield: Sheffield Academic Press, 1990.

Schecter, Solomon. *Aboth de-Rabbi Nathan: Edited from Manuscripts with an Introduction, Notes and Appendices.* New York: Philipp Feldheim, 1967 [reprint of Vienna: Hildesheim 1887].

Scheftelowitz, E. *The Jewish law of Family and Inheritance and its Application in Palestine.* Tel Aviv: Martin Feuchtwanger, 1947 [1941].

Schiffman, Lawrence. "The Conversion of the Royal House of Adiabene in Josephus and Rabbinic Sources." In *Josephus, Judaism and Christianity,* ed. Louis Feldman and Gohei Hata. Detroit: Wayne State University Press, 1987.

Schneemelcher, Wilhelm, ed. *New Testament Apocrypha.* 2 vols. Louisville, Ky.: Westminster/John Knox Press, 1963.

Scholem, Gershom. "The Science of Judaism—Then and Now." In *The Messianic Idea in Judaism and Other Essays on Jewish Spirituality.* New York: Schocken, 1971.

Schoub, Myra. "Jewish Women's History: Development of a Critical Methodology." *Conservative Judaism* 34 (1982): 33–47.

Schultz, Vicki. "Telling Stories about Women and Work: Judicial Interpretations of Sex Segregation in the Workplace in Title VII Cases Raising the Lack of Interest Argument." *Harvard Law Review* 103 (1990): 1750–1844.

——. "Women 'Before' the Law: Judicial Stories about Women, Work, and Sex Segregation on the Job." In *Feminists Theorize the Political*, ed. Judith Butler and Joan W. Scott. New York: Routledge, 1992.

Schürer, Emil. Rev. and ed. Geza Vermes and Fergus Millar. *The History of the Jewish People in the Age of Jesus Christ*. 3 vols. Edinburgh: T & T Clark, 1973.

Schüssler-Fiorenza, Elizabeth. *In Memory of Her: A Feminist Theological Reconstruction of Christian Origins*. Tenth anniversary edition. New York: Crossroad, 1994 [1983].

Scott, Joan Wallach. *Gender and the Politics of History*. New York: Columbia University Press, 1988.

——. "Experience." In *Feminists Theorize the Political*, ed. Judith Butler and Joan W. Scott. New York: Routledge, 1992.

Segal, J. B. "The Jewish Attitude towards Women." *Journal of Jewish Studies* 30 (1979): 121–37.

Seidman, Naomi. "Carnal Knowledge: Sex and the Body in Jewish Studies." *Jewish Social Studies* 1 (1994): 115–46.

Seller, O. R., and D. C. Baramki. *A Roman-Byzantine Burial Cave in Northern Palestine*. New Haven, Conn.: American Schools of Oriental Research, 1953.

Sellers, Ovid, et al. *The 1957 Excavation at Beth-Zur*. Cambridge, Mass.: American Schools of Oriental Research, 1968.

Shamir, Orit. "Nol ha-Mishkolot." *Moreshet Derech* 39 (1991): 32–34.

Shanks, Michael. "Conclusion: Reading the Signs: Responses to Archaeology after Structuralism." In *Archaeology After Structuralism: Post-structuralism and the Practice of Archaeology*, ed. Ian Bapty and Tim Yates. New York: Routledge, 1990.

Shapira, Abraham. "Work." In *Contemporary Jewish Religious Thought: Original Essays on Critical Concepts, Movements and Beliefs*, ed. Arthur Cohen and Paul Mendes-Flohr. New York: Free Press, 1987.

Shapiro, Susan. "Voice from the Margins: Women and Jewish Studies." *Association for Jewish Studies Newsletter*, 2d ser., 4 (1990): 1–2, 4.

——. "Écriture judaïque: Where Are the Jews in Western Discourse." In *Displacements: Cultural Identities in Question*, ed. Angelika Bammer. Bloomington: Indiana University Press, 1994.

——. "A Matter of Discipline: Reading for Gender in Jewish Philosophy." In *Judaism Since Gender*, ed. Miriam Peskowitz and Laura Levitt. London: Routledge, 1997.

Sheffer, Abigail. "The Use of Perforated Clay Balls on the Warp-Weighted Loom." *Tel Aviv* 8 (1981): 81–83.

Shohat, Ella, and Robert Stam. *Unthinking Eurocentrism: Multiculturalism and the Media*. New York: Routledge, 1994.

Silberman, Neil. *Between Past and Present: Archaeology, Ideology and Nationalism in the Modern Middle East*. New York: Anchor Books, 1990.

Silberstein, Laurence. "Toward a Postzionist Discourse." In *Judaism Since Gender,* ed. Miriam Peskowitz and Laura Levitt. London: Routledge, 1997.

Sinclair, Lawrence. *An Archaeological Study of Gibeah (Tell el-Ful).* New Haven, Conn.: American Schools of Oriental Research, 1960.

Skinner, Marilyn, ed. *Rescuing Creusa: New Methodological Approaches to Women in Antiquity.* Lubbock, Tex.: Texas Tech, 1987.

Slavitt, David. *Ovid's Poetry of Exile.* Baltimore, Md.: Johns Hopkins University Press, 1990.

Smallwood, Mary. *The Jews Under Roman Rule: From Pompey to Diocletian.* Leiden: Brill, 1976.

Smith, R. H. *Pella of the Decapolis.* Vol. 1, *The 1967 Season of the College of Wooster Expedition to Pella.* Wooster, Ohio: College of Wooster, 1973.

Smith, R. H., and L. P. Day. *Pella of the Decapolis.* Vol. 2, Final Report on the College of Wooster Excavations in Area IX, the Civic Complex, 1979–1985. Wooster, Ohio: College of Wooster, 1989.

Snyder, Jane. "The Web of Song: Weaving Imagery in Homer and the Lyric Poets." *Classical Journal* 76 (1980–1981): 193–6.

Sokoloff, Michael. *A Dictionary of Jewish Palestinian Aramaic of the Byzantine Period.* Ramat-Gan: Bar Ilan University Press, 1990.

Spacks, Patricia Meyer. *Gossip.* Chicago: University of Chicago Press, 1986.

Sperber, Daniel. "On Social and Economic Conditions in Third Century Palestine." *Archiv Orientali* 38 (1970): 1–25.

———. *Roman Palestine 200–400. Money and Prices.* Ramat-Gan, Israel: Bar-Ilan University, 1974.

———. *Roman Palestine 200–400. The Land. Crisis and Change in Agrarian Society as Reflected in Rabbinic Sources.* Ramat-Gan, Israel: Bar-Ilan University, 1978.

Spivak, Gayatri Chakravorty. *Outside in the Teaching Machine.* New York: Routledge, 1993.

Stehle, Eva. "Venus, Cybele, and the Sabine Women: The Roman Construction of Female Sexuality." *Helios* 16 (1989): 143–64.

Stern, David. "Midrash and Indeterminacy." *Critical Inquiry* 15 (1988): 132–61.

Stern, Menahem. *Greek and Latin Authors on Jews and Judaism.* 3 vols. Jerusalem: Israel Academy of Sciences and Humanities, 1984.

Stewart, Charles, and Rosalind Shaw, eds. *Syncretism/Anti-syncretism: The Politics of Religious Synthesis.* London: Routledge, 1994.

Strack, Hermann, and Gunter Stemberger. *Introduction to the Talmud and Midrash.* Edinburgh: T. & T. Clark, 1991.

Strange, James F. "Archaeology and the Religion of Judaism in Palestine." *Aufsteig und Niedergang der Römischen Welt* 2.19.1. Berlin: de Gruyter, 1977.

Sukenik, E. L. "Kever Yehudi Zafonit-Maarvit Le-yerushalayim." *Tarbiz* 1 (1930): 122–24.

Sulzberger, Mayer. *The Status of Labor in Ancient Israel.* Philadelphia: Dropsie College for Hebrew and Cognate Learning, 1923.

Sussman, Varda. "A Tomb at Naḥf." ʿAtiqot, Hebrew ser., 8 (1982): 31–32.

Taubenschlag, Raphael. *The Law of Greco-Roman Egypt in the Light of the*

Papyri. 332 BC—640 AD. 2d ed. Warsaw: Panstwowe Wydawnictwo Naukowe, 1955.

Taylor, J. du Plat. "Roman Tombs at 'Kambi,' Vasa," in *Report of the Department of Antiquities, Cyprus, 1940–1948, 1950.* Nicosia, Cyprus: Department of Antiquities, 1950.

Thebert, Yvon. "Private Life and Domestic Architecture." In *A History of Private Life.* Vol. 1, *From Pagan Rome to Byzantium,* ed. Paul Veyne. Cambridge, Mass.: Harvard University Press, 1987.

Thomas, Y. "The Division of the Sexes in Roman Law." In *A History of Women in the West.* Vol.1, *From Ancient Goddesses to Christian Saints,* ed. Pauline Schmitt Pantel. Cambridge, Mass.: Harvard University Press, 1992.

Thompson, Cynthia. "Portraits from Roman Corinth: Hairstyles, Headcoverings and St. Paul." *Biblical Archaeologist* 51 (1988): 99–115.

Thompson, Wesley. "Weaving: A Man's Work." *Classical Weekly* 75 (1982): 217–22.

Tibullus. *Elegies. Introduction, Text, Translation and Notes,* ed. G. Lee. 2d ed. Liverpool: F. Cairns, 1982.

Tilly, Christopher. *Reading Material Culture: Structuralism, Hermeneutics, and Post-Structuralism.* Oxford: Basil Blackwell, 1990.

Toynbee, J. M. C. *Death and Burial in the Roman World.* Ithaca: Cornell University Press, 1985 [1971].

Trebilco, Paul. *Jewish Communities in Asia Minor.* New York: Cambridge University Press, 1991.

Treggiari, Susan. "Domestic Staff at Rome in the Julio-Claudian Period, 27 B.C. to A.D. 68." *Histoire Sociale* 6 (1973): 241–55.

———. "Family Life among the Staff of the Volusii," *Transactions of the American Philological Association* 105 (1975): 393–401.

———. "Jobs in the Household of Livia." *Papers of the British School at Rome* 43 (1975): 48–77.

———. "Jobs for Women." *American Journal of Ancient History* 1 (1975): 76–104.

———. "Lower-Class Women in the Roman Economy." *Florilegium* 1 (1979): 65–86.

———. "Women as Property in the Early Roman Empire." In *Women and the Law: a Social History Perspective,* Vol. 2, ed. D. Kelly Weisberg. Cambridge, Mass.: Schenkman, 1982.

———. *Roman Marriage: Iusti Coniuges from the Time of Cicero to the Time of Ulpian.* Oxford: Clarendon Press, 1991.

Trigger, Bruce. *A History of Archaeological Thought.* New York: Cambridge University Press, 1989.

Trinh T. Minh-ha. *When the Moon Waxes Red: Representation, Gender and Cultural Politics.* New York: Routledge, 1991.

Trouillot, Michel-Rolph. *Silencing the Past: Power and the Production of History.* Boston: Beacon Press, 1995.

Tzaferis, Vasileios. *Excavations at Capernaum. Vol. 1: 1978–1982.* Winona Lake, Ind.: Eisenbrauns, 1989.

Ucko, Peter. "Ethnography and Archaeological Interpretation of Funerary Remains." *World Archaeology* 1 (1969): 262–80.

Ulbert, Gunter. *Cáceres el Viejo. Ein Spätrepublikanisches Legionslager in Spanisch Extremadura.* Mainz am Rheim: Verlag Philipp von Zabern, 1984.

Varro. *De Lingua Latina.* 2 vols. Cambridge, Mass.: Harvard University Press, 1938.

Veyne, Paul. "The Roman Empire." In *A History of Private Life.* Vol. 1, *From Pagan Rome to Byzantium.* Cambridge, Mass.: Harvard University Press, 1987.

Visotzky, Burton. "Midrasch Mishle: A Critical Edition Based on Manuscripts and Early Editions." Ph.D. diss., Jewish Theological Seminary of America, 1982.

———. *The Midrash on Proverbs.* New Haven: Yale University Press, 1982.

Waithe, M. E., ed. *History of Women Philosophers.* Vol. 1, *Ancient Women Philosophers.* Boston: Kluwer Academic Publishers, 1987.

Walby, Sylvia. *Patriarchy at Work: Patriarchal and Capitalist Relations in Employment.* Cambridge: Polity Press, 1986.

Walker, Susan. *Memorials to the Roman Dead.* London: British Museum, 1985.

Wallace-Hadrill, Andrew. "Pliny the Elder and Man's Unnatural History." *Greece and Rome,* new ser. 37 (1990): 80–96.

Wasserstein, A. "A Marriage Contract from the Province of Arabia Nova: Notes on Papyrus Yadin 18." *Jewish Quarterly Review* 80 (1989): 93–130.

Waterman, Leroy. *Preliminary Report of the University of Michigan Excavations at Sepphoris, Palestine, in 1931.* Ann Arbor: University of Michigan Press, 1937.

Watson, Alan. *Roman Law and Comparative Law.* Atlanta: University of Georgia Press, 1991.

Webber, J. "Between Law and Custom: Women's Experience of Judaism." In *Women's Religious Experience: Cross-Cultural Perspectives,* ed. Pat Holden. London: Croom Helm, 1983.

Wegner, Judith Romney. *Chattel or Person? The Status of Women in the Mishnah.* New York: Oxford University Press, 1988.

———. "Tragelaphos Revisited: The Anomaly of Woman in the Mishnah." *Judaism* 37 (1988): 160–72.

———. "Public Man, Private Woman: The Sexuality Factor and the Personal Status of Women in Mishnaic Law." *Jewish Law Association Studies* 4 (1990): 23–54.

———. "Philo's Portrayal of Women: Hebraic or Hellenic?" In *Women Like This: New Perspectives on Jewish Women in the Greco-Roman World,* ed. Amy-Jill Levine. Atlanta, Ga.: Scholars Press, 1991.

Weinberg, Gladys. *Excavations at Jalame. Site of a Glass Factory in Late Roman Palestine.* Columbia: University of Missouri Press, 1988.

Weinberg, Gladys, and Dorothy Burr Thompson. "Small Objects from the Pnyx I." *Hesperia Supplement* 7. Cambridge, Mass.: American School of Classical Studies, 1943.

Weir, S. *Spinning and Weaving in Palestine.* London: Trustees of the British Museum, 1970.

Weisberg, D. "Some Observations on Late Babylonian Texts and Rabbinic Literature." *Hebrew Union College Annual* 39 (1968): 71–80.

Weisfeld, Israel H. *Labor Legislation in the Talmud.* Chicago: University of Chicago Library, Department of Photographic Reproductions, 1946.

Weiss, Ze'ev. "Social Aspects of Burial in Beth Shearim: Archaeological Finds and Talmudic Sources." In *The Galilee in Late Antiquity,* ed. Lee Levine. New York: Jewish Theological Seminary of America, 1992.

White, Kevin. *Greek and Roman Technology.* Ithaca, N.Y.: Cornell University Press, 1984.

Whitehead, Harriet. "The Bow and the Burden Strap: A New Look at Institutionalized Homosexuality in Native North America." In *Sexual Meanings: The Cultural Construction of Gender and Sexuality,* ed. Sherry Ortner and Harriet Whitehead. New York: Cambridge University Press, 1981.

Wicker, Kathleen O'Brien. "First-Century Marriage Ethics: A Comparative Study of the Household Codes and Plutarch's Conjugal Precepts." In *No Famine in the Land: Studies in Honor of John L. McKenzie,* ed. James W. Flanagan and Anita Weisbrod Robinson. Atlanta, Ga.: Scholars Press, 1975.

———. "Mulierum Virtutes." In *Plutarch's Ethical Writings and Early Christian Literature,* ed. Hans Dieter Betz. Leiden: Brill, 1978.

Wild, J. P. "The Gynaceum at Venta and Its Context." *Latomus* 26 (1967): 648–76.

———. *Textile Manufacture in the Northern Roman Provinces.* New York: Cambridge University Press, 1970.

———. "Roman Textiles from Vindolanda, Hexham, England." *Textile Museum Journal* 18 (1979): 19–24.

———. "Roman and Native in Textile Technology." In *Invasion and Response: The Case of Roman Britain,* ed. Barry Burnham and Helen Johnson. Oxford: British Archaeological Reports, 1979.

———. "The Roman Horizontal Loom." *American Journal of Archaeology* 91 (1987): 459–71.

———. *Textiles in Archaeology.* Aylesbury: Shire Publications, 1988.

Willett, Tom. *Eschatology in the Theodicies of 2 Baruch and 4 Ezra.* Sheffield: Sheffield Academic Press, 1989.

Williams, Patricia. *The Alchemy of Race and Rights.* Cambridge, Mass.: Harvard University Press, 1991.

———. "And We Are Not Married: A Journal of Musings on Legal Language and the Ideology of Style." In *Some Consequences of Theory,* ed. Barbara Johnson and Jonathan Arac. Baltimore, Md.: Johns Hopkins University Press, 1991.

Wilson, Lillian. "Loomweights." In *Excavations at Olynthus.* Pt. 2, ed. D. M. Robinson. Baltimore, Md.: Johns Hopkins University Press, 1930.

———. *The Clothing of the Ancient Romans.* Baltimore, Md.: Johns Hopkins University Press, 1938.

Wilson, William, trans. *The Writings of Clement of Alexandria.* The Anti-Nicene Christian Library. Edinburgh: T & T Clark, 1867.

Winkler, John. *The Constraints of Desire: The Anthropology of Sex and Gender in Ancient Greece.* New York: Routledge, 1990.

Wipszycka, Ewa. *L'industrie textile dans l'Egypte romaine*. Wroclaw: Zactad Naradowy im Ossolinskich, 1965.

Wistrand, Erik. *The So-Called Laudatio Turiae: Introduction, Text, Translation, Commentary*. Gothoburg: Acta Universitatis Gothoburgensis, 1976.

Woolf, Virginia. *Collected Essays*. New York: Harcourt Brace Jovanovich, 1966.

Wordelman, Amy. "Everyday Life: Women in the Period of the New Testament." In *The Women's Bible Commentary*, ed. Carole Newsom and Sharon Ringe. Louisville, Ky.: Westminster/John Knox Press, 1992.

Wyke, Maria. "Mistress and Metaphor in Augustan Elegy." *Helios* 16 (1989): 25–47.

———. "Woman in the Mirror: The Rhetoric of Adornment in the Roman World." In *Women in Ancient Societies*, ed. Léonie Archer, Susan Fischler, and Maria Wyke. New York: Routledge, 1994.

Yadin, Yigael. *The Finds from the Bar Kokhba Period in the Cave of Letters*. Jerusalem: Israel Exploration Society, 1963.

———. "The Excavation of Masada 1963/1964: Preliminary Report." *Israel Exploration Journal* 15 (1963): 1–120.

Yardeni, A. "The Aramaic and Hebrew Documents in Cursive Script from Wadi Murabba'at and Nahal Hever and Related Material, a Paleographic and Epigraphic Examination." Ph.D. diss., Hebrew University, 1991.

Yarnall, Judith. *Transformations of Circe: The History of an Enchantress*. Urbana and Chicago: University of Illinois Press, 1994.

Yaron, Reuven. *Introduction to the Law of the Aramaic Papyri*. Oxford: Clarendon Press, 1961.

Yeivin, Shmuel. "The Origin of an Ancient Jewish Burial Custom" (in Hebrew). *Bulletin of the Jewish Palestine Exploration Society* 8 (1940): 22–27.

Yeivin, Ze'ev. "Excavations at Khorazin." *Eretz Israel* 11 (1973): 144–57.

———. "Korazin: A Mishnaic City." *Bulletin of the Anglo-Israel Archaeological Society* 1982: 46–48.

Young, Kate et al., eds. *Of Marriage and the Market*. New York: Routledge, 1981.

Zandy, Janet. "Women Have Always Sewed: The Production of Clothing and the Work of Women." Special Issue: Working Class Studies. *Women's Studies Quarterly* 23.1–2 (1995): 162–68.

Zerubavel, Yael. "The Death of Memory and the Memory of Death: Masada and Holocaust as Historical Metaphors." *Representations* 45 (1994): 72–100.

Zimmer, Gerhard. *Römische Berufsdarstellungen*. Berlin: Mann, 1982.

Zlotnick, Dov. *The Tractate 'Mourning'*. New Haven: Yale University Press, 1966.

Zuckermandel, M. S. *Tosephta Based on the Erfurt and Vienna Codices, with Parallels and Variants*. Jerusalem: Wahrmann, 1970.

Index

Compositor: J. Jarrett Engineering, Inc.
Text: 10/13 Sabon
Display: Sabon
Printer and binder: Thomson-Shore, Inc.